INTER-STATE CONFLICTS AND CONTENTIOUS ISSUES IN SOUTH ASIA:

CHALLENGES AND PROSPECTS FOR SAARC

INTER-STATE CONFLICTS AND CONTENTIOUS ISSUES IN SOUTH ASIA:

CHALLENGES AND PROSPECTS FOR SAARC

Edited By

Emanual Nahar

KALPAZ

ISBN: 978-93-5128-169-6

Price : ₹ 825

First Published, 2016

Published by

Kalpaz Publications
C-30, Satyawati Nagar,
Delhi – 110052
E-mail: kalpaz@hotmail.com
Ph.: 9212142040
Printed at: G. Print Process, Delhi

Cataloging in Publication Data—DK
Courtesy: D.K. Agencies (P) Ltd. <docinfo@dkagencies.com>

Inter-state conflicts and contentious issues in South Asia challenges and prospects for SAARC / edited by Emanual Nahar.
pages cm
Includes bibliographical references.
ISBN 9789351281696

1. Conflict management—South Asia. 2. National security—South Asia. 3. South Asia—Politics and government. 4. South Asian cooperation. I. Nahar, Emanual, editor.

JZ5584.S64I58 2015 DDC 327.170954 23

Contents

List of Contributors

1. **Professor Mohammed Khalid** is Professor in Political Science, Department of Evening Studies Panjab University, Chandigarh.
2. **Professor K.S. Sidhu** is Professor in Defence Studies (Retd.) Punjabi University, Patiala.
3. **Dr Rajesh Kumar** is Assistant Professor in Political Science, School of Social Sciences, Guru Nanak Dev University, Amritsar.
4. **Professor Surinder K. Shukla**, Professor in Political Science-USOL, Panjab University, Chandigarh.
5. **Dr Mathew Joseph**, Associate Professor, M.M.A.J. Academy of International Studies, Jamia Millia Islamia, New Delhi.
6. **Professor Davinder Kumar Madaan** is Professor of Economics & Head-School of Social Sciences, Punjabi University, Patiala .
7. **Professor Emanual Nahar,** Fellow and Professor in Political Science- USOL, Panjab University, Chandigarh.
8. **Dr Kuldeep Singh,** (Fellow P.U.) Associate Professor, PG dept. of Political Science, G.N.N. College, Doraha.
9. **Dr Pushpinder Kaur**, Assistant Professor, University Institute of Legal Studies, Panjab University, Chandigarh.
10. **Dr Gurnam Chand**, Associate Professor and Head Department of Political Science, M.R. Govt. College, Fazilka.
11. **Kanwar Deep Singh** is a Research Scholar, Department of Political Science, Panjab University, Chandigarh.
12. **Dr Rajnish Saryal,** Assistant Professor in Political Science, Panjab University Regional Centre, Ludhiana.
13. **Dr Hari K. Sharma,** Assistant Professor in Political Science, NCWEB, Hansraj College, University of Delhi.

14. **Dr Bawa Singh** is teaching as Assistant Professor in the Centre for South and Central Asian Studies, School of Global relation, Central University of Punjab, Bathinda.
15. **Dr Madhu Chopra** is Assistant Professor, Department of Defence and Strategic Studies Kurukshtra University, Kurukshetra.
16. **Dr Sujit Lahiry** is Assistant Professor in Political Science, Panjab University Regional Centre, Sri Muktsar Sahib, Punjab.
17. **Harinderjit Kaur** is Assistant Professor, Department of Political Science, Government College, Sri Muktsar Sahib, Punjab.
18. **Rajiv Kumar** is Assistant Professor Department of Political Science Panjab University Constituent College Nihal Singh Wala, Moga, Punjab.
19. **Shayama Bangar** is a Research Scholar, Department of Political Science, Panjab University, Chandigarh.
20. **Priyanka** is an Assistant Professor, Rayat and Bahra College, Ropar (Punjab).
21. **Reema Duggal** is a Research Scholar, Department of Political Science, Panjab University, Chandigarh.
22. **Anjna Malhotra** is Assistant Professor in Political Science, S.D.A.M. College, Dinanagar, Punjab.
23. **Dr Sheveta Sehgal** is Assistant Professor of in Political Science, A.S. College, Khanna (Punjab).
24. **Vipin Sharma,** Research Scholar, Deptt. Of Evening Studies-MDRC, P.U., Chandigarh.
25. **Dr Vinod Kumar**, Assistant Professor, P.U. Regional Centre, Sri Muktsar Sahib

Foreword

Richness in material and human resources has warranted a constant interaction between countries in South Asia and the outside world. South Asian states have also been aware of their geopolitical advantages and the perceptions. Efforts were made early to create institutional mechanisms for regional integration to enable the fostering of a common regional identity and a cooperative growth strategy making optimum use of inter-regional trade and social and political development. A culmination of such an understanding was the creation of the South Asian Association for Regional Cooperation (SAARC).

The organisation of eight South Asian nations, namely Afghanistan, Bangladesh, Bhutan, India, the Maldives, Nepal, Pakistan and Sri Lanka, with observer nations, Myanmar, China, Iran, the European Union (EU) and the United States, to name a few, is known as the South Asian Association for Regional Cooperation (SAARC). It was established at the first summit in Dhaka on December 7-8, 1985. India, significantly, constitutes 70 per cent or more of SAARC's area and population. Seven of them have common borders with India but not each other. All have a shared culture, ethnicity and experienced long interactive historical events including British imperialism and its consequences.

Over the years, SAARC has attempted to address several regional problems, for instance drug and human trafficking, economic cooperation among south Asian states and the forging of a south Asian social identity and most recently efforts have been made to tackle the menace of terrorism in the region. Despite its stated intentions SAARC as a regional body has for years grappled with inter-state, intra-state and regional conflicts. Since its existence in 1985, SAARC has been criticised for its failure to forge an effective regional identity. Inter-state conflicts and the bilateral interests of member states have a decisive influence on the achievements of

SAARC; the regional body has also been influenced by external players and other regional organisations. In an interdependent and swiftly globalising world, it would be unrealistic to believe that SAARC can prosper in isolation. South Asian integration efforts are often influenced either directly or indirectly by great power politics and alliances in other regions. It has now become necessary for SAARC to rise above bilateral conflicts and to foster closer relationships with other regional and international organisations, in order to evolve into an effective regional organisation.

SAARC, regrettably, has yet to develop into a conflict-mediating or conflict-resolving institution both on multilateral and bilateral issues. It has succeeded however in evolving as a forum and a framework but one which does not have the capacity to devise instruments and techniques for consultations on bilateral and multilateral political and security problems. While it is common to lay the blame at the door of Indo-Pakistani rivalry, the reasons for SAARC's failure are in fact deeper and structural in nature. A constellation of geographical, ethnic, historical and political factors have gridlocked SAARC. International borders in South Asia are still not all settled beyond dispute, and conventional conflicts are not decreasing in shared border areas. The destiny of South Asian nations today is to either swim together or risk sinking separately in the battle against poverty and unemployment as well as in meeting the challenges of the environment, national security, and globalisation.

This publication is a by-product of a very successful ICSSR sponsored National Seminar organised by the Department of Political Science — University School of Open Learning, Panjab University, Chandigarh. The book comprises of papers presented during the National Seminar from learned and distinguished experts, academicians, and research scholars. This study evaluates SAARC, as a living and developing organisation and efforts have been made to cover all the aspects in an objective manner.

This edited work is an attempt to bring to light the debilitating effect of inter-state conflicts in South Asia on regional cooperation. Analyses has focused primarily on the negative association of interstate conflict and regionalism in South Asia, however this study also discusses how other regional cooperation mechanisms in South Asia have coped with such challenges to promote a vibrant regional identity. The edited work also offers some solutions in the form of recommendations, to contribute in the process of regional cooperation in South Asia. It gives an in-depth historical and analytical account of conflicting issues and security concerns in the South Asian region. The study also analyses various development policies and confidence building measures initiated by the respective governments, and provides useful suggestions and policy recommendations to tackle the concerned challenges in South Asia. The objective of this book is to highlight various trends, problems and also the peace processes in operation in South Asian Region. Thus, this book should serve as an import ant source as it provides a wealth of information about the existing issues of contentious prevailing in South Asia, that have been continuously hampering the process of regional economic cooperation and integration under the forum of SAARC. It will be highly useful for all the individuals engaged in research and teaching work related to issues, problems and conflicts in South Asia.

Vice- Chancellor
Panjab University
Chandigarh

Preface

Problems in South Asia have become more acute not only because of the historical and political relations but also due to many other factors such as different attitudes and perceptions of SAARC members, economic disparities, political set up of institutions, preponderance of India in South Asia, super-powers rivalry in South Asia.

The disparities in the economic field are hindrance in the way of SAARC. SAARC members have neither equal per capita income nor equal growth rate in the industrial and agricultural sector. The Pattern of development, rather underdevelopment is more or less the same.

The problems concerning small nations of SAARC is even greater because they do not have sufficient productive capacity in the fields of agriculture and industry. They lack the economic strength to make significant contribution to the programme activities.

There are many critical problems among South Asian countries related to the difference in their perception about nature, role and structure of SAARC. Most of these differences arise because of different vintage points determined by their respective national interests with which each nation views SAARC.

Bangladesh is primarily interested in management of river water, Pakistan's approach is mainly political and it seems to be the least interested in regional interactions. Nepal joined the SAARC only to demand that it should be a zone of peace. Sri Lanka's main interest is to solve domestic problems with the cooperation of SAARC countries.

Most of the crucial problems faced by South Asian countries are internal and structural in nature. Wide disparities in the economic and political set-up do not provide favourable ground for useful regional cooperation.

However, SAARC is an essential regional organisation for the overall development of the South Asian Region. The most important factor needed to make SAARC a successful Regional Model is to remove fear and distrust among the member states. The success of SAARC will depend on whether the member nations will show prudence and wisdom to resolve bilateral disputes and differences, and thereby creating a state of regional cooperation, peace and stability.

—Emanual Nahar

Introduction

In the Inaugural Address of the Seminar, Professor A.K. Bhandari, DUI, Panjab University Chandigarh highlighted that Regional Cooperation has been assuming greater significance in International Politics. It is a multi-dimensional phenomenon and its understanding requires comprehensive approach. It usually appears under certain economic conditions and its aim is to improve the economic efficiency and expand the horizons of regional cooperation in International Politics.

The idea of Regional Cooperation in South Asia was first moved by the President of Bangladesh- Ziaur Rehman. From 1980 to 2013, SAARC has completed thirty two years of its formal institutional existence, and has passed through two distinct phases. The first phase extention was preparatory phase, based on gradual and step by step approach for initiating regional cooperation, mostly in non-controversial and peripheral areas, such as Confidence Building Measures (CBM'S). In the second phase of its evolution, SAARC moved into the expansionary phase , when regional cooperation was expanded both in social and core economic sectors. Many major steps have been taken by their members for considerable success.

No doubt, regional cooperation is constructing mutual trust and understanding among the member states on economic areas which would result into political cooperation too. Even as SAARC member countries has signed a number of conventions and agreements in different areas. Such types of developments can be expected to provide the necessary impetus to economic cooperation in the region.

SAARC has been able to build up an extensive set of connections via different associations and institutions. The establishment of SAFTA has boosted the economic cooperation between member states of the region. This has led to closer people to people contact, and created a network of friendly relationships. It has already made some progress in establishing bilateral relationship with ASEAN, European Union and Arab League.

Professor Kuldip Singh, renowned Professor in Political Science, while delivering his Keynote Address pointed out that Bilateral Disputes among member states have created major hindrance in the successful working of SAARC. The tensions between India and Pakistan are a key factor in the slow growth of regional cooperation in South Asia. Secondly, the issue of terrorism has been one of the important agenda of SAARC, since its first Summit held in 1985. With the passage of time, the issue of terrorism has taken a more **complex character in South Asia.** Due to various political conflicts and terrorist activities in South Asia, the trade between all the nations is far below their potential. SAARC has showed inability to tackle inter-state conflicts. Although the SAARC countries have agreed upon SAFTA but nations like Pakistan are reluctant to restore normal trading relations with India.

Professor R.S. Yadav, Chairperson: Department of Political Science, Kurukshetra University, Kurukshetra in his Presidential Address emphasised that SAARC might pass a resolution expressing the determination of all members to fight terrorism, and set up a committee to pursue the matter. It will be in the advantage of all the members of SAARC, if they do not allow their political conflicts come in the way of the regional cooperation and if they make their efforts towards cooperation in possible areas. Such cooperation may eventually lead to the solution of political objects. SAARC is a good beginning in this regard; it can take the issue of trade in few commodities like tea, jute, cotton, etc.

This regional cooperation can be more meaningful if all the countries of the region work together on one platform. They can achieve more negotiating power for their products in the international markets.

Professor Kuldip Singh from GNDU, Amritsar chaired the first technical session of the National Seminar. **Prof. Mohammed Khalid** from Panjab University, Chandigarh presented the paper on **"SAARC and Indian Ocean: An Agenda for Action".** In his paper he said that during the Cold War SAARC Members have been demanding to make 'Indian Ocean a Zone of Peace' and 'Nuclear Free Zone'. During its existence of about 29 years, the SAARC Countries have not devised or discussed to make a common Ocean Policy. There are many challenges facing the South Asian nations emanating from the Indian Ocean and these calls for a joint SAARC effort and approach to work towards cooperation. The paper strives to point out the possible areas of cooperation at SAARC level as regard to the Indian Ocean.

Professor K.S. Sidhu from Punjabi University, Patiala in his presentation of paper on **"Dynamics of South Asian Security and Role of SAARC"**, pointed out that SAARC was envisioned initially as an organisation that would facilitate peace, economic integration and prosperity in the region. In the past, any initiative within the framework of SAARC to discuss cooperation on issues of traditional and non-traditional security threats was not possible since it was argued that discussion of such issues was outside the terms of reference of SAARC. An overview of South Asia in relation to crucial security issues and a critical analysis of traditional and non–traditional security risks, based on the ground realities of South Asia, may precede an analysis of the recent initiatives undertaken by SAARC to mitigate these risks. Countries in South Asia are beginning to comprehend the inadequacy of national security apparatuses in countering traditional and non-traditional risks and there is a fundamental need for co-operative security system to mitigate these growing traditional and non-traditional security threats.The proposed security system in South Asia ought to be based on developing multilateral cooperation based on open diplomacy to counter the broad range of security threats being faced by the region, individually or the region as a whole. Such an initiative ought to be part of strengthening the process of regional cooperation on energy, trade and infrastructure as economic integration can facilitate and compliment collaboration on security issues.

Professor Mathew Joseph C. from Academy of International Studies, Jamia Millia Islamia, New Delhi, presented paper on **"Small States and Regional Organisations: Case Study of Bhutan and SAARC".** He highlighted that when the idea of an organisation for regional cooperation for South Asian countries was mooted by late Gen. Ziaur Rehman of Bangladesh, Bhutan was very enthusiastic about it. Bhutan even hosted a ministerial level preparatory meeting of South Asian countries in Thimphu in 1985 as a prelude to the formation of SAARC. Apart from the economic and trade benefits accruing from an organisation for regional cooperation, SAARC has provided Bhutan an opportunity to open up to the regional space and the larger world outside. For Bhutan, joining in SAARC was a positive step in the direction of modernisation and interaction with the larger world.

Professor Mohammed Khalid from Panjab University, Chandigarh chaired the third technical session of the Seminar. **Dr Rajesh Kumar**, from GNDU, Amritsar, explained through his paper on **"SAARC: Challenges of Human Trafficking, Illegal Migration and Human Security"**, conceptualises changing notions of security right from the emergence of world order in 1945 through cold war period to the present globalised world. Dr Rajesh addresses the new insecurities like trafficking in persons and illegal population movements introduced or worsened by globalisation from a human security perspective by identifying factors that heighten the insecurity of persons within countries of origin, transit and destination. He analyses various challenges and prospects of cooperation among SAARC nations who have several bilateral outstanding problems and also examines responses to the problems in countries confronting them.

Dr Gurnam Chand, Associate Professor and Head Department of Political Science, M.R. Govt, College, Fazilka in his presentation on **"Strengthening SAARC: India-Sri Lanka Experience"**, pointed out that to make SAARC vibrant, a qualitative change is required among SAARC members to improve the form and content of bilateral relations among members. In this context, he discusses the growth of India Sri Lanka relations during the last two and half decades as an interesting example of building win-win relationship. It will help create better understanding among members to appreciate the nuances of collective cooperation.

Dr Hari K. Sharma from Delhi University, presented a paper on **"Trends of Regional Integration and SAARC".** He explored that ever since the inception of SAARC in 1985, the regional grouping has failed to achieve any breakthrough both in terms of improving trade or reducing political tensions. The region has witnessed political instability, military takeovers, ethnic clashes, arms race, nuclear weapons, terrorism, conflict on borders and even possibility of wars; rather than economic integration. It is not that South Asian economies didn't achieve progress but SAARC has played a very limited role in that. In comparison to other regional groupings SAARC has failed both at the operational and deliverance level. Dr Hari attempts to locate SAARC in the galaxy of other regional groupings and highlight the short-sightedness of its political and institutional leadership which still presents a contrasting picture in the face of a global wave of economic cooperation.

Dr Bawa Singh, Assistant Professor, Central University of Punjab, Bathinda in his paper **"Mapping SAARC's Role in the Changing Geopolitical and Geostrategic Landscape"**, discusses that Geostrategic challenges are posing serious security concerns for SAARC. Many serious charges have already been leveled against SAARC not being fully realised its regional cooperation potential as well as not been able to check the strategic challenges. He analyses that how an emerging geopolitics and geostrategic challenges has been making it ineffective in realising its regional cooperation as well as failed to achieve its set goals and objectives.

The third Technical session of the Seminar was chaired by **Dr Deepak Kumar Singh** from Panjab University, Chandigarh. **Dr Rajnish Saryal**, Assistant Professor in Political Science, Panjab University Regional Centre, Ludhiana in his presentation discusses that the South Asian region that comprises of seven developing countries is one of the highly vulnerable regions of the world due to its unique topographical, climatic and costal conditions. The climate change has further aggravated this situation particularly by making costal countries more vulnerable in the event of sea rise due to global warming. His paper intends to explain the potential role of SAARC to articulate a common agenda on climate change of SAARC members. The paper further seeks to unravel the capacity of SAARC as a negotiating agent in the collective bargaining on post Kyoto regime vis-à-vis European Union. Dr Saryal argues that the South Asian Association for Regional Cooperation (SAARC), showcases a great potential for such collective bargaining in the climate change discourse.

Dr Madhu Chopra from Kurukshetra University, Kurukshetra, through her paper on **"Terrorism in South Asia and its impact on Indian Security"**, raised the concern that South Asia has been the major target areas of terrorism, insurgencies and separatist movements in comparison with other parts of Asia. Afghanistan, Pakistan, India and Bangladesh have been facing serious terrorist activities of the highest form in the world; internecine ethnic, communal and separatist conflicts pose a serious threat to stability and inter-state relations in this region. The worst part of this scourge is that the increasing coordination of the terrorists, insurgents and radical groups with their counterparts in neighbouring countries has added a critical dimension to the entire management of militancy or terrorism in South Asia. Dr Madhu has made an attempt to discuss the meaning and some of the important definitions of terrorism and how this phenomenon has affected the security of India. And some steps are suggested for fighting against the problem of terrorism such as interacting with religious groups, developing institutionalised strategic system, addressing problems of youth, developing Effective Intelligence System.

Dr Emanual Nahar, Fellow and Professor, Panjab University in his paper **"Indo-Pak Disputes: Bumpy Road Ahead For SAARC"**, highlights the importance of Indo-Pak relations for successful working of SAARC. He examines that even after the completion three decades of establishment of SAARC, neither South Asian nations have been able to push the process of integration into full swing nor the organisation itself has become viable enough to promote peace, harmony and economic integration or prevent conflicts in the region. Indo-Pak bilateral disputes and conflicts accompanied by suspicion and mistrust have severely hampered the process of much needed regional cooperation. Dr Nahar argues that SAARC can prove to be a highly beneficial organisation for South Asian Nations, only if all the members, especially India and Pakistan work together on one platform. Considering the vast natural and human potential of South Asian Nations, harmonious economic cooperation between India and Pakistan could develop South Asian region as competitive International market.

Kanwar Deep Singh, Research Scholar, Panjab University, in his presentation on **"Curbing Transnational Terrorism in South Asia:** A Regional Concern", dwells upon the the cross-border dimension of many of the internal, often interrelated, security crises that seriously affect South Asian states and inter-state relations. Kanwar Deep Singh, examines that South Asia has the highest number of conflict-afflicted people in the world, and the highest number of deaths related to terrorism in the world. He argues that despite various declarations regarding the need for greater collaboration among states on issues related to border security, mutual legal assistance, and law enforcement, this cooperation has been slow to materialise in South Asia. His paper is an excellent analysis of the trends of transnational terrorism in South Asia and to assess the regional approach to counter it.

Dr Sujit Lahiry Assistant Professor of Political Science, Panjab University in his paper, Regional Centre. Sri Muktsar Sahib " Mapping SAARC: Towards a Cooperative Security Framework in South Asia", explains it that the domestic politics of these seven South Asian states, i.e., India, Pakistan, Bangladesh, Sri Lanka, Nepal, Bhutan and Maldives had led to the formation of SAARC. Accordingly, SAARC was institutionalised on December 8, 1985 with the signing of the Dhaka Declaration and adoption of the SAARC Charter. Afghanistan was included as the eighth member of SAARC on November 13, 2005. His paper also discusses the emerging frontiers of SAARC, like, SAPTA and SAFTA. He concludes by arguing that there is an urgent need to move towards a cooperative security framework in South Asia, which will concomitantly lead to the creation of a South Asian identity as well as a strengthened SAARC.

The fourth technical session of the Seminar was jointly chaired **by Dr Matthew Joseph C.**, Associate Professor, Jamia Millia Islamia, New Delhi, **Dr Kuldeep Singh. Harinderjit Kaur**, in her paper **"Indo-Pak Disputes: Impact on Regional Cooperation in South Asia"**, explores that how Indo-Pak bilateral disputes and conflicts accompanied by suspicion and mistrust have severely hampered the process of much needed regional cooperation in the South Asia. She argues that the realisation of durable peace and the future of economic integration through SAARC depend upon the ability and interest of India and Pakistan to resolve domestic as well as long-standing differences through peaceful deliberations.

Rajiv Kumar in his presentation on **"Regionalism in the Age of Globalisation: Reinventing the SAARC through New Regional Approach",** explained that SAARC as an institution is still working in old regionalism framework which is very state-centric in nature. The association has allowed the political logic to dominate over economics and therefore lags far behind several other regional and multilateral initiatives. Thus it has failed to provide adequate responses to globalisation. It has remained an inter-governmental mechanism which had little relevance for people of South Asia. He suggests the strong need for SAARC to redefine and reorient itself from old regionalism to new regionalism where it becomes more people-centric.

The Valedictory Session was chaired by the chief guest, **Professor M.M. Puri**, former Vice-Chancellor, Panjab University, Chandigarh. Renowned **Professor Baljit Singh**, Professor in Political Science, University of Jammu, Jammu delivered the Valedictory Address. He dwelled on the various crucial aspects of regional cooperation in South Asia. He critically discussed and explained the problems and prospects before SAARC. While summing up, Professor Baljit Singh suggested some excellent measures to be adopted for the successful regional cooperation and integration in South Asia.

I wish to thank the honourable chief guest Professor M.M. Puri for his esteemed presence. I also express my sincere thanks to all the dignitaries, students and research scholars for their active participation and presence in the seminar. I express my gratitude to **Professor Arun Kumar Grover, Honorable Vice-Chancellor, Panjab University, Chandigarh,** for his kind support and guidance.

SAARC and Indian Ocean: An Agenda for Action

— ***Mohammed Khalid***

Abstract

Founded in 1985 at Dhaka, the South Asian Association for Regional Cooperation (SAARC) came into existence on the basis of respect for sovereignty, territorial integrity, political equality and independence of all member states. Its member states viz., Afghanistan, Bangladesh, Bhutan, India, the Maldives, Nepal, Pakistan and Sri Lanka have committed themselves to 16 areas of cooperation and have signed many agreements and conventions so far. Incidentally these efforts have not made SAARC a strong regional organisation like for example ASEAN, GCC or European Union. SAARC countries including Pakistan, India, Maldives, Sri Lanka and Bangladesh have a total estimated coastline of about 11,129 km. on the Indian Ocean. Their trade and commerce is largely dependent on the waters of the Indian Ocean. During the Cold War they were among the countries demanding to make 'Indian Ocean a Zone of Peace' and 'Nuclear Free Zone'. During its existence of about 29 years, the SAARC Countries have not devised or discussed to make a common Ocean Policy. There are many challenges facing the South Asian nations emanating from the Indian Ocean and these calls for a joint SAARC effort and approach to work towards cooperation. The paper strives to point out the possible areas of cooperation at SAARC level as regard to the Indian Ocean.

* Professor of Political Science, Department of Evening Studies, Panjab University, Chandigarh.

Founded in December 8, 1985 the South Asian Association for Regional Cooperation (SAARC) comprises eight member countrie's *viz.*, Afghanistan, Bangladesh, Bhutan, India, Maldives, Nepal, Pakistan and Sri Lanka. The Association is dedicated to economic, technological, social, and cultural development of the South Asian nations. The Organisation based itself on the respect for sovereignty, territorial integrity, political equality and independence of all member states; non-interference in the internal matters; cooperation for mutual benefit; take all decisions unanimously; keep aside all bilateral issues and discuss multilateral concerns. Its members have committed themselves to 16 areas of cooperation such as agriculture, biotechnology, culture, energy, environment, economy and trade, finance, funding mechanism, human resource development, poverty alleviation, people to people contact, security aspects, social development, science and technology; communications and tourism.[1]

To promote cooperation, SAARC works at the summit level, through Charter Committee, Standing Committee, and Programming Committee. From Dhaka in 1985 to Addu (Maldives) in 2011 there have been 17 Summit declarations so far. SAARC countries have taken steps some areas to build close cooperation. A SAARC Disaster Management Centre (SDMC) was established in New Delhi in October 2006 to provide policy advice and facilitates capacity building including strategic learning, research, training, system development, expertise promotion and exchange of information for effective disaster risk reduction and management. They have worked on climate issues and set up the Intergovernmental Expert Group on Climate Change (IGEG.CC). They have addressed to poverty related issues and to suggest strategies and measures. At the Sixth Summit (Colombo, 1991) an Independent South Asian Commission on Poverty Alleviation (ISACPA) was established. A South Asian University has been established to provide world class facilities and professional faculty to students and researchers drawn from every member country. To promote tourism, the Tourism Ministers met at Cox's Bazar (Bangladesh) in May 2006 and adopted the Cox's Bazar SAARC Action Plan on Tourism. They have also built cooperation in the field of sports, arts and culture.

However, during 29 years of its existence, the member countries have not been able to make it a vibrant regional organisation like for example ASEAN or OIC, GCC or SADC. At Thimpu Summit in 2010, Prime Minister of Bhutan Jigme Thinley in his address, said, **"Saarc's journey has not been one of outstanding success"** and "We are losing focus. He further said that the squabbles and tensions between the bloc's member-states had prevented implementation of its numerous, but ultimately toothless, commitments to change. Concluding his address he warned that **"Fractious and quarrelsome neighbours do not make a prosperous community."**[2]

The organisation faces problem of cohesion due to many reasons. There are tensions in India-Pakistan relations and feeling of insecurity among smaller countries given to India's overwhelming presence. SAARC leaders admitted a collective failure to develop their conflict-ridden region and to forge a united front against the threats of climate change and terrorism.[3] Apart from tensions in Indo-Pakistan relations there are geographical, ethnic, historical and political factors that have gridlocked SAARC. Differences in political systems, historical differences, pangs of bloody partition of British India, which had left unresolved partition disputes and problems of ethnic Indian minority communities in Sri Lanka, have not been tackled successfully so far. Member countries of the Organisation have differential development levels and conspicuous economic inequalities in areas of trade, industry and service sectors which have made it difficult for them to go together.

Apart from the commonly known and discussed failures of SAARC, it has not shown the dynamism to live up to the fast changing regional and global situation. For instance, the SAARC countries signed SAFTA in 2004 which came into force on 1 January 2006. India has several trade pacts with Maldives, Nepal, Bhutan and Sri Lanka. But some SAARC members are yet not willing to sign a free trade agreement. Intra-SAARC trade flows under SAFTA remain far below its potential. As of 2013, the total value of exports by Member States under SAFTA had reached just about US$ 3 billion.[4]

Apart from numerous failures, there is another important area —the Indian Ocean—which is important to all the major SAARC countries but has not been paid proper collective attention it deserved. These countries have set up SAARC Coastal Zone Management Centre in the Maldives to promote cooperation in planning, management and sustainable development of the Coastal Zones, including research, training and promotion of awareness in the region. The work done seems negligible and ineffective given to the emerging challenges from the Indian Ocean and growing importance of its waters for the safety and development of South Asian nations. In this regard, here is proposed an agenda for action by SAARC.

Of the eight SAARC countries, Pakistan, India, Maldives, Sri Lanka and Bangladesh are either on the Indian Ocean littoral or its islands. Total estimated coastline of SAARC countries comes to about 11,129 km. This includes 1,050 km coastline of Pakistan, 7,517 km of India, (including 6100 km of Indian mainland) 644 km. of Maldives, 1,340 km of Sri Lanka and 580 km of Bangladesh.[5] These countries have a large Exclusive Economic Zone (EEZ) full of resources. Such as Pakistan has an EEZ of about 2,40,000 sq. km, India has 2.01 million sq. km. Sri Lanka 5,32,619, Maldives, 9,23,322, and Bangladesh 86,392 sq km.[6]

Their dependence on the sea for trade is enormous. About 96 per cent of Pakistan's trade, about ninety per cent of India's trade, more than 80 per cent of Bangladesh, the entire trade of Maldives and Sri Lanka is dependent on the waters of the Indian Ocean.[7] Substantial amount of Nepalese and Bhutanese trade depends on sea which is carried through the Kolkata, Haldia ports. The trading ships of these countries in adjoining South Asian waters need to be protected.

Fishing industry plays an important role in their national economy providing employment to millions of fishermen directly and providing jobs to a large number of people in ancillary industries. It is also a major source of export earnings. Pakistan marine fishing employed 1,46,917 persons and its potential was estimated at 1 million tons per year from the marine subsector alone. India has 8,118 km of marine coastline, 3,827 fishing villages, and 1,914 traditional fish landing centres and its fish catch is estimated at 8 million metric tonnes per year. Second largest industry in Maldives is fishing and its total fish catch per annum amounted to 1, 84,158 tonnes in 2006. The fisheries sector of Sri Lanka employs around 1,80,000 active fishers and another 4,00,000 in support services and the total yield over the last ten years was recorded 3,40,000 tonnes in 2009. In Bangladesh fishing contribute around 8 per cent to national income, which also is 32 per cent of the total agricultural income.[8]

Some of the most critical sea lanes connecting the oil rich Middle East, to East Asia have become highways of international trade and they pass through the vicinity of South Asia. Passing through the Gulf of Harmuz and Sea of Oman, Lakshadweep Sea, and the Andaman Sea, these Sea Lanes of Communication (SLOCS) have become life lines for the nations. As the bulk of their trade depends on the Indian Ocean, security of SLOCS can be addressed collectively.[9] Without ensuring the security of SLOCs no SAARC country can dream of the safety of their trading ships. All the SAARC countries heavily import oil from different countries of the Middle East and thus dependent on trouble free supplies. In all its deliberations during the last 29 years since the inception in 1985, SAARC has not discussed any collective initiative to protect these SLOCS.

Piracy in the Indian Ocean has become the greatest threat to the movement of maritime traffic. Threat is very real as the ships have to cross through the narrow straits. South Asia has two major choke points—the Strait of Hormuz, and the Strait of Malacca—near its borders. Rising from Somalia coast the pirates have attacked or hijacked hundred of ships in the Arabian Sea including super tankers for ransom. Piracy threat emerged in the late 1980s and nearly 2,700 piracy related incidents have been recorded since 1984 which occurred mostly in territorial waters while ships were at anchor or berthed. Rising pirate attacks have led to a 12 to 15 per cent rise in insurance premiums and a hike from US $500 to US $20,000 of the special risk insurance for each ship passing through the Gulf of Aden.[10] In the days of growing trade and commerce, this menace needs to be tackled collectively by the SAARC countries. SAARC as an organisation has least discussed about the need for a collective initiative in this regard. This can also be a prospective agenda for future collective action.

Sea Terrorism was not given much importance in the 1980s. The enormity of its threat became clear in the 1990s, as there was a sudden rush in the number of sea attacks. Such attacks are more devastating in the ports when most crews of cargo ships are unarmed and defenseless to an armed attack. In such attacks, the disabling of a ship at port is enough to halt all activity at that port for some time, especially if the disabled ship is blocking the movement for other vessels. Such an attack has disastrous economic impact. Although there are many government sponsored agencies involved with port security in each country, but a collective protection shield to secure ports can also be considered at the SAARC level.

Surveillance of Indian Ocean is another important initiative which needs a serious consideration by SAARC countries. These countries can set up common monitoring stations or launch intelligence satellite intended to keep an eye on ship movements in the waters around South Asian coast. Data collected from this surveillance system can be immediately relayed to member states if an unusual ships movement is detected. Satellite ocean surveillance can be effectively used to strengthen security of seas around the long South Asian Coast. Monitoring stations around the coastal areas of South Asia is an option to keep watch on ship movement. As an organisation, SAARC needs to take this initiative.

The two largest opium producing countries in the world —Myanmar and Afghanistan–are either part of SAARC or in its vicinity. Drugs like heroin are cultivated in these areas and the money accruing from this illegal trade is often laundered through illegal means. This contraband is sent to other parts of the world using drug mules, fishing boats, container ships etc. SAARC has addressed to this problem in its various summit declarations but has not so far developed any collective mechanism to control the ocean routes used for drug and arm trafficking. There is strong funding link between terrorist groups and drug trafficking. Waters of the Indian Ocean surrounding South Asian sub-continent have been frequently used for this purpose.[11] SAARC countries are particularly affected because the region is infested with all kind of terrorist and insurgent groups. There are a number of terrorist groups active in India. Pakistan has many domestic and trans-national terrorist outfits which are a big threat not only for Pakistan but also for the neighbouring India. Bangladesh, Nepal and Sri Lanka also have active terrorist groups in their respective countries. These outfits use sea routes clandestinely to import small arms to carry out their activities. This area needs a collective effort on the part of SAARC to stem the menace.

The Exclusive Economic Zone (EEZ) Pakistan's is enormously rich both in living and non-living resources. Pakistan established its Pakistan Maritime Security Agency (PMSA) to protect its vast sea resources in its Maritime Zone. India has a sprawling EEZ which measure about two-third of the landmass of the country and has rich living and non-living resources. Similarly, the Maldives, Sri Lanka and Bangladesh have large EEZ with rich resources.[12] The EEZ has the potential to meet the energy needs of the respective countries of South Asia. Apart from EEZ, Indian Ocean seabed is estimated to have a whopping 10-18 million sq km. area full of poly-metallic nodules containing minerals like cobalt, nickel and copper. These are resources of the future.[13] Exploration and exploitation of these resources can be commonly taken up by the countries of South Asia. However, such an important issue has never been discussed at the SAARC forum. This must be made an agenda for the future.

Indian Ocean, the third largest Ocean in the world is inextricably interwoven with and has huge and growing strategic significance for South

Asia. The Region's history, economies and security is greatly dependent on the Indian Ocean. To develop cooperation the countries of South Asia formed SAARC with some determined areas of cooperation. They signed many agreements and conventions forging collaboration in different fields. The Organisation has not lived up to the changing geopolitical environment in the Indian Ocean. With the rising spate of terrorist activities in the Indian Ocean and growing menace of sea piracy a new set of security threats is looming on South Asia. SAARC as an organisation has not addressed this issue collectively. There is need to counter the terrorists and pirates, stem drug trade, secure their ports, trading ships and SLOCS collectively. Apart from the other declared areas of cooperation, this needs to be prospective agenda for action for SAARC in future.

References

1. Charter of the South Asian Association for Regional Cooperation, Article 1.
2. Giles Hewitt, "*South Asian leaders admit to collective failures*", (AFP). Available at, http://www.google.com/hostednews/afp/article/ALeqM5g9hlUugreKBToYFgHuXj7HU62XuQ
3. "SAARC leaders admit collective failures", The Nation, April 29, 2010, p.1.
4. "Intra-SAARC Trade Flows under SAFTA", posted on SAARC official website, available at http://saarc-sec.org/
5. Khalid Mohammed, "*SAARC: Emerging Security Challenges and need for strategic initiatives in the Indian Ocean*", in, edited by R. Sidda Goud, Manisha Mookherjee: India-Sri Lanka Relations Strengthening SAARC, Allied, Hyderabad, 2013, p. 51.
6. See, "Exclusive Economic Zone", From Wikipedia, the free encyclopedia, at, http://en.wikipedia.org/wiki/Exclusive_ economic_zone
7. Khalid Mohammed, "SAARC: Emerging Security Challenges and need for strategic initiatives in the Indian Ocean", op, cit., p. 52.
8. See, "Feel Bangladesh"- fishery projects, at, http://feelbd.org/index.php?page=upcoming_projects&&data_id=85
9. Gupta, Sourabh, "Abe's quest for collective self-defence: will Asia's sea lanes bind or divide?", EAST ASIA FORUM, May 25, 2014.
10. Kimani, Mary, "Tackling piracy off African shores, More regional cooperation needed for peace and security", Africa Renewal, January 2009, p. 3; also see, "Economic Impact of Piracy in the Gulf of Aden on Global Trade", Working Paper of Department of Transportation United States of America, at, http://www.marad.dot.gov/documents/Economic_Impact_ of_Piracy_2010.pdf

11. See, "Links between Terrorism, Drug Trafficking, Illegal Arms Trade Stressed in Continuing Third Committee Debate on Crime", Press Releases of United Nations Information Service, UNIS/GA/SHC/302 dated October 5, 2000.
12. For the importance of living resources see, Zhen Sun, "Conservation and Utilisation of the Living Resources in the Exclusive Economic Zone –How Far Can We Go?", Proceedings from the 2012 LOSI-KIOST Conference on 'Securing the Ocean for the Next Generation', held in Seoul, Korea, May 2012.
13. Ibid.,

South Asian Security Perspective (Role of SAARC)

— ***K.S. Sidhu***

Abstract

The end of the Cold War and the subsequent transformation of the global distribution of power from a bipolar to a multi-polar structure had profound ramifications on the perception of security, which resulted in 'regionalism' receiving a renewed impetus as a means of sustaining peace and stability. South Asia is one of the 'critical regions with complex security' in the world primarily due to the fact that most of the South Asian states are engulfed with varying degrees of intra-state and inter-state conflicts and disputes. Inter-state conflicts in South Asia probably are highest compared to any other regional blocs. Although recent initiatives by SAARC to tackle regional security issues are encouraging, the lack of a security system comparable with the ASEAN Regional Forum (ARF) or African Union (AU) renders many of its recommendations to fail in crossing over from deliberation to application. SAARC was envisioned initially as an organisation that would facilitate peace, economic integration and prosperity in the region. In the past, any initiative within the framework of SAARC to discuss cooperation on issues of traditional and non-traditional security threats was not possible since it was argued that discussion of such issues was outside the terms of reference of SAARC. An overview of South Asia in relation to crucial security issues and a critical analysis of traditional and non–traditional security risks, based on the ground realities of South Asia, may precede an analysis of the recent initiatives undertaken by SAARC to mitigate these risks.

Countries in South Asia are beginning to comprehend the inadequacy of national security apparatuses in countering traditional and non-traditional risks and there is a fundamental need for cooperative security system to mitigate these growing traditional and non-traditional security threats. The proposed security system in South Asia ought to be based on developing multilateral cooperation based on open diplomacy to counter the broad range of security threats being faced by the region, individually or the region as a whole. Such an initiative ought to be part of strengthening the process of regional cooperation on energy, trade and infrastructure as economic integration can facilitate and compliment collaboration on security issues.

Introduction

The end of the Cold War and the subsequent transformation of the global distribution of power from a bipolar to a multi-polar structure had profound ramifications on the perception of security, which resulted in 'regionalism' receiving a renewed impetus as a means of sustaining peace and stability. Despite sharing a common history, cultural and religious similarities, South Asia remains one of the least integrated regions in the world, both in terms of security cooperation as well as economic integration.

In the past, the critical regional issues of human security were enough to overcome decades of mistrust and launch this region towards cooperative security system. The concurrence of positive trends in regionalism and prevalence of non-traditional security threats should culminate in the visualisation of a comprehensive security apparatus in South Asia. Although recent initiatives by SAARC to tackle regional security issues are encouraging, the lack of security system akin to the ASEAN Regional Forum (ARF) or African Union (AU) renders many of its recommendations to fail in crossing over from deliberation to application. An overview of South Asia in relation to crucial security issues and a critical analysis of traditional and non–traditional security risks, based on the ground realities of South Asia, may pave the way for an analysis of the recent initiatives undertaken by SAARC to mitigate these risks.

Regional Scenario in South Asia

The South Asian region, comprising of Afghanistan, Bangladesh, Bhutan, India, the Maldives, Nepal, Pakistan, and Sri Lanka has about 23 per cent of the world's population and 15 per cent of the world's arable land, but receives less than 1 per cent of global foreign investment and tourism revenues, only 2 per cent of global GDP. Compounding the formidable economic and social challenges facing South Asia are numerous traditional and non-traditional security threats. South Asian countries confront both military and human security dilemmas and their national budgets tend to favour increase in military spending which tend to have an adverse impact on the capacity of the countries in the region to provide adequate resources to spend on human security programs, *therefore,* the level of poverty remains so high. Far from mitigating security threats, the extensive diversion of resources has made South Asia one of the major flashpoints in the world, with domestic compulsions and threat perceptions further fueling the existing arms race between some of the South Asian countries. Threat perceptions in the region are also influenced by the fear of nuclear weapons falling into the hands of terrorists, or even an accidental use of nuclear weapons or a false alarm provoking a nuclear conflict between regional rivals.

Security Threats in South Asia

The 'Security' concept in the 1990s, has four dimensions, **first**: the concept of security is extended from the security of nations to the security of groups and individuals, **second**: it is extended from security of nations to the security of the international system, **third**: the concept of security is extended horizontally ... from military to political, economic, social, environmental and 'human' security and **fourth:** political responsibility for ensuring security is itself extended; it is diffused in all directions from nation states to international institutions, downwards to regional or local government, and sideways to non-governmental organisations, to public opinion and the press, and to the abstract forces of nature or of the market.'[1] South Asia is plagued, perhaps more than ever before, by multiple security threats. In many cases, traditional security threats have been aggravated by Non-Traditional Security threats.

Traditional Security

The lack of confidence among member states has been the main obstruction to regional security in South Asia. Long history of mistrust and confrontation has rendered South Asian states to be a deeply divided and compartmentalised region susceptible to volatility and instability. The South Asian region is over-involved by mistrust, confrontation and conflict which are further aggravated by poor governance and misunderstandings. South Asia is almost perpetually plagued by various inter and intra-state conflicts and crisis stemming from the lackadaisical approach of the ruling elites toward resolution of such problems based on narrow considerations of caste, religion, ethnicity, language, community etc. The persistence of multifarious problems, both within and between the South Asian states hampers the sustenance of an environment wherein basic essential needs of the common man are fulfilled.[2]

Intra state conflicts

South Asia is an area of tremendous political complexities. States like Pakistan and Bangladesh have been largely ruled by authoritarian military rulers. The political and governing institutions in most of the South Asian countries are weak while the political parties themselves lack vigour, organisation, discipline, and commitments. Taken individually, each of the South Asian states suffer from some kind of instability and consequently projects varying intensities of human deprivation.

Sri Lanka had its internal problems. Democracy in this tiny island nation has remained overshadowed by the civil war emanating from Tamil-Singhalese ethnic conflicts. The conflicts in Sri Lanka have pushed successive governments on the brink of collapse. Ruling elites in Sri Lanka failed to reform economic policies due to polarised political debate.

The society in Pakistan faces sporadic bursts of violence derived from ethnic, sectarian and religious differences in its diverse community. The conflict in the Sindh province between ethnic Sindhis and those residents who migrated from India following partition has made the province, especially its capital Karachi, ungovernable. Conservative religious elements are also very powerful in Pakistan leading to tensions and conflicts over religious differences, which has also played a major role in sustaining the Indo-Pakistan altercations over Kashmir. Religious orthodoxy is evident in Bangladeshi society manifesting itself in attacks on women's groups, prominent non-governmental organisations and the intellectuals.

Bhutan and Maldives have their own arrays of internal problems. The emerging internal political problems in Bhutan and the fallout of attempted coup in Maldives in 1987 have varying affects in uniting the country for the cause of development.

In Nepal, the series of democratically elected government have failed to produce any better result than the old royal regime due to widespread corruption and crisis of governance. The political fundamentalists such as Maoists and mainstream political parties are posing major threat to democracy in Nepal. In addition to creating law and order problems, increased human rights violations and a heavy reliance on security forces have undermined the question of legitimacy of governance in Nepal.

India, *per se*, faces several unresolved issues that result from internal as well as external sources. These include ethnicity, border disputes, separatist demands, terrorism and subversive activities, communalism, religious problems and so on. All these issues flout the basic ideals of nation building in India, that is, the ideals of democracy, secularism, socialism and federalism. Moreover, the very fact that narrow-minded sub-national interests are considered prior to the socio-economic and political well being of the country as a whole is detrimental for the development of genuinely democratic policy. No wonder the perpetuance of these problems prevent India from becoming a 'nation' in a true sense of the term, which adversely affects the imperatives of order, welfare and legitimacy. Moreover, the problem of civil violence in recent years has emerged as a more serious security issue than the problem of inter-state warfare in South Asia. India has been variously preoccupied with quelling separatists and religious conflicts.

Divergences are also manifest in values and principles followed in governance and statecraft. The Indian political system has been professedly a blend of democracy, federalism, secularism, and until its global collapse, socialism. Bangladesh and Pakistan are Islamic states where the influence of religion runs very high as an instrument of political profiteering rather than indicator of prevailing public opinion. Maldives is an Islamic society with relatively lesser influence of religion in politics. Nepal remains under Hindu influence while Bhutan and Sir Lanka are Buddhists societies. Not surprisingly, a leading scholar of South Asia remarked that 'South Asia. Nepal fell under the grip of Maoist movement in 1996 and since then more than 10000 people have been killed in the insurgency.

Inter-state conflicts

South Asia is one of the 'critical region with complex security' in the world primarily due to the fact that most of the South Asian states are engulfed with varying degrees of conflicts and disputes. Inter-state conflicts in South Asia probably are highest compared to any other regional blocs. Bilateral relations are defined by antagonism and mistrust. The differences between India and Pakistan over Kashmir, between Sri Lanka and India over the nationality of Tamilian, where Sri Lanka accused India, especially state government of Tamil Nadu for supplying arms and providing trainings to the Tamil terrorists in its Southern areas are only two of the most outstanding examples in this regard.[3] The problems between India and Nepal on open border and the Indo-Nepal treaty of peace and Friendship of July 1950 tend to present an unresolved relationship. Dispute between India and Bangladesh over illegal migration from the Chittagong Hill Tracts (CHT) and the demarcation of boundaries involving fertile islands and enclaves and also in sharing the water of river Ganges continue to persist.[4]

Non-Traditional Security

I. Food and Water
II. Health
III. Environmental Security & Climate Change
IV. Illegal Migration & Human Trafficking
V. Energy Security
VI. Transnational Crime & Transnational Terrorism

Food & Water Security

Substantial increases in food prices are forcing governments and development agencies in South Asia to reassess the policies for agriculture, food security, and international trade that they have pursued over the past three decades. In South Asia, food costs constitute the major portion of the average household's spending. If food prices continue to rise without a matching increase in salaries and incomes of people at the bottom of the economic ladder, it is estimated that approximately 100 million people could be pushed back into poverty, generating a host of political, social, economic, and environmental challenges. A well-coordinated approach is clearly required to tackle the problem of food security at both the national and the regional level.

Along with the issues related to food, access to safe water and sharing of water resources between the countries in South Asia have become matters of critical importance. Nearly 63 per cent of the South Asia's population has no access to sanitation facilities, while 11 per cent of the population does not have access to safe drinking water.

Health Security

The AIDS epidemic poses a crucial security threat in South Asia, particularly to India. Since India shares a porous border with its neighbours, cross border movement of infected patients poses severe threats to Bangladesh, Bhutan, Nepal, Pakistan, and Sri Lanka. Adding to this threat is the re-emergence of new strains of older diseases such as tuberculosis (TB) and cholera that are increasingly resistant to medical treatment. The unprecedented scale of movement of people and goods, along with the misuse or over-use of antibiotics, rapid urbanisation, poor sanitation and weak health care infrastructures, exacerbates the possibility of a global pandemic and threatens to overwhelm the health care capacities of many South Asian states.

Environmental Security and Climate Change

South Asia is among the world's most vulnerable regions to both natural and man-made disasters. Over the last 25 years, disasters have killed nearly half a million people in South Asia and inflicted colossal financial damages. India had by far the highest number of disaster events, but flooding in Bangladesh claimed the most lives. The importance of environmental security is not confined to man made and natural disasters but is also reflected on issues of environmental degradation and sustainability. South Asia as a region is characterised by extremely high environmental stress resulting from floods, scarcity of water, high urban population density, energy shortages, deforestation, and air pollution.

Climate change is expected to exacerbate the existing vulnerabilities in South Asia, leading to the further depletion of scarce food and water resources, augmenting migration and increasing the number of internally displaced people.

Irregular Migration and Human Trafficking

Regional migration has risen to the top of the security agenda in South Asia, due in part to concerns that irregular migration flows could result in extremist elements entering in to a country in a clandestine way and then engage in acts of terrorism or organised crime results in undermining the security of the country Concerns relating to migration although in most cases are played up and exaggerated to serve the interest of some political parties, specially prior to elections, given the impact of migration patterns on national security interests and interstate political relations. This important development within South Asia, has become a highly emotive issue and will need to be addressed. Some may even argue that migration management has become a critical issue in South Asia. It should also be stressed that throughout South Asia two types of migration is taking place, across borders and within individual countries.

Energy Security

Access to efficient and clean energy has become a critical issue for the functioning of economies. Not only are South Asian economies growing rapidly, but the demand for energy is also growing at an unprecedented rate. The uneven distribution of energy supplies among South Asian countries has generated significant vulnerabilities for their economies. Threats to energy security in South Asia are predominantly caused by lack of political will among several energy producing countries to share resources with neighbouring countries, as well as by the lack of regional cooperation in distributing energy. Apart from regional issues, rising costs of fossil fuels (specifically, oil and gas) and environmental hazards caused by coal-generated power plants will be a source of energy insecurity in the foreseeable future.

Transnational Crime and Terrorism

The absence of regional security cooperation has led to the proliferation of terrorism and transnational criminal elements throughout South Asia, with severe consequences. The bulk of transnational criminal activities in South Asia comprises of smuggling and human trafficking. Despite the negative economic impact of smuggling of consumer goods, the most nefarious form of smuggling are arms and drugs. The exploitation of poor local people as 'drug mules', the corruption of border security and the social costs of drug compound to create a significant human security concern.

Recent terror attacks have exemplified the ability of transnational terrorist organisations to instigate volatility and insecurity in an entire region by igniting confrontation between two of the largest military powers. Evidence exists of collaboration between terrorist groups from regional countries, as well as extremists seeking safe haven or expanding their bases by residing in neighbouring states.

Initiatives by SAARC

SAARC was envisioned initially as an organisation that would facilitate peace, economic integration and prosperity in the region. In the past, any initiative within the framework of SAARC to discuss cooperation on issues of traditional and non-traditional security threats was not possible since it was argued that discussion of such issues was outside the terms of reference of SAARC. However, the subject of combating terrorism within South Asia has been given the highest priority. Both traditional and non-traditional security issues are now being addressed by several SAARC member states within the framework of SAARC itself.

The inclusion of Afghanistan in SAARC has further highlighted the importance of the need for a platform to discuss security issues. India's emergence as a major global power, combined with the security challenges, particularly terrorism, faced by South Asia as a region and by each of its member states individually, has led to the realisation, at the highest political level, that an effective regional security system has now become necessary to ensure the security and development of South Asia.

Contours of Security System in South Asia

The proposed System is envisioned as independent from SAARC as incorporating it within SAARC would require modification of its charter. In the future, provided that structural and legislative amendments are undertaken to facilitate the incorporation of the system within SAARC, it could act as the overseeing body. The constituents of the ASEAN Regional Forum (ARF), particularly its annual security dialogue can be implemented within this system. Since several member states of SAARC are discussing security issues under the ARF, it is only viable that a forum should exist for the discussion of South Asian security issues.

The dynamics of security system in South Asia ought to be based on developing multilateral cooperation based on public diplomacy to counter the wide range of security threats being faced by the region, individually or the region as a whole. Such an initiative ought to be part of strengthening the process of regional cooperation on energy, trade and infrastructure as economic integration can facilitate and compliment collaboration on security issues.

Cooperative Security in South Asia

To ensure peace and stability in the least integrated South Asian region, the socio-economic development route has to be followed by increasing trade, investment and energy cooperation, ensuring equitable sharing of resources, sustainable growth and prosperity to create a safe and stable environment in South Asia which will be conducive to robust security cooperation. Security collaboration is thus inherently linked to economic integration and addressing both issues under a single architecture which has both Track 1 and 2 elements, but is not constrained by the modalities of SAARC, is, in my opinion, the most practical approach to collectively address the diverse range of issues facing our region. One of the fundamental steps in achieving cooperative security is the formation of a holistic security system which would espouse security cooperation between politically diverse nations through a wide network of institutions.

To view security in the narrow perspective of settling issues through war is an outmoded and preposterous proposition. While accounting for the severe constraints and impediments in overcoming deeply entrenched regional acrimonies, it may be logical to conclude that a regional security system is an important step towards regional cooperation on security issues and economic integration. Confidence building, preventative diplomacy, conflict prevention are all steps, which if undertaken through an institutional mechanism, may eventually draw all the regional countries to collectively fight the common threats as well as benefit from each other's economies. Filtration with extra-regional power, therefore, has considerably crippled the prospects of co-operation in the South Asian Region, thereby, undermining both security and prosperity.

A new paradigm of development, is needed which 'puts people at the centre of development, regards economic growth as a means and not as an end, protects the life opportunities of future generations as well as the present generations and respects the natural system on which all life depends.'[5] 'This paradigm will help build society where the right of food is as revered as the right to vote, where the right to a basic education is as deeply enshrined as the right of free press and when the right to development is considered one of the fundamental human rights.'[6] The states of the region have to give up emotional approach to resolve mutual issues.

Obstructions in co-operative security

There are issues like Siachin, Wuler Barrage and Demarcation of Sir Creek etc., to be resolved, but it appears peace in South Asia primarily hinges on the resolution of Kashmir imbroglio. How to achieve it, ought to be the central focus of SAARC, which unfortunately has evaded, pooling collective insight of the member countries, to arrive at a consensus to act as moral force on both India and Pakistan to start a dialogue, with the explicit commitment on both sides, that taking a rigid stance would only unleash violence and catastrophe. 'Resolving the Kashmir issue will require restraint from, and dialogue between, New Delhi and Islamabad...on searching for such a framework, it is worth looking at other peace process models'.[7]

The hasty retreat of the British Raj and the bitterness generated between the ruling elites of the two major south Asian states gravely disrupted the traditional complementarities and cohesion. Indeed, the legacy of state formation in South Asia bestows a unique complexity to the entire region. Thus, some of the contentious issues that inhibit cooperation in South Asia include those resulting from colonial legacies, issues of political and ideological character, issues of strategic conflict and military balance, issues that arise from the spill-over effect of internal conflicts and turmoil in a given country on its neighbours and issues that arise out of resource and developmental conflicts. The most pronounced security dilemma, however, stems from escalating arms race in South Asia, particularly between the two military powers – India and Pakistan. These disputes among countries further complicate the scenario and have created a lot of problems among the leaders for friendly talks.

Similarly, the cultural diversity based on languages, religions and ethnicities is another factor that disabled region to unite. Rather it frequently exerts a negative impact on inter-state relations in South Asia due to religious differences. For example, Pakistan's deep commitment to create an Islamic state and Bharatiya Janata Partiy's (BJP's) commitment to make India purely a Hindu state are two this kind of school of thoughts that hampers state making in South Asia. The area is characterised by countries with widely differing political systems – democracies, military dictatorships and monarchies. Though most of the South Asian states have emerged with shared colonial pasts, similar political experiences, common social values divergences, however, are still significant. India and Sri Lanka are said to have performed better than other functioning democracies with varying degrees of success. Pakistan and Bangladesh, at the beginning of the 1990s witnessed a sweeping democratic transition in their domestic scenarios. But in a long-term perspective, both have yet to institutionalise democracy and confirm the capability of the political system to keep the military out of politics. Nepal's transition to democracy is at the crossroad following the Maoist movement. Bhutan retains the authority of monarch as the dominant institution while the Maldives has yet to experience multiparty political systems.

Almost manifestly, South Asian nations, despite their apparent adherence to the ideal of non-alignment, have pursued extremely dis-consonant foreign policies. Consequently, the major global powers have played their roles in aggravating the intra-regional cleavages of South Asia. Finally, India's overwhelming regional preponderance creates certain basic insecurities and sharp differences between India and its neighbourhood. 'South Asia presents as different political order and powers structures as one seldom finds in any other geopolitical region of the world'.[8]

The security dilemma in South Asia, its endemic tensions, mutual distrust and occasional hostilities, is largely considered products of the contradictions of India's security perception with that of the rest of the countries of the area. India's neighbours perceive threats to their security coming primarily from India whereas India considers neighbours as an integral part of its own security system. The pre-eminence of India in the South Asian power configuration given its geography, demography, economics, and ecology is something about which neither India nor its neighbours can do nothing but accept. But the image of India in South Asia is that of a power that demands habitual obedience from its neighbours. This has also been the main cause of failure of the SAARC to evolve as true regional bloc.

As it is, serious misgivings about the SAARC developing into a vehicle of purposeful and effective cooperation among the member countries are created by the history of the sub-continent, which has been replete with conflicts and discords. On top of this, since its inception in 1985 there have also been serious differences among member countries over the aims and functioning of SAARC. Such differences have been pronounced in verbal bickering in several SAARC meetings. This is in the face of the fact that closer social, economic and cultural ties (the espoused ideals of SAARC) are considered the one and only hope for building regional cooperation efforts in South Asia in the coming years. Indeed, increasing rationalisation of world trade and the fluidity of the emerging global system has increased trade within each trade blocs and those countries that do not belong to any trade blocs are likely to be the losers.[9]

The failure of SAARC arises precisely out of the effort to use the institution to focus attention away from serious disagreements within the member countries and establish some arrangements despite these disagreements. The assumption that peace can be achieved through SAARC without addressing the political problems of the region has neither been able to cultivate peace nor to invigorate the SAARC process successfully. Though since its very inception, it has been regularly able to hold Summit meetings but there are interruptions, in between owing mainly to intrastate conflicts between the member countries.

Economic cooperation yields peace and prosperity if the differences among the member states are put aside. Current level of cooperation in South Asia, however, is manifested by historical legacy of state formation; economic well-being and the size and power of individual states. It seems that powerful nations of South Asia are not interested to accelerate economic integration towards its stipulated goals. South Asia also holds the dubious distinction of lacking economic incentives for regional cooperation. History shows that regional economic integration can be successful only if the countries concerned establish a commonality of political purpose. The driving forces behind regionalism should be to forge closer links between historical rivals to prevent the occurrence of wars.

Problematical variables

The first is the management of security affairs in the face of a possible deterioration of the integrity of South Asian states. Bangladesh, India, and Pakistan each reveal a different facet of the problem.

A second problematic variable is the uncertainty surrounding the intentions of various superpowers towards the region. Even with the region's low intrinsic value, a substantial Soviet and American military presence could be established in the Indian Ocean purely on the basis of extra-regional considerations.

The South Asian security system is an insecurity system, and the trade-offs for each regional government involves minimising insecurity, not maximising security. Insecurity, whether due to internal disorder or external conflict, has become the norm after long years of independence, and one cannot honestly say that the situation will radically change for the better in the foreseeable future. The overwhelming pattern of defense relationships within South Asia has been bilateral. SAARC has acted as a forum for confidence-building measure over and above the limited bilateral measures agreed between member nations and summits have helped to diffuse bilateral tensions on a number of occasions.

On state security, the SAARC has to undertake confidence building measures such as regular dialogue and consultations at the ministerial and senior officials levels, publication of defense white papers, promotion of a regional arms registry, promotion of joint military exercises, disaster relief and search and rescue cooperation between civilian and military personnel, training for peacekeeping operations in support of the United Nations and cooperation among defense colleges on state security issues.

The efforts to promote multilateral security cooperation in the region would be more effective, when simultaneously pursued with comprehensive security cooperation efforts, which would also include non-traditional security issues. Therefore, consolidating confidence building measures in a "more traditional" political and military sense seem to be more crucial at least in advancing South Asian security cooperation. It would be important to develop a concrete strategy for systematic, multilateral and regular security cooperation efforts based on on-going bilateral cooperation efforts. Plans to promote confidence-building would also be important as a prerequisite to security cooperation.

Indian Perspective

With regard to peace, security and development in South Asian Region, India faces three dimensional out-look. One, "India is demographically and militarily the most powerful state in the region. India also in a unique position where it shares borders each neighbouring state, but most the neiighbours do not share a border with each other. The asymmetry has led to a second conundrum. India often gets enmeshed in the internal politics of neighbouring countries. It is seen as having taken sides in political battles in Dhakka, Male, Kathmandu, and Colombo, and even Thimpu- and those who feel delhi is not with them turn resentful. The third issue is the unique India-Pakistan dynamic which often holds the rest of the region hostage".[10]

Conclusion

South Asia has emerged as a regional entity in the international political system with the creation of SAARC but it failed to strengthen regional cohesiveness. Regional cooperation in South Asia cannot be said to have evolved into a complete bloc in terms of 'regionalism and economic integration' due to mainly to the prevalence of conflict over the desire of peace and stability. Given the historical legacy and contemporary reality of endemic conflicts and mistrust in the region, the fact that the formal cooperation process in the region has survived recurrent setbacks is testimony of resilience of the organisation. The antagonistic nature of relations with large sets of outstanding issues, low levels of intra-SAARC trade and joint economic ventures, inadequate information and infrastructure facilities; independent and largely uncoordinated economic policies pursued by each country in the sub-continent and increasing 'militarisation' and 'religionisation' of the region are all indicators of lack of 'region-ness' and herald a bleak future for any type of sustainable economic integration.

The realisation of durable peace and the future of economic integration through SAARC lie on the ability and interest of South Asian leaders to resolve domestic as well as long-standing differences. Any realistic assessment of the prospects for the growth of economic integration depends on as how individual country address existing contentious issues and their commitment in promoting regional cooperation given the extensive heterogeneity of state formation and economic dynamics in South Asia.

The South Asian experience has demonstrated that political factors can cause longlasting breakdown of establishment of economic links. Moreover, if peace is to be achieved through integration or vice-versa a new paradigm of forward looking process needs to be employed by the South Asian nations wherein they can discuss contentious issues such as Kashmir; border problems; distribution of natural resources with freely and fairly. Despite religious and cultural heterogeneity there is no problem at the public level in South Asia – whether one comes from India or Pakistan, Hindu or Muslim they can hug each other without any problem.[14] The centre of the problem lies with 'politics' of the nation states and its agencies.

The dilemma with South Asian states is that they are not ready for full scaled economic integration for the fear of either is being swamped up into Indian economy due to its hegemonic behaviour or losing their sovereignty to some extent. They are also literally not ready to solve long standing political conflicts due mainly their desire to maintain supremacy one over another. At this outset, the concept that full-scale economic integration will lead peace and hence 'peace dividend' thereof is far from reality at least in the present setting in the case of South.

Regional Cooperation in South Asia (SAARC) was conceived by the founding fathers, with very laudable objectives and its launching in 1985 did augur well for South Asia, which by any reckoning, is the most pitiable region, both in terms of economic and demographic indices and the lingering morbidity of inter-state tension, conflicts and prejudices, resulting in four wars within a span of half a century between two of its arch rivals — India and Pakistan, and running battles on the lines of control (LOC) in the wake of colossal insurgency in the Indian occupied Kashmir. This has intensified during the past decade to a proportion which has all the dangerous portents to escalate into a worst possible conflagration in the region, particularly keeping in view the stark reality that both India and Pakistan are now nuclear powers.

If South Asian Nations could steer a relationship based on accommodation and tolerance for each other's cultural aspirations, the region would indeed be free from Cold-War-fixation. A new paradigm of development, is needed which 'puts people at the centre of development, regards economic growth as a means and not as an end, protects the life opportunities of future generations as well as the present generations and respects the natural system on which all life depends.'

With very few exceptions South Asians accept their present levels of arms spending is necessary. The nuclear explosion program in India was a domestic political triumph, and Pakistan's response has merely been to threaten emulation. There is thus a difference in perspective between regional elites and outside observers, especially those in the West, about the necessity of national security. That this difference is not recent, but rooted in the very origins of India and Pakistan, is made evident by even a cursory examination of the history of strategic thought on the sub-continent.

Despite obstacles, efforts should continue to develop a regional community for security cooperation. It is likely that these efforts will develop into a "bi-multilateral cooperation framework," which will be a multilateral mechanism to complement existing bilateral relations and alliances. South-Asian states have to address contentious issues to remove mistrust so as to create environment conductive to growth to promote co-operative culture in the region and project SAARC as an effective organisation, conducive to cooperation and trust, with India as leading driver would help the regional cohesiveness grow.

References

1. S.M. Rahman, 'Report on Culture of Peace in Central South Asia', UNESCO Sub-Regional Workshop. Nov. 20-22, 1995. P..28 (FRIENDS Publication) 'quoted from Emma Rothsetild, what is Security, Daedalus, Vol. 24, No. 3, Summer 1995. p. 53.
2. Monica Bhanot; 'Challenges to Regional Cooperation in South Asia: A New Perspective' *Online Journal of Peace and Conflict* at http://www.trinstitute.org/ojpcr/toc2 3.htm; (Issue 2.3, August, 1999)
3. Zaglul Haider, Crisis of Regional Cooperation in South Asia, *Security Dialogue*, (Sage Publications: 2001, Vol.32 (4) p. 427.
4. Monica Bhanot; 'Challenges to Regional Cooperation in South Asia: A New Perspective' *Online Journal of Peace and Conflict* at http://www.trinstitute.org/ojpcr/toc2 3.htm; (Issue 2.3, August, 1999)
5. Human Development Report, 1994, Published for the United Nations Development Programme, Oxford University Press 1994. p. 11.
6. 'Ibid', p. 6.
7. Sumantra Bose, "Kashmir: Sources of conflict, Dimensions of Peace", *Survival* ,Vol. 41 No. 3, Autumn 1999, p.149.
8. Rajan Mahan, 'The Nature of South Asian Region: Assonant Affinities, Dissonant Diversities' in Kaushik Mahan and Rampant (eds.), *India and South Asia*, (New Delhi: South Asian Publishers, 1991), pp. 24-25.
9. B.S. Shreekantaradhya, 'Globalisation of Indian Economy: Strategies and Constraints', in S. Murty, The Changing Indian Economic Order, (New Delhi; Indus Publications, 1993), p. 151.
10. Prashant Jha, "New Delhi and the Neighbours", Hindustan Times, Chandigarh, June 29, 2014.

SAARC: Challenges of Human Trafficking, Illegal Migration and Human Security*

— *Dr Rajesh Kumar*

Abstract

Studies on SAARC focus on traditional threats such as military aggression, nuclear proliferation, proxy wars and terrorism. This paper examines changing notions of the term security in international relations and the scope and dimensions of a broadened regional security agenda that focuses upon human security which is under strain because of human mobility within the SAARC region. It focuses on two specific issues affecting human security that can be attributed to human mobility: trafficking and illegal population movements across India, Nepal, Sri Lanka and Bangladesh borders. The paper conceptualises changing notions of security right from the emergence of world order in 1945 through cold war period to the present globalised world. The paper addresses the new insecurities like trafficking in persons and illegal population movements introduced or worsened by globalisation from a human security perspective by identifying factors that heighten the insecurity of persons within countries of origin, transit and destination. It analyses various challenges and prospects of cooperation among SAARC nations who have several bilateral

* Paper presented by Dr Rajesh Kumar, Asstt. Professor of Political Science, School of Social Sciences, GURU NANAK DEV UNIVERSITY, AMRITSAR in ICSSR-NWRC sponsored Conference on "SAARC : Problems and Prospects" on 24th - 25th March, 2013 being organised by USOL, Deptt. Of Political Science, Panjab University, Chandigarh. Email: rkumargndu@gmail.com MobileNo: +91-9815949829.

outstanding problems, which require much efforts and resources on part of scholars and policy makers for finding solutions to problems and realising the goal of peace and human security in the region. Finally, the paper examines responses to the problem in countries confronting them.

Key Words: *Human Trafficking, Illegal Migration and Human Security.*

Introduction

Most studies of SAARC focus on traditional threats such as military aggression, nuclear proliferation, proxy wars and terrorism. This paper examines changing notions of the term security in international relations and the scope and dimensions of a broadened regional security agenda that focuses upon human security which is under strain because of human mobility within the South Asian region. It focuses on two specific issues affecting human security that can be attributed to human mobility: trafficking and illegal population movements across India, Nepal, Sri Lanka and Bangladesh borders. The paper addresses the new insecurities like trafficking in persons and illegal population movements introduced or worsened by globalisation from a human security perspective by identifying factors that heighten the insecurity of persons within countries of origin, transit and destination. It analyses various challenges and prospects of cooperation among SAARC nations in realising the goal of peace and human security in the region. Finally, the paper examines responses to this vexed problem among SAARC nations.

Challenges Faced by SAARC Countries

In last few decades, SAARC countries have witnessed rise in human mobility and they all have been affected by human security challenges, and such issues continue to remain relevant for these South Asian countries in many respects. First, they represent a subset of the transnational issues as a growing threat to national and regional stability (such as transnational human trafficking and illegal migration). Second, they have, in varying degrees, undermined and distorted institutional state capacity, trade and (legitimate) economic growth in a region that is of geostrategic importance to India. Third, all carry significant implications for the lives, welfare and safety of ordinary citizens of South Asia. Fourth, they have often raised political tension and increased inter-state hostility and rivalry. Finally, because these challenges have not been addressed by established international and regional frameworks, they necessarily require innovative and novel countermeasures—something that none of the South Asian governments including Indian Government is not so well placed to facilitate, both by virtue of its resources and leadership role.

India's neighbourhood has serious ethnic or provincial fault, which results in their blaming "foreign hand" (read India) for their internal problems. Violence in Karachi, suicide terrorism in Lanka; failurc of nation building processes, due to faulty policies adopted by successive governments and regimes, are routinely blamed on India. Ironically, both the Maoists and non-Maoist political groups in Nepal blame New Delhi for the domestic instability. In Sri Lanka, both the Sinhalese and Tamils are apprehensive regarding the role played by New Delhi; while the Sri Lankan Tamils feel, that they have been "backstabbed" in not being supported by New Delhi, the Sinhalese fear that New Delhi is secretly supporting the Tamils. Bangladesh is a classic example of how anti-Indian sentiments have become a national pastime, with Bangladeshi believing that India cannot and will never do anything positive vis-a-vis Dhaka. Worse, even if the regimes take any decisions on merits, they will be suspected of being either pro-Indian or worse, an Indian stooge. This is hardening of public sentiment, prevents governments in Dhaka from pursuing any policy that is even remotely perceived as being pro -Indian. In short, this is the regional problematique which India is facing today and is likely to face in the foreseeable future.[1]

India's bilateral relations with neighbouring countries remain strained over the issue of illegal movements of people across its borders. The problems in North-East India has been simmering on for past several years. Census Reports of Government of India substantiate this fact that substantive changes in the demographic profile of north-eastern states have taken place which has led to precipitation of the illegal migrants' crisis. The recent ethnic conflicts in Assam is attributed to the long pending problem of illegal migrants (having entered Assam after 31-03-1971) staying in the state. India's neighbouring country; Bhutan is accused of having uprooted several thousand people of Nepalese origin from their country and forcibly evicted them back to Nepal. A very large influx of Indians within Nepal has always been bone of contention between India-Nepal bilateral relations. Influx of large number of people from Pakistan Occupied Kashmir to Indian State of Jammu and Kashmir has complicated the Kashmir problem and made it very difficult for the return of 'Hindu Kashmiris' back to their homes in Kashmir in last few decades. Presence of Tamilians of Indian origin in Sri Lanka and the demand for a separate Tamil Elam and the victory of Sri Lankan forces against LTTE continue to remain a very contentious issue between India and Sri Lanka. The problem continues even as on today over the issue of rehabilitation of remaining Tamils on Sri Lankan soil guaranteeing human security to them. Undoubtedly, South Asian countries continue to have strained relationship with each other because of the movement of people across each other's borders in search of better livelihood. Except Sri Lanka, all other South Asian countries have very poor records in terms of human development index report prepared by UNDP annually. They continue to struggle very hard in meeting the targets of Millennium Developments Goal (MDGs) as envisaged under UN Millennium Development Goals Declaration in the year 2000.

Changing Paradigms of Security: National Security to Human Security

From the 1980s onwards, and especially after the collapse of the Soviet Union, scholars of international relations increasingly began to emphasise the need for a broader understanding of security. They argued that these traditional threats have not disappeared, but that other, non-military sources of threat now seemed more pressing. One of the most prominent attempts to widen the security agenda has been provided by Barry Buzan[2] and his colleagues. They stress that the security of human collectivities is affected by factors in five major sectors: military, political, economic, societal and environmental. Generally speaking, military security concerns the two-level interplay of the armed offensive and defensive capabilities of states, and states' perceptions of each other's intentions. Political security concerns the organisational stability of states, systems of government and the ideologies that give them legitimacy. Economic security concerns access to the resources, finance and markets necessary to sustain acceptable levels of welfare and state power. Societal security concerns the sustainability, within acceptable conditions for evolution, of traditional patterns of language, culture, religious national identity and custom. Environmental security concerns the maintenance of the local and the planetary biosphere as the essential support system on which all other human enterprises depend. To Buzan, these five sectors do not, stresses, operate in isolation from one another. Buzan's concept of security, even with the formulation in terms of five sectors, has the state (and state sovereignty) as the core referent object of security.[3]

The 1990s witnessed a proliferation of works that focused on the individual and societal dimensions of security (for example, Buzan 1991;

Sorensen 1996; Bilgin, Booth, and Jones 1998; Buzan, Waever, and Wilde 1998; Krause and Williams 1998). Academics who were critical of established ways of thinking about security called for dropping the traditional assumption that security could be understood and practiced within an interstate framework. Post-Cold War approaches turned toward frameworks that looked at the threats faced by nonstate actors (individuals, social groups, and the global society) as well as states. In the post-Cold War era, the academic debate on security was accompanied by practitioners' increasing interest in "human security," which in turn was warranted by a series of developments that were visible during the Cold War but became more apparent in its aftermath. These developments included—

(a) growing disparities in economic opportunities both within and between states;

(b) increasing hardships faced by peoples in the developing world who found themselves on the margins of a globalising world economy;

(c) diminishing nonrenewable resources leading families and groups to become refugees;

(d) rising anti-foreigner feelings and violence in reaction to migration pressures from the developing to the developed world; and

(e) proliferating intrastate conflicts increasing public interest in, and pressure for, humanitarian intervention.

Furthermore, it was not only an increase in public awareness of the aforementioned developments but also growing consciousness of the costs incurred as a result of the kinds of security practices produced by the established ways of thinking that provided the impetus for an alternative approach. In the post-Cold War era, a range of actors including academics, the United Nations, and non-governmental organisations explored individual and societal dimensions of security. [4]

In 1990s United Nations Development Program (UNDP) further developed this concept of human security. The UNDP report pointed out two ways in which the concept of security should be changed:

(1) the stress put on territorial security should be shifted toward people's security, and

(2) security should be sought not through armaments but through sustainable development.

The report made four points concerning the need to move away from a national security approach toward an approach that emphasises human security. **First**, the authors of the UNDP report presented human security as a universal concern that is relevant to people across the world regardless of geographical location. The process of globalisation has created a third world within the first world as well as a first world within the third world. **Second**, the report maintained that the components of security are interdependent; distress in one part of the world is likely to affect other parts of the world. **Third**, human security is best ensured through prevention rather than intervention after the crisis takes its toll. **Fourth**, the report argued that the referent for security (that is, the focus for security thinking and practices) should be the people rather than states.[5]

The UN Human Development Report 1994 defined human security as to include "safety from chronic threats such as hunger, disease, and repression as well as protection from sudden and harmful disruptions in the pattern of daily life."[6] Later the concept was expanded to include economic, health and environmental concerns as well as physical security of the individual. Advocates of human security tend to be dismissive of old concepts of "geo-politics" and "nation-state" and stress on the need to confront and resolve challenges created by the changing nature of state system rather than on armed conflict, power balancing etc… Human security, however addresses 'world system' is based on the key human security postulate that peace and security need to be refocused away from the state toward human rights and equality in resources, health and environment, among other things.[7] It is also very much present in the report drawn up by Koffi Annan, the UN Secretary-General, in preparation for the September 2000 Millennium Summit.[8] Today, human life and dignity are the keywords. The UNDP lists seven dimensions of security: economic, food, health, environmental, personal, community and political. This very broad and therefore unwieldy definition, with 'vulnerability' as its defining feature, is supported by Japan, one of the proponents of human security.[9]

Nowadays governments are giving more stress on issues such as drugs, health and global warming, which fall under the 'comprehensive security'. A comprehensive security strategy starts with the recognition that there are various security dimensions in the current international environment. The concept is based on the idea that security is comprehensive in nature and should not be restricted only to military issues. It however did not exclude military capabilities. Later on in 1990s the concept of cooperative security emerged, it carried a few of elements of all others and included cooperative efforts for achieving security. These efforts would be towards issues of common concern. This has become a attractive security concept as it works around the welfare of all parties going for cooperative measures.[10]

In recent years a variety of scholars have argued for a widening of the security agenda to cover a variety of economic, social, ecological and demographic issues. Among the most discussed non-traditional security issues are transnational terrorism, human trafficking as part of organised crime, international migration, asylum seekers and environmental degradation.

In the 1998 text book *World Security* a wide range of 'new categories' of security challenges are examined, including arms proliferation, international migration, transnational crime including human trafficking, ethnic warfare and environmental degradation. According to the editors, Klare and Chandrani, who identified seven issues that are commonly associated with contemporary sources of transnational instability: internal war and conflict; terrorism; heroin and cocaine trade; piracy; the transnational diffusion of infectious disease; environmental degradation; and unregulated mass population movements.[11]

Politically, globalisation has changed the concept of security from all dimensions, making the world to remain a dangerous and highly uncertain to live in. By and large, all nations within the region including India will continue to face a number of significant challenges to its security. For example, if one or more governments in the region lose their ability to contain internal political conflict and humanitarian crisis, the maintenance of public order are simply failed to provide for the immediate need of their people. It will create conditions for a catastrophic civil unrest. Thus in recent times with fast pace of globalisation and complicated issues being faced by states, the understanding of security have become crucial for betterment of humanity. These contemporary concerns in SAARC region include human trafficking, illegal movement of people (migration), terrorism, 'naxalism-maoism', poverty, population growth, health, environment, cultural, religious and ethnic. The next few sections deal with the human mobility and emerging threats to human security being faced by people and governments of SAARC countries and the challenges and prospects of their cooperation on such vexed issues.

Human Trafficking and Illegal Movement of People (Migration) as Threats to Human Security in South Asia:

South Asian countries do feel the necessity of dealing effectively with the increasingly wide-spread phenomenon of human trafficking.

There is also a greater realisation of having effective partnerships involving all stakeholders–governments, lawmakers, media, NGOs, regional and international organisations for getting this problem ended. This form of contemporary slavery violates the notion of universal human rights as well as social work ethics. Support for these values is well articulated in the Universal Declaration of Human Rights, Article 4, the International Covenant on Civil and Political Rights, Article 8, and the International Covenant on Economic, Social, and Cultural Rights, Article 7. The SAARC Convention on Prevention of Trafficking in Children and Women[12] defines severe forms of trafficking to include sex trafficking, peonage, debt bondage, and involuntary servitude and slavery, all of which are based upon violent and abusive criminal means of control. All of these declarations have been well supported in the social work literature and codes of ethics, thus compelling social workers to strive to uphold and protect the rights of this vulnerable population. India is a major destination country for sex-trafficked girls (Human Rights Watch, 1996; USDOS, 2008) with large numbers of Nepalese, Bangladeshi, and rural Indian females trafficked to Indian cities, particularly Mumbai (Bombay; India Department of Census, 2007). There is no accurate figure of the numbers trafficked. Many of the girls are compelled by a combination of economic hardships, obligations to family and, at the same time, inability to break out of a narrow gender-based role.[13] It is necessary to mention here that numbers mentioned above must have increased substantially as they are taken from previous year reports and census.

Trafficking in persons is a particularly egregious criminal activity in which perpetrators intentionally seeks out the weakest and most vulnerable members of a society in order to exploit them for personal gain, frequently by exploiting conditions of poverty or forced migration due to civil unrest or the collapse of economic systems. It is important to include trafficking in persons as a distinct manifestation of globalisation in a discussion of human security for several reasons. First, the growth of trafficking in humans has reached such proportions as to present a significant human rights crisis in countries of origin, transit and destination. The second is the degree to which certain populations are specifically at risk for being exploited because of their particular vulnerabilities, economic, political and social factors can all contribute to creating a heightened status of insecurity among certain segments of a population. Traffickers identify and target individuals who are characteristically vulnerable, thereby ensuring greater success for themselves. And finally, although a crime against individuals, trafficking in persons relies heavily upon the complicity of government institutions and their employees.[14] Tragically, many of these institutions are designated guardians of vulnerable populations. Consequently, women and children are increasingly at risk in environments that are traditionally considered safe, their communities, families, and public places of business and commerce. A human security framework will therefore provide a basis for specific policy and institutional changes necessary to protect vulnerable populations from the risk of being trafficked in their countries of origin as well as in countries of transit and destination.[15]

Recent Trends in Human Trafficking

Over the last decade, the issue of human trafficking has moved from the margins to the mainstream of international legal and political discourse. Globalisation has complicated and added potency to internal conflict and terrorism. While creating wealth and better opportunities for many people, it has often negatively influenced the vulnerable members of society. The diffusion of information technology, the advancement in transportation and communication, and the free flow of financial capital, have all accelerated the movement of people. However, those who have been marginalised or deprived by poverty and inequity have up to now found it difficult to even voice their protest, except with extreme acts of terror like suicide bombings.

In this paper, trafficking is understood to be the movement of people, through coercion or deception, for the purpose of putting them into exploitative or slavery-like conditions (such as forced prostitution, sweatshop labour, and domestic work, to name a few examples). *The U.N. Report of Year 2000, estimates that 600,000-800,000 people are* trafficked across borders each year, with 60,000 to 70,000 people trafficked into the South *Asia alone.* As for the number of people trafficked within national borders, current estimates place that number between two to four million people per year. A high-profit, low-risk crime and human rights violation, human trafficking is now widely recognised as a major source of revenue for transnational organised crime syndicates, which use their established networks for arms and drug trafficking to engage in this increasingly sophisticated and brutal trade in people. As the more pernicious effects of globalisation come to bear through augmented poverty and increased inequality in many parts of the world, we can expect a rise in trafficking. More and more migrants who choose to migrate for basic survival will become increasingly susceptible to the trafficker's deceptive promises of a better life abroad. Despite universal condemnation of this practice, concerns regarding the tension between, on the one hand, state obligations under international law to protect and promote trafficked persons' human rights and, on the other hand, state desires to restrict irregular migration and combat transnational organised crime are playing out in a rapidly evolving legal environment. **The first international agreement on trafficking** in over fifty years the **Palermo Protocol** (a protocol to the UN Convention against Transnational Organised Crime) was concluded in 2000 and entered into force in 2003. **The Rome Statute** of the International Criminal Court recognises trafficking and related exploitation as war crimes and crimes against humanity. A number of regional instruments have also developed over the past few years, including the South Asian Association for Regional Cooperation Convention (covering South Asia) and the EU Framework Decision on Combating Trafficking in Human Beings.[16] The UN Protocol covers three types of human trafficking: sex, labour, and organ trafficking. Henceforth, the following abbreviations are used here: HT for human trafficking, LT for labor trafficking, and ST for sex trafficking. Despite the existence of a legal framework, world over concerns are getting expressed about the worsening of the problem, especially the South Asian countries who have one of the worst records on this account.

Illegal Movement of Population (Migration)

Migration is a form of human movement through space, its initial definition is within the context of all human developments. Cavalli-Sfoerza has suggested a morphological classification of human movements that consist of two broad categories. The first include reciprocal movements of individuals which begin at home or dwelling, proceed to one or more specific locations, and return to home. A reciprocal movement cycle is defined by aggregating all reciprocal movements of a person over a period of time. In contrast to these reciprocal moves, human displacements that are essentially one-way and relatively permanent may be identified as a second major movement category. These movements are defined as migration and involves residential shift.[17]

The last two decades saw India embarking on a major move towards industrialisation. For past one decade, the Indian economy grew by an average of eight per cent a year. This was largely attributed to the stable political situation and sound government economic and industrial policies. The continuous economic development of the country has generated immense employment opportunities in all important sectors of the economy. This has placed a high demand on the local labour market, which could not cope with the requirements especially in the construction and infrastructure sectors. India has always been attractive to workers from nearby neighbouring countries like Nepal, Bangladesh and Sri Lanka. With Nepal India has open borders hence inflow of wrong kind of persons specially of criminal backgrounds takes place through this border. However, due to various reasons such as the geographical proximity of India and adaptability to the culture, a significant number of Bangldeshi workers have resorted to illegal entry. As per one of the estimates more than 3 million people travelled to India on valid documents and did not go back to their country. Smaller countries like Bhutan and Bangladesh also face similar problems like Rohingya refugees from Myanmar, Sri Lanka always had the influx of Tamil refugees in their country, however after the end of war with LTTE India has been receiving refugees from Sri Lanka in very large number. Nepal also has a floating population of Bhutanese refugees on their soil of Napalese origin. Thus, it is necessary for all the governments to embark upon on a major exercise to eradicate this problem. All South Asian countries need to learn a lot from the European Union countries regarding managing the illegal movement of people across each other's borders as well as the menace of human trafficking.

The Role of The United Nations:

The United Nations General Assembly held a thematic debate on human trafficking at the United Nations Headquarters, New York on 3 June 2008. The focus of the debate was on the prevention, protection and prosecution as defined in the United Nations Protocol to Prevent, Suppress and Punish Trafficking in Persons, Especially Women and Children, supplementing the United Nations Convention against Transnational Organised Crime. The debate consisted of an opening session and two interactive panels, one entitled "Enhancing multilateral cooperation to prevent trafficking in persons" and another "Protecting victims of trafficking and cross-border cooperation in prosecuting traffickers in persons". Non-governmental representatives from regional organisations, the private sector, media, and civil society were active participants at the thematic debate.[18] In order to combat human trafficking, the Vice President of UNGA called for the universal ratification of the United Nations Protocol to Prevent, Suppress and Punish Trafficking in Persons and the inclusion of an additional "P" – partnership – to the three "P" agenda of prevention, protection and prosecution and also referred to the Global Initiative to Fight Human Trafficking (UN.GIFT) and the Vienna Forum held in 2008.[19] Thus human trafficking includes the connections of human trafficking to economic globalisation and transnational crime. As discussed, the UN General Assembly adopted two international treaties (protocols) to fight international trafficking, which supplemented the United Nations Convention Against Organised Crime; the one protocol cited above dealt with trafficking and the other with smuggling. They are part of a package designed to address transnational organised crime. The trafficking protocol attempts to create a global language as the basis for subsequent legislation to define trafficking, assist victims of trafficking, and prevent trafficking in persons. The protocol also attempts to establish judicial cooperation and information exchange among countries.

Saarc Convention on Preventing and Combating Trafficking in Women and Children for Prostitution

The SAARC Convention on preventing and combating trafficking in Women and Children[20] for Prostitution entered on 05 January 2002 at Kathmandu, Nepal has been very historic document that offers concrete proposals for tackling this menace affecting not only the human security goals of people living in the region, rather also have affecting the bilateral relations of SAARC member countries. Under Article VIII suggests, Measures to Prevent and Interdict Trafficking in Women and Children:

1. The State Parties to the Convention shall provide sufficient means, training and assistance to their respective authorities to enable them to effectively conduct inquiries, investigations and prosecution of offences under this Convention.
2. The State Parties to the Convention shall sensitise their law enforcement agencies and the judiciary in respect of the offences under this Convention and other related factors that encourage trafficking in women and children.
3. The State Parties to the Convention shall establish a Regional Task Force consisting of officials of the Member States to facilitate implementation of the provisions of this Convention and to undertake periodic reviews.
4. The State Parties to the Convention may also by mutual agreement set up bilateral mechanisms to effectively implement the provisions of the Convention, including appropriate mechanisms for cooperation to interdict trafficking in women and children for prostitution.
5. The State Parties to the Convention shall exchange, on a regular basis, information in respect of agencies, institutions and

individuals who are involved in trafficking in the region and also identify methods and routes used by the traffickers through land, water or air. The information so furnished shall include information of the offenders, their fingerprints, photographs, methods of operation, police records and records of conviction.

6. The State Parties to the Convention may consider taking necessary measures for the supervision of employment agencies in order to prevent trafficking in women and children under the guise of recruitment.
7. The State Parties to the Convention shall Endeavour to focus preventive and development efforts on areas which are known to be source areas for trafficking.
8. The State Parties to the Convention shall promote awareness, *inter-alia*, through the use of the media, of the problem of trafficking in women and children and its underlying causes including the projection of negative images of women.[21]

The Article IX- Care, Treatment, Rehabilitation and Repatriation of the Victim simposes important obligations on part of member nations and it says;

1. The State Parties to the Convention shall work out modalities for repatriation of the victims to the country of origin.
2. Pending the completion of arrangements for the repatriation of victims of crossborder trafficking, the State Parties to the Convention shall make suitable provisions for their care and maintenance. The provision of legal advice and health care facilities shall also be made available to such victims.
3. The State Parties to the Convention shall establish protective homes or shelters for rehabilitation of victims of trafficking. Suitable provisions shall also be made for granting legal advice, counseling, job training and health care facilities for the victims.
4. The State Parties to the Convention may also authorise the recognised non-governmental organisations to establish such protective homes or shelters for providing suitable care and maintenance for the victims of trafficking.
5. The State Parties to the Convention shall encourage recognised non-governmental organisations in efforts aimed at prevention, intervention and rehabilitation, including through the establishment of such protective homes or shelters for providing suitable care and maintenance for the victims of trafficking.[22]

Finally under Article X it has been stated that the State Parties to the Convention shall adopt, in accordance with their respective Constitutions, the legislative and other measures necessary to ensure the implementation of the Convention.[23] However, going by the past records of SAARC's functioning a deep suspicion gets cast over the willingness of member countries to address these issues within the sub-continent. The strained relationship between India and Pakistan often overshadows the smooth functioning of SAARC that raises serious doubts about the implementation of provisions under SAARC Convention on Preventing and Combating Trafficking in Women and Children for Prostitution.

Conclusion

Globalisation has resulted into bringing countries and people closer to each other. At the same time it has raised the aspirations of people for better living standards world over, especially, in Third World countries. As a result of procedural lapses and absence of human face in the implementation of norms of globalisation, a huge schism has been created within the society. It has led to prosperity of few and misery of masses and created a sort of first world and third world like situation within the respective countries itself. If the world has witnessed an astonishing technological revolution that has expedited the process of globalisation, it has also resulted in giving rise to transnational organised crimes exponentially. Those who are involved in committing of organised crimes are making use of those very technologies for perpetrating such crimes like human trafficking and enticing people for migration and making fullest use of the potential vulnerabilities of poor people in regions like South Asia which continues to be faced with socio-economic challenges of monstrous nature. Though, economic disenfranchisement and the violation of human rights in particular are areas that must be addressed by states' governance and integrated into comprehensive prevention and protection programs. Another area of concern is the extent to which anti-trafficking programs in countries of origin and transit are supported by the influx of outside funds and get paralysed once these funds are spent, there is a danger that antitrafficking programs will cease. South Asian countries, which have been facing severe economic challenges, and have less than satisfactory records in human rights protection, one remains skeptical those SAARC countries, will assume an aggressive role in protecting potential victims of trafficking or illegal migration. Fostering an international climate where trafficking in persons is universally perceived as a form of slavery and a violation of human rights, in countries of origin, transit and destination, is vital to any enduring progress in the eradication of human trafficking.

References

1. D. Subba Chandran, "Alternative Regional Strategy for India: A Charm Offensive to Win the Hearts and Minds", *Institute of Peace and Conflict Studies*, New Delhi, JANUARY 2011 NO 161. Accessed from www.ipcs.org.com.
2. Buzan, Barry, Ole Waever and Jaap de Wilde (1998), Security: A New Framework for Analysis, Boulder, Co.: Lynne Rienner and also see Buzan, Barry (1991a), People, States and Fears: An Agenda for International Security Studies in the Post Cold War Era, 2nd Edition, Boulder, Co.: Lynne Rienner cited in Notions of Security :Shifting Concepts and Perspectives 15 February 2007 Deliverable 1, accessed from www. ttsrl.com *Transnational Terrorism, Security and the Rule of Law* (TTSRL)
3. Weaver, Ole et al (eds) (1993), *Identity, Migration and the New Security Agenda in Europe*, London: Pinter, p.23.
4. Pinar Bilgin, " Individual and Societal Dimensions of Security", *International Studies Review, Vol. 5, No. 2 (Jun., 2003), pp. 203-222 Published by: Blackwell Publishing* on behalf of The International Studies Association Stable URL: http://www.jstor.org/stable/3186403 .Accessed: 25/01/2011 07:27
5. *Ibid.*,
6. For details see United Nations, *Human Development Report 1994*, as cited in the report of the *Commission on Global Governance, Our Global Neighbourhood* (Oxford: Oxford University Press, 1995).
7. Arabinda Acharya and Amitav Acharya, *Human Security in Asia: Conceptual Ambiguities and Common Understandings*, (Centre for Peace and Development Studies, Orissa, India, with York University, Toronto, Canada) accessed from URL: http://www.jstor.org/stable/3186403 Accessed: 25/01/2011 07:27.
8. Kofi Annan, '*We the Peoples. The Role of the United Nations in the 21st Century'*, New York, UN, 2000.
9. *UNDP, 'Human Development Report 1994'*, New York, UN, 1994. *Commission on Human Security*, 'Human *Security Now'*. New York, UN, 2003.
10. Dipankar Banerjee, *Security in South Asia*, (New Delhi, Manas Publications, 1999), pp. 293-297.
11. Klare, M.T., and Y. Chandrani (1998) 'Preface', in M.T. Klare and Y. Chandrani (eds.) *World Security: Challenges for a New Century*, Third Edition, New York; St. Martin's Press cited in *Notions of Security: Shifting*

Concepts and Perspectives, 15 February 2007 Deliverable 1, Work package 2 'Citizens and governance in a knowledge-based society' COT Institute for Safety, Security and Crisis Management (ML, Project Co-ordinator) Netherlands Organisation for Applied Scientific Research TNO accessed from www. ttsrl.com Transnational Terrorism, Security and the Rule of Law (TTSRL).

12. The Document is accessed from www.saarc.org.com.
13. Nairruti Jani and Scott P. Anstadt (2013) Contributing Factors in Trafficking from South Asia, Journal of Human Behavior in the Social Environment, 23:3, 298-311, DOI:10.1080/10911359.2013.739010 accessed from : http://dx.doi.org/10.1080/10911359.2013.739010
14. Michele Anne Clark (2003) Trafficking in Persons: An issue of human security, Journal of Human Development: A Multi-Disciplinary Journal for People-Centered Development, (4) (2), 247-263, DOI: 10.1080/1464988032000087578 accessed from : http://dx.doi.org/10.1080/1464988032000087578
15. Michele Anne Clark (2003) Trafficking in Persons: An issue of human security, Journal of Human Development: A Multi-Disciplinary Journal for People-Centered Development, (4) (2), 247-263, DOI: 10.1080/1464988032000087578 accessed from : http://dx.doi.org/10.1080/1464988032000087578
16. See U.N. GAOR, 55th Sess., Protocol to Prevent, Suppress and Punish Trafficking in Persons, Especially Women and Children, Supplementing the UN Convention Against Transnational Organised Crime, at 53, U.N. Doc. A/55/383 (2000) (entered into force Dec. 25, 2003), reprinted in 40 ILM 335 (2001).This content downloaded from 203.134.215.216 from www.jstor.com on Wed, 21 Aug 2013 00:57:10 AM .
17. H. Cavalli-Sforza, " The Distribution of Migration Distances: Modes and Applications to Genetics," in J. Sutter, ed., *Human Displacements* (Monaco, 1962), p.140, cited in Curtis C. Roseman, "Migration as a Spatial and Temporal Process," *Annals of the Association of American Geographers, Vol. 61. No. 3 (Sep., 1971) pp. 589-598* accessed from http://www.jstor.org/stable/2569235 on 05/02/2009 *03:47.*
18. **Summary of The General Assembly Thematic Debate on Human Trafficking,** New York, 3 June 2008, accessed from ***htrafficking summary280708.pdf***
19. *Ibid.*
20. SAARC Convention On Preventing And Combating Trafficking In Women And Children For Prostitution accessed from www.saarc.org.com.
21. *Ibid.*
22. *Ibid.*
23. *Ibid.*

Afghanistan: 8th Member of SAARC

— ***Surinder K. Shukla****

Abstract

Afghanistan is seen as a viable doorway for South Asian countries for access to the oil and gas of Central Asian Republics like Tajikistan, Turkmenistan, and Uzbekistan. Thus, in order to promote economic growth and reduce poverty in Afghanistan, enhancing its cross-border and transit trade with neighbouring countries is a must. It has already been five years since Afghanistan joined the SAARC but it has still not been possible to chart out concrete ways to help the country come out of the shackles of civil war. The decade of 2010–2020 has been declared as the 'Decade of intra-regional connectivity'. Instead of major powers wasting time and resources on framing strategic equations inside the country, they need to see what Afghanistan has to offer to the region and vice versa, and try capitalise on that. The region also has an equally big stake in Afghanistan's stability.

Introduction

Significance of SAARC is much clear both in the regional context and in the global context if the two speeds with which global politics is confronted are taken into cognisance. One is the slow speed in Europe and the west, the other is the fast speed of development in South Asia and the activities of ASEAN. As Narendra Modi took oath as India's fifteenth prime minister in May 2014, SAARC neighbours were invited as special guests to the ceremony. This is the first time India has invited all SAARC (South Asian Association for Regional Cooperation) which includes India, to attend a swearing-in ceremony of the prime minister. With the invitations, Modi had signaled the primacy of neighbourhood in the foreign policy that is focused on regional integration and peace. South Asia home to 1.6 billion people remains one of the least integrated regions in the world. The invitation to swearing-in ceremony of the prime minister reflects the significance that is attached by the new government to the neighbourhood policy. This will further foster the socio-economic integration within the region where India is set to play a major role.

The 14th Summit conference of the South Asian Association of Regional Cooperation (SAARC) opened in New Delhi (3rd April 2007) marking the expansion of the organisation with the formal induction of Afghanistan as its eighth member and inclusion of five other countries as observers. For the first time in its 22-year-old history that the association that groups Bangladesh, Bhutan, India, Maldives, Nepal, Pakistan and Sri Lanka has expanded its membership. The 13th SAARC Summit in Dhaka in November 2005 had approved Afghanistan's request for membership. During the inaugural session at Vigyan Bhavan all SAARC member states welcomed the admission of Afghanistan into the regional grouping as they did the inclusion of China, Japan, South Korea, European Union and the United States as observers.

I

Prime Minister of Pakistan Shaukat Aziz at the summit declared Afghanistan "a natural and indispensable member" of the SAARC community. "I am sure that Afghanistan would play its valuable role to enrich and strengthen our organisation." The Indian Prime Minister was of the view that the admission of Afghanistan in SAARC completed South Asia's regional identity. India considers Afghanistan a valuable member of the SAARC fraternity and the region's gateway to Central Asia and beyond. At the outset of the summit, a Joint Declaration was signed by Afghan President Hamid Karzai and leaders of existing SAARC member states, formalising Afghanistan's entry into SAARC. Indian ruling Congress Party President Mrs Sonia Gandhi also attended the inaugural session at which Bangladesh handed over the SAARC chairmanship to India which is hosting the summit for the third time. With the signing of the Joint Declaration, Afghanistan becomes a party to all existing SAARC agreements, declarations and legal documents.

President Karzai in his maiden address said Afghanistan's full membership in SAARC would maximise benefits to people of the whole region and underlined the need for greater economic cooperation within member states. As a new member, he said that he looked up to SAARC for development of his country that had suffered two decades of economic and political isolation. He specifically mentioned the proposed Turkmenistan-Afghanistan-Pakistan-India gas pipeline project and said it should be a priority. Mr Karzai also called for an end to extremism and terrorism, saying it impeded progress of the region and was detrimental to its security. "It is our duty to ban extremism and terrorism in all forms and sources, including political sponsorship and financing," was his fervent plea.

The issue of terrorism was also raised by the Indian prime minister and Sri Lankan President Mahinda Rajapaksa and they called for bold and effective measures to combat it. Japanese Foreign Minister Taro Aso announced that his country had contributed an additional US $7 million to the 'SAARC-Japan Special Fund' for advancing social and cultural exchanges. He also offered support to work with SAARC for improving regional connectivity. The Chinese foreign minister also spoke on the occasion. United States was represented by its Assistant Secretary of State for South and Central Asia Richard Boucher. However, he remained a silent observer and did not speak on the occasion. Only ministerial-level representatives were asked to make a statement. All the South Asian leaders shared the view that it was time for SAARC to move from rhetoric to action and implementation to realise its enormous potential. The emphasis was on tangible benefits for the people of the region. Heads of delegations from Bangladesh, Bhutan, Maldives, Nepal and Sri Lanka also made statements after adoption of the agenda. The SAARC secretary-general also addressed the summit.

CAR RALLY: The summit was preceded by a cheerful flagging-off of the SAARC Car Rally by the South Asian leaders outside the Vigyan Bhavan here on Tuesday. A team from Afghanistan also joined the car rally but it will not go to Afghanistan. The motto of the car rally is: "Connecting people, strengthening ties" and this was specially mentioned by the Indian prime minister in his inaugural address to make a case for connectivity. "The SAARC rally that we have just flagged off and the popular response that it has evoked are graphic reminders of the potential of connectivity," he noted. The rally, being conducted in partnership with the Confederation of Indian Industry, started from Cox's Bazaar in Bangladesh on March 15, 2007. It reached India after travelling through Bhutan, Nepal and Pakistan. It will now proceed to Sri Lanka and conclude in the Maldives on April 14.

Anarkali Honaryar, the only non-Muslim woman member of parliament of the Afghan lower house received the prestigious UNESCO Madanjeet Singh Prize for Tolerance and Non-Violence. She was recognised by the world body for her pivotal role in helping women who suffer from domestic abuse, forced marriages and gender discrimination and for her commitment to promote the ideals of human dignity, mutual respect and tolerance in her country. An Afghan lady receiving such a distinguished honour is a matter of pride for all South Asians. What is even more noteworthy is the fact that Afghans are slowly emerging on the regional and global stage.

It has already been five years since Afghanistan joined the SAARC but it has still not been possible to chart out concrete ways to help the country come out of the shackles of civil war. The decade of 2010–2020 has been declared as the 'Decade of intra-regional connectivity'. Afghanistan's geo-strategic location at the crossroads of the Silk Route made it the meeting point of great philosophic and cultural traits with influences of the Indian and Zoroastrian traditions and the Persian Greek and Roman empires. Its role as a connecter and as a land-bridge between Central Asia, the Middle East and South Asia needs to be thoroughly re-examined. Economic issues, primarily trade and investment, must be given due focus in any discussion and debate on the reconstruction of Afghanistan, Afghanistan can reap benefits from entrepot trade between Central Asian countries and the rest of SAARC. Moreover, even today, Afghanistan is seen as a viable doorway for South Asian countries for access to the oil and gas of Central Asian Republics like Tajikistan, Turkmenistan, and Uzbekistan. Thus, in order to promote economic growth and reduce poverty in Afghanistan, enhancing its cross-border and transit trade with neighbouring countries is a must. Road and railway connectivity must be promoted on a burden-sharing basis wherein neighbours share the costs.

According to India's former envoy to Kabul, Jayant Prasad, "Peace and stability in Afghanistan is the most important global security challenge for the world." The way to go about it therefore is for the international community to recognise the crucial role that trade, transit and better connectivity can play in this regard.

SAARC regional centres can also be set up in Afghanistan just like in other member countries. The SAARC development fund can be earmarked for the education of Afghan girls, technical assistance, capacity-building, and making the country self-reliant. It is a heartening fact that the South Asia Foundation has established a UNESCO Madanjeet Singh Centre for Preservation of Afghanistan's Cultural Heritage in Kabul where subjects such as archaeology, history of art and civilisation, museology, epigraphy and so on are being taught to students. Among other activities, the Centre will conduct a suitable training programme for Afghan specialists in cultural heritage conservation. Additionally, how swiftly Afghanistan can renovate and promote the historical site of the Bamiyan has a bearing on Buddhist pilgrims and tourists visiting the country. It can be inserted into the popular Buddhist pilgrim circuit of Lumbini-Bodhgaya-Sarnath-Kushinagar. This will give a boost to tourism as it can attract Korean, Chinese, Japanese, Thai, Sri Lankan and Singaporean Buddhists.

There has been a lot of talk about a "regional solution' for Afghanistan's problems. However, no country has a concrete definition of what constitutes this solution. It is extremely important for all immediate neighbours to be on the same page regarding this solution. Post-2014, Afghanistan needs to focus on the reintegration and rehabilitation of the thousands of fighters belonging to various armed groups as this is critical for ensuring durable peace. India, Pakistan, Bangladesh and Nepal are among the five largest contributors to the UN peacekeeping operations. There is no reason why they cannot contribute to peace and reconstruction in their own region. Following the American withdrawal, an idea of a South Asian peacekeeping contingent can also be mulled over but only after a certain degree of stability has been established and after receiving the mandate from the UN. Internal security challenges stemming from ethno-linguistic or religious zeal, prevalence of small arms and narcotic smuggling, ambiguous power relationships, and weak political structures will discourage SAARC member states to commit ground troops. However, in the longer term, the idea of a regional solution cannot be taken forward without having the rest of South Asia on board.

Erecting a gigantic security force itself cannot guarantee peace and stability in countries with a long history of deadly conflicts. People must be given employment opportunities, schools need to re-opened, focus must be given to women empowerment, and corruption needs to be controlled urgently. Instead of major powers wasting time and resources on framing strategic equations inside the country, they need to see what Afghanistan has to offer to the region and vice versa, and try and capitalise on that. The region also has an equally big stake in Afghanistan's stability.

II

Foreign Affairs Afghanistan

Afghanistan or the Islamic Republic of Afghanistan, is a landlocked country that is located approximately in the center of Asia. It is variously designed as geographically located within Central Asia, South Asia, and the Middle East. It is bordered by Pakistan in the South and east, Iran in the South and west, Turkmenistan, Uzbekistan and Tajikistan in the north, and China in the far northeast. Afghanistan is a crossroads between the East and the West, and has been an ancient focal point of trade and migration. It has an important geostrategical location, connecting south and Central Asia and Middle East. The foreign relations of Afghanistan, like those of any country, have changed along with the political, sociological, and economic state of the various parts of Afghanistan.

Prior to the Soviet invasion, Afghanistan pursued a policy of neutrality and non-alignment in its foreign relations, being one of a few independent nations to stay neutral in both World War I and World War II. In international forums, Afghanistan generally followed the voting patterns of Asian and African non-aligned countries. During the 1950s and 60s, Afghanistan was able to use the Russian and American need for allies during the Cold War as a way to receive economic assistance from both countries. However, given that unlike Russia, America refused to give extensive military aid to the country, the government of Mohammed Daud Khan developed warmer ties with the USSR while officially remaining non-aligned.

Following the Marxist coup of April 1978, the Taraki government developed significantly closer ties with the Soviet Union and its communist satellites. After the December 1979 invasion, Afghanistan's foreign policy mirrored that of the Soviet Union. Afghan foreign policymakers attempted, with little success, to increase their regime's low standing in the non-communist world. With the signing of the Geneva Accords, President Najibullah unsuccessfully sought to end the Democratic Republic of Afghanistan's isolation within the Islamic world and in the Non-Aligned Movement. Most Western countries, including the United States, maintained small diplomatic missions in' the capital city of Kabul during the Soviet occupation. Many countries subsequently closed their missions due to instability and heavy fighting in Kabul after the Soviet withdrawal in 1989.

Notably, Afghanistan participated in the 1991 –Gulf War against-Iraq. Many countries initially welcomed the introduction of the Taliban, who they saw as a stabilising, law-enforcing alternative to the warlords who had ruled the country since the fall of Najibullah's government in 1992. The Taliban soon became alienated of those countries' positive feelings due to enforced Shariat Law in Taliban-controlled territories spreading around the world. The brutality towards women who attempted to work, learn, or leave the house without a male escort caused outside aid to the war-torn country, to be limited. Repeated Taliban efforts to occupy Afghanistan's seat at the UN and OIC were unsuccessful. By 2001, only Pakistan, Saudi Arabia, and the United Arab Emirates recognised the Taliban as the legitimate government of Afghanistan.

All three countries withdrew recognition to the Taliban in the months following the September 11, 2001 terrorist attack on the United States. Following the American Invasion and the Bonn Agreement the new government under the leadership of Hamid Karzai started to re-establish diplomatic relationships with many countries who had held close diplomatic relations before the communist'coup d'etat and the subsequent civil war. Afghan war and forced migration from Afghanistan are divided into four phases.

1. April 1978;
2. 1989
3. 1996 after Taliban
4. September 2001

The government of President Hamid Karzai continued to focus on securing continued assistance for rebuilding the economy, infrastructure, and military of the country. It has continued to maintain close ties with the United States, India, Iran, the European Union, and the Islamic world.

III

With Pakistan

Notably, two areas—NWFP and Baluchistan—have long complicated Afghanistan's relations with Pakistan. Controversies involving these areas date back to the establishment of the Durand Line in 1893 dividing Pashtun and Baluch tribes living in Afghanistan from those living in what later became Pakistan. Afghanistan vigorously protested the inclusion of Pashtun and Baluch areas within Pakistan without providing the inhabitants with an opportunity for self-determination. Since 1947, this problem has led to incidents along the border, with extensive disruption of normal trade patterns.

The most serious crisis lasted from September 1961 to June 1963, when diplomatic, trade, transit, and consular relations between the countries were suspended. The 1978 Marxist coup further strained relations between the two countries. Pakistan took the lead diplomatically in the United Nations, the Non-Aligned Movement, and the Organisation of the Islamic Conference in opposing the Soviet occupation. During the war against the Soviet occupation, Pakistan served as the primary logistical conduit for the Afghan resistance.

Pakistan, aided by UN agencies, private groups, and many friendly countries, continue to provide refuge to several million Afghans. Pakistan developed close ties to the Taliban regime, which it believed would offer strategic depth in any future conflict with India, and extended recognition in 1997. Following the 2001 invasion and overthrow of the Taliban, Pakistan recognised the transitional administration led by Hamid Karzai and offered significant amounts of aid and continued relief to Afghan refugees living in Pakistan. As of 2006, Afghan-Pakistani relations continue to fluctuate due to continued controversy over the Durand Line and Afghanistan's close relationship with India. Much of Afghanistan has long relied on Pakistani links for trade and travel to the outside world, and Pakistan views Afghanistan as eventually becoming its primary route for trade with Central Asia, though these plans will of necessity await establishment of secure conditions. On the other hand, Pakistan has a two faced policy for Afghanistan. That is because of Durand Line Opposition between these two countries, the situation is becoming worse day by day. Many many Afghans believe that Pakistan is an agent of Western countries, strengthening the diplomatic attempts of them.

Others however are more pragmatic and seek to form a confederation with Pakistan. Such a confederation would in essence, re-establish the original Afghanistan minus Nishapur in Iran as created by the founder Ahmed Shah Abdali. Prominent European and North American scholars believe that such a union would bring peace and stability to both countries and in lieu of history would be the natural route to go for the better interest of both these countries, their peoples and the region as a whole.

IV

With Iran

Remarkably, Afghanistan shares a long history with Iran, as the nation was once a part of ancient Persia. There are also deep ties in language and culture, as an eastern dialect of Persian (Dari Persian) is the dominant language of Afghanistan, especially in terms of education and business. Despite such close ties, Afghanistan's relations with Iran have fluctuated over the years, with periodic disputes over the water rights of the Helmand River as the main issue of contention. Following the Soviet invasion of Afghanistan, which Iran opposed, relations deteriorated. The Iranian consulate in Herat closed, as did the Afghan consulate in Mashad. The Iranians complained of periodic border violations following the Soviet invasion. In 1985, they urged feuding Afghan Shia resistance groups to unite to oppose the Soviets. Iran supported the cause of the Afghan resistance and provided limited financial and military assistance to rebel leaders who pledged loyalty to the Iranian vision of Islamic revolution. Iran provides refuge to about 2 million Afghans, though it has refused to accept more in recent years and, indeed, tried to force many to repatriate- Following the emergence of the Taliban and their harsh treatment of Afghanistan's Shia minority, Iran stepped up assistance to the Northern Alliance- Relations with the Taliban deteriorated further in 1998 after Taliban forces seized the Iranian consulate in Mazari Sharif and executed Iranian diplomats, who were accused of being secret spies.

Following this incident, Iran almost went to war with the Taliban by massing up troops and tanks on the border with Afghanistan. As a response, the Taliban immediately began gathering and recruiting great number of men along the border with Iran. Many foreign fighters from Pakistan and Arab nations were also arriving. Iranian politicians decided to call it off because Afghans are known to raid cities and loot them, a similar event that occurred in early 1700s when all major Iranian cities were sacked and huge numbers of Iranians killed. This as well as intervention by the United Nations Security Council and the United States prevented an imminent Iranian war with the Taliban. Since 2001, the new government has engaged In cordial relations with both Iran and the United States, even as relations between the two countries have grown strained due to American objections to Iran's nuclear program. Relations very recently in 2007 and 2008 grew when Iran donated much aid to Afghan infrastructure and Afghan President Hamid Karzai vowed to stand by his ally, Ahmadinejad. Most of the Afghan people supported the Iranian government and most Iranians wish to see Afghanistan developed. In fact, the two nations have stated they wish to create a trade league in an effort to improve standards. Iran has also declared their support for the Afghan Republic in' the tense Afghan- Pakistani stiff drop in relations.

V

With Russia

In the nineteenth century, Afghanistan served as a strategic buffer state between Czarist Russian and the British Empire in the subcontinent. Afghanistan's relations with Moscow became more cordial after the Bolshevik Revolution in 1917. The Soviet Union was the first country to establish diplomatic relations with Afghanistan after the Third Anglo-Afghan war and Signed an Afghan-Soviet nonaggression pact in 1921, which also provided for Afghan transit rights through the Soviet Union. Early Soviet assistance included financial aid, aircraft and attendant technical personnel and telegraph operators. The Soviets began a major economic assistance program in Afghanistan in the 1950s, Between 1954 and 1978, Afghanistan received more than US $1 billion of Soviet aid, including substantial military assistance. In 1973, the two countries announced a US $200-million assistance agreement on gas and oil development, trade, transport, irrigation, and factory construction. Following the 1979 invasion, the Soviets augmented their large aid commitments to shore up the Afghan economy and rebuild the Afghan military. They provided the Kannal regime an unprecedented $800 million. The Soviet Union supported the Najibullah regime even after the withdrawal of Soviet troops in February 1989.

Today, unresolved questions concerning Soviet MIA/POWs in Afghanistan remain an issue between Russia and Afghanistan. Tajik rebels based of Afghanistan in July 1993 attacked a Russian border outpost in Tajikistan, killing 25 Russians and prompting Russian retaliatory strikes, which caused extensive damage in northern Afghanistan. Reports of Afghan support for the Tajik rebels led to cool relations between the two countries. Russia became increasingly disenchanted with the Taliban over their support for Chechen rebels and for providing a sanctuary for terrorist groups active in Central Asia and in Russia itself. Russia provided military assistance to the Northern Alliance, who eventually proved a major force in the efforts to overthrow the Taliban regime following U.S. intervention in 2001. In October 2005, Russian defense officials stated they will be giving helicopters and other military equipment to 'Afghanistan's army' worth US $30 million.

VI

With India

India has traditionally enjoyed good relations with the Afghan government. Historically, the region was tied to the civilisation of South Asia, and the ancient Hindu kingdom of Gandhara may have covered what is now the Kabul province. President Hamid Karzai graduated from a University in India. However India's support to the Soviet invasion and occupation of Afghanistan was cause of distrust between the two countries. It also supported the Afghan Northern Alliance "unofficially" against the Taliban. Relations deteriorated after the Taliban took power. During the course of the hijack of Indian Airlines Flight 814, the Taliban requested recognition by India in exchange for help in negotiations.

The request was not acted upon by the Indian Government. After the fall of the Taliban, India resumed previous ties. India has helped Afghanistan in the Reconstruction Process donated buses, aircraft and has imparted training to its fledgling police force. During President Hamid Karzai's visit to New Delhi, Indian Prime Minister Manmohan Singh pledged an additional $50 million in assistance to Afghanistan, bringing the total Indian pledge to $650 million — of which $200 million has already been spent. India is also reconstructing a road in the remote southwestern Afghan province of Nimroz. The project is being carried out by state-owned Border Roads Organisation (BRO), the mission statement of which states that the BRO is India's "most reputed, multifaceted, transnational, modern construction organisation committed to meeting the strategic needs of the armed forces." The killing of a BRO employee by the neo-Taliban in November 2005 prompted the Indian authorities to dispatch approximately 200 Indo-Tibetan Border Police commandos to Afghanistan in March 2006 to provide security for Indians working in various construction projects in the country.

VII

With United States of America

Notably, relations with the United States can be traced back to over 150 years, to the early 1800s, when the first recorded person from America was visiting Afghanistan.

In fact, the 1940s, the United States established its first official embassy in Kabul. The first U.S. Ambassador to Afghanistan was

Cornelius Van Engert. The first official Afghanistan Ambassador to the United States was Habibullah Khan Tarzi who served from 1948 to 1953. Since the 1950s the U.S. extended an economic assistance program focused on the development of Afghanistan's physical infrastructure which included roads, dams, and power plants. Later, U.S. aid shifted from infrastructure projects to technical assistance programs to help develop the skills needed to build a modern economy. Dwight D. Elsenhower visited Kabul in December 1959, becoming the first U.S. President to travel to Afghanistan; The Peace Corps was active in Afghanistan between 1962 and 1979. During the early 1960s former King of Afghanistan, Zahir Shah, visited the United States and met with John F. Kennedy. After the April 1978 coup, relations deteriorated. In February 1979, U.S. Ambassador Adolph "Spike" Dubs was murdered in Kabul after security forces burst in on his kidnappers. The U.S. then reduced bilateral assistance and terminated a small military training program.

All remaining assistance agreements were ended after the Soviet invasion of Afghanistan. Following the Soviet invasion, the United States supported diplomatic efforts to achieve a Soviet withdrawal. In addition, generous U.S. contributions to the refugee program in Pakistan played a major part in efforts to assist Afghans in need. U.S. efforts also included helping Afghans living inside Afghanistan.

This cross-border humanitarian assistance program aimed at increasing Afghan self-sufficiency and helping Afghans resist Soviet attempts to drive civilians out of the rebeldominated countryside. During the period of Soviet occupation of Afghanistan, the U.S. provided about 3 billion US dollars in military and economic assistance to the Afghan Mujahideens.

Following the September 11 attacks, the United States launched an attack on the Taliban government as part of Operation Enduring Freedom. Following the overthrow of the Taliban, the U.S. supported the new government of Afghanistan and continues to station thousands of U.S. troops in the country. Their aim is to help the new government of President Hamid Karzai establish authority all across Afghanistan and hunt down insurgents that are launching attacks. Afghanistan supported the 2003 'Invasion of Iraq'.

The United States is also the leading nation in the rebuilding or reconstruction of Afghanistan. It has been providing multi-billion US dollars in weapons and aid, as well as infrastructure development. In 2005, the United States and Afghanistan signed a strategic partnership agreement committing both nations to a long-term relationship. U.S.

President George W. Bush and First Lady Laura Bush made a surprise visit to Afghanistan on March 1, 2006. Hamid Karzai is hailed as an example of a great leader by most U.S. politicians, universities and media outlets each time he visits the USA.

VIII

With Germany

The German-Afghan relationship is long and has been mostly cordial. Many Afghan academics studied in Germany, many more sought refuge in Germany during the years of civil war. There has been significant cultural exchange over the years. Several of the best secondary schools in Kabul are founded and supported by the German government. Germany remains one of the most significant donors of foreign aid and partners in the rebuilding of Afghanistan. The Bonn agreement for the post Taliban governance of Afghanistan was debated and signed in the former seat of government of Western Germany.

X

United Nations

During the Soviet occupation, the United Nations was highly critical of the U.S.S.R.'s interference in 'the internal affairs of Afghanistan and was instrumental in obtaining a negotiated Soviet withdrawal under the terms of the Geneva Accords. In the aftermath of the Accords and subsequent Soviet withdrawal, the United Nations had assisted in the repatriation of refugees and has provided humanitarian aid such as health care, educational programs, and food and has supported mine-clearing operations. The UNDP and associated agencies have undertaken a limited number of development projects. However, the UN reduced its role in Afghanistan in 1992 in the wake of fierce factional strife in and around Kabul.

The UN Secretary General has designated a personal representative to head the Office for the Coordination of Humanitarian Assistance to Afghanistan (UNOCHA) and the Special Mission to Afghanistan (UNSMA), both based in Islamabad, Pakistan. Throughout the late 1990s, 2000, and 2001, the UN unsuccessfully strived to promote a peaceful settlement between the Afghan, factions as well as provide humanitarian aid; this despite increasing Taliban restrictions upon UN personnel and agencies.

Conclusion

Prior to the Soviet invasion, Afghanistan pursued a policy of neutrality and non-alignment in its foreign relations, being one of a few independent nations to stay neutral in both World War I and World War II. In international forums, Afghanistan generally followed the voting patterns of Asian and African non-aligned countries. Afghanistan is a crossroads between the East and the West, and has been an ancient focal point of trade and migration. It has an important geostrategical location, connecting south and Central Asia and Middle East. The foreign relations of Afghanistan, like those of any country, have changed along with the political, sociological, and economic state of the various parts of Afghanistan. It has already been five years since Afghanistan joined the SAARC but it has still not been possible to chart out concrete ways to help the country come out of the shackles of civil war.

References

Hindustan Times, 22 May 2014, p.1.

Magnus, Ralph H (1998) Afghanistan, Mullah and Mujahid, Harper Collins, India.

Mandelbaum, Michael (1994) 'The Reluctance to Intervene' Foreign Policy, Number 95, 1994, pp. 3-18

Afghanistan Significance of Guatanamo in solving 9/11 Celebration and Closure of 9/11- Is it a Closure?

Cornwell, Rupert (2008) 'No Justifying Guatanamo', *The Tribune*, 14 February, p. 11 Guatanamo Bay System.

Wikileaks: How India kept Kashmir out of US Af-Pak envoy's brief? Accessed by The Hindu through Wikileaks, *The Hindu*, 21 May 2011, p. 9.

Osama's death hotly discussed on Social Networking Sites, *The Hindu*, 8 May 2011, p1. Particularly websites like Twitter and Facebook debated and discussed the killing of Osama bin Laden in the internet-based social media. But bloggers focused their attention on the events that unfolded after the death of the al-Queda leader.

Taliban Betrayed Me,says Osama, *The Hindu*, 27 October 2002, p. 14

Kabul's Long Winter, *The Economic Times*, New Delhi,16 February 1996, p. 9.

Conflicting Reports of presence of Taliban in Kashmir, *The Times of India*, 15 December, 1998, p. 1.

Daullah, 'wild beast' of Taliban killed. The one-legged commander was involved in numerous hostage beheadings and training suicide bombers, *Times International*, 14 May 2007.

Small States and Regional Organisations: Case Study of Bhutan and SAARC

— *Mathew Joseph*

There are many small states in the world. However, according to the received wisdom their destiny is tied to that of big states and middle level states neighbouring them. Most of the small states are either islands or land-locked states. Their status as small islands and landlocked states make them depending on the nearby states for almost everything. In fact, the relations between small states and neighbouring big or middle level states are not of interdependence, but absolute dependence. The small states generally do not count in the power calculations of International Politics unless they are located in a strategic zone. These general principles are universally applicable in the case of small states all over the world. Bhutan is no exception to this. It actually rather confirms the above mentioned principles of the existence of the small states.

According to a widely accepted definition, a small state is one having a population of less than 1.5 million.[1] According to this definition 45 countries in the comity of nation-states can be termed as small states.[2] Small states face multiple challenges in terms of their security, trade and economic relations in their respective regions and with the rest of the world. To overcome their limitations they either tend to form regional organisations along with their neighbouring small states (eg. Caribbean Community or CARICOM and the PICTA - Pacific Island Countries Trade Agreement) or join with other neighbouring states despite the difference in size to form regional organisations like the South Asian Association for Regional Cooperation (SAARC).

Going by the definition mentioned above, Bhutan is one of the small states in the South Asian region, the other being Maldives. Bhutan is a land-locked country sandwiched between India and China. Bhutan has a population of 750, 821.[3] It perfectly fits into the category of "small states". The land-locked status of Bhutan creates many hurdles in its economic growth and relations with other countries in the region and beyond. For long, Bhutan remained as an isolated country located in the eastern Himalayas. Bhutan was a theocracy in which spiritual and temporal realms of authority were shared between the institutions of *Je Khenpo* (Secular rular of Bhutan) and *Druk Desi*.[4] Druk (Thunder Dragan) Druk Deri (regent) Political stability was a distant dream under the theocracy and that led the British imperial power to introduce monarchy into Bhutan.

The monarchy was established in Bhutan only in 1907.[5] In the first half of the 20th century, Bhutan followed a policy of isolationaism. Bhutan started opening up in the 1960s and now the country is a member of many regional and international organisations. Politically Bhutan was an absolute monarchy till 2005. Under the fifth king of Bhutan King Jigme Khesar Namgyal Wangchuck Bhutan now is a constitutional monarchy with an elected government.

When the idea of an organisation for regional cooperation in South Asia was mooted by late Gen. Ziaur Rahman of Bangladesh in 1980, six the fourth king of Bhutan King Jigme Singye Wangchuck whole heartedly welcomed it. In fact, the small countries in the region were more enthusiastic than India and Pakistan regarding the formation of an organisation for regional cooperation.

Bhutan hosted a ministerial level preparatory meeting of South Asian countries in Thimphu in 1985 as a prelude to the formation of the SAARC. This incident show the enthusiasm expressed by Bhutan in the very idea of the formation of an organisation for regional cooperation. Bhutan had her own reasons to join in the SAARC. Apart from the economic and trade benefits accruing from an organisation for regional cooperation, SAARC has provided Bhutan an opportunity to open up to the regional space and the larger world outside. For Bhutan, joining in SAARC was a positive step in the direction of modernisation and interaction with the larger world. In this regard King Jigme Singye Wangchuck said the following in the First Summit of SAARC themself:

It has always been an important objective in the foreign policy of Bhutan to develop close ties of friendship and co-operation with all neighbouring countries in our quest for peace and stability. We see in SAARC a process to facilitate the realisation of this aim and fulfilment of the hopes and aspirations of the people of Bhutan.[7]

Bhutan largely remained an isolated country till the late 1950s. The state policy of isolationism underwent a change in the context of the Chinese conquest of Tibet in late 1950s. Tibet was considered to be the spiritual heartland of the Lamaist world of which Bhutan is a part.[8] In fact, Nawang Namgyal, the legendary founder of Bhutan was a politicoreligious refugee from Tibet.[9] The ruling elite of Bhutan, *Ngalongs,* are linked to Tibet genealogically. Lose of the independent identity of Tibet triggered Bhutan to move away from the traditional policy of isolationism and embark on the path of modernisation.

Bhutan's foreign relations were determined by the India-Bhutan Friendship Treaty of 1949 (Treaty of Perpetual Peace and Friendship between the Government of India and the Government of Bhutan) till it was revised in 2007.[10] As per the Article II of the 1949 Treaty Bhutan needs to consult with India regarding her foreign relations. Article II reads as follows: "The Government of India undertakes to exercise no interference in the internal administration of Bhutan. On its part the Government of Bhutan agrees to be guided by the advice of the Government of India in regard to its external relations."[11] This article put severe restrictions on Bhutan to engage with the outside world.

However, in the context of the Chinese incursions in Tibet, India also wanted Bhutan to have relations with the outside world. This led Bhutan to take membership in international organisations like the Universal Postal Union (UPU) in the late 1969.[12] In 1971, Bhutan got membership in the United Nations Organisation (UNO) with the insistence and active support of India and it became an active member of the Non-Aligned Movement (NAM) in 1973.[13] These developments established Bhutan as a member in the comity of nations. Though Bhutan got membership in the UN, her relations with other countries in the region were practically nil. Diplomatic relations of Bhutan was restricted only to India and Bangladesh. Bhutan's intention to broaden her ties with the outside world did not materialise in the 1970s.

The merger of Sikkim, another Mahayana Buddhist country in the Himalayas, with India was a major political development that affected the national psyche of Bhutan in more than one way.[14] This development made Bhutan as the only remaining Mahayana Buddhist country in the world. The Bhutanese monarchy and the ruling elite were very much concerned about how to protect the unique identity of the country as an independent entity. The Bhutanisation drive within the country is started as a response to this and it led to the discriminatory practices towards the people of Nepali origin in Bhutan. The enactment of rules and regulations to protect the unique *Drukpa Kagyuppa* cultural identity of the country led to the forceful eviction of the people of Nepali origin from Bhutan in the late 1980s and early 1990s. These circumstances provided adequate reasons for Bhutan to welcome the initiative for the establishment of SAARC. It is explained as follows:

> The late 1950s witnessed Bhutan's growing suspicion of China; added to this the conflict between India and Pakistan exposed this small nation-state to an unsettling environment where the threats of territorial integration, internal destabilisation and political crisis loomed large. When Sikkim was merged as a state of the Indian Union in 1974 (sic), Bhutan's desire to protect its identity as a sovereign Himalayan Buddhist Kingdom intensified. One of the steps that Bhutan took towards fulfilling this objective was to become a member of SAARC. Bhutan was convinced that joining this forum would counteract external threats while expanding its relation with neighbouring South Asian countries.[15]

Apart from getting recognised as an independent sovereign country in South Asia, joining in SAARC was considered to be a necessary step by Bhutan to improve her economy through trade and economic cooperation. Bhutan is rich in natural resources. However, as a small state Bhutan does not have the wherewithal to harness them for national development. Bhutan hoped that an organisation for regional cooperation will provide opportunities to exploit the abundant natural resources for the development of the country. The Bhutanese perspective of regional cooperation is articulated by a study as follows:

> Bhutan views regional economic cooperation as a viable alternative strategy to bring about collective economic self-reliance and mutual prosperity to uplift the poorer nations. As a landlocked country, Bhutan proposed the immense need to develop air links and telecommunication between the member states, to facilitate increased trade and joint economic ventures in harnessing the rich natural resources and manpower. The changing economic situation in the world has made Bhutan

> realise new challenges posed by major economies on smaller developing nations. SAARC is seen as a forum to enhance economic cooperation and bring about greater liberalisation and privatisation in nations with smaller economies.[16]

One of the operational principles of SAARC, that there is no scope for raising bilateral issues in the SAARC platform helped Bhutan to overcome a major political crisis erupted in the country. As mentioned earlier, the Bhutanisation drive which was initiated by King Jigme Singye Wangchuck in the late 1970s and early 1980s led to the enactment of many discriminatory laws like the Citizenship Acts of 1977 and 1985, Marriage Act of 1980 and the promulgation of *Driglam Nam Za* in 1989.[17] These discriminatory laws and practices led to the marginalisation of the people of Nepali origin and finally forced the expulsion of more than one lakh people to India and Nepal. The refugee issue between Bhutan and Nepal was one of the major challenges faced by the Government of Bhutan in the last twenty five years. In this issue SAARC could not do anything due to the stipulation that it can not intervene in a bilateral issue. Now most of the refugees are relocated in third countries through the process of third country resettlement. The SAARC remained as a mute spectator to the entire episode. The inability of SAARC to intervene in contentious issues in the region is certainly a weakness of the organisation.

In the last twenty eight years of the existence of SAARC, Bhutan hosted the SAARC summit meeting only once. The sixteenth SAARC Summit was held in Thimphu on 28-29 April 2010.[18] It was the silver jubilee summit of SAARC. The central issue of the summit was the problem of climate change. The exact theme of the summit was "Towards a green and happy South Asia." The Thimphu summit endorsed of the claims made by Bhutan on behalf of the ideology and success of GNH in the following words:

> The Leaders emphasised on a greater focus to pursue people-centric development with due emphasis on socio-cultural progress and upholding traditions and values and in that regard, noted the concept of Gross National Happiness (GNH) pursued by Bhutan, inter alia, in ensuring people-centric development, culture, preservation of environment, better governance.[19]

Similarly the summit voiced its concern regarding environmental degradation in South Asia and underlined the importance of "...sustainably managing the environment and development through adoption of eco-friendly approaches and technologies and that South Asia should become a world leader in low-carbon technology and renewable energies."[20] The successful completion of the silver jubilee summit of SAARC at Thimphu has enhanced the prestige and status of Bhutan in the South Asian region.

Bhutan was one of the staunch supporters of the South Asia Preferential Trade Agreement (SAPTA).[21] Along with other Least Developed Countries (LDCs) in South Asia in SAPTA, Bhutan gets deeper tariff cuts. Bhutan is trying her level best to expand trade with other members of SAARC. Through this it is hoped that overdependence on India will gradually reduce and that will improve her relations with other countries in the region.

When compared to other regional organisations, the achievements of SAARC are very meagre. SAARC has completely failed in evolving a regional framework on all pertinent issues that affect the entire region like the problem of climate change. Despite the Charter, every country in the region is willing to pursue its national interests through individual efforts. Still, the member states of SAARC could not establish worthwhile relations with each other. According to Christopher Snedden, "The fact that SAARC has existed since 1985 is an achievement in itself."[22]

The small-states in the region benefited a lot from SAARC than the big countries. SAARC has played a major role in bringing them and their problems in to the regional space and framework. It also helped the small states in the region to think about the basic principle of modern state system, the notion of sovereign equality. This in itself is a significant achievement for SAARC. It has enhanced the status and affirmed the peculiar identity of small states in the region. The overall experience of Bhutan in SAARC was positive from the Bhutanese angle. Bhutan's entry into SAARC has helped her to mark her very presence and existence in the comity of nations and provided a vast regional space to operate.

References

1. See World Bank, "Small States: Meeting Challenges in the Global Economy", Report of the Commonwealth Secretariat/World Bank Joint Task Force on Small States, April 2000, p. 3, URL: http://www.cpahq.org/cpahq/cpadocs/meetingchallengeinglobaleconomyl.pdf (accessed on 2 August 2014).
2. *Ibid.*
3. This is the current population of Bhutan. See the Website of the national Statistical Bureau (NSB), Bhutan, URL: http://www. nsb.gov.bt/main/main.php#&slider1=4 (accessed on 8 August 2014).

4. Mathew Joseph C, *Ethnic Conflict in Bhutan* (Nirala Publications, New Delhi: 1999), p. 57.
5. Manorama Kohli, *From Dependence to Interdependence: A Study of Indo-Bhutan Relations*, New Delhi: Vikas Publishing House, 1993), p. 6.
6. Kishore C. Dash, "The Political Economy of Regional Cooperation in South Asia", *Pacific Affairs*, Vol.69, No. 2, Summer 1996, URL: https://www.mtholyoke.edu/acad/intrel/dash.htm (accessed on 8 August 2014). For a comprehensive account of the origin and development of the idea of regional cooperation in South Asia see S.D. Muni and Anuradha Muni, *Regional Cooperation in South Asia* (New Delhi: National, 1984).
7. Cited in Shashi Upadhyay, "Bhutan and SAARC" in Ramakant and R.C. Misra (eds.), *Bhutan: Society and Polity* (New Delhi: Indus Publishing Company, 1996), pp. 321-322.
8. Dorji Penjore, "Security of Bhutan: Walking between the Giants", *Journal of Bhutan Studies* (Thimphu), Vol. 10, 2004, p.115.
9. Joseph C., *Ethnic Conflict in Bhutan*, p. 57.
10. "India, Bhutan sign friendship treaty", *Hindustan Times* (Internet Edition), 9 February 2007, URL: http://www.hindustantimes.com/world-news/india-bhutan-sign-friendship-treaty/article1-193104.aspx (accessed on 10 August 2014).
11. See the text of the Treaty of Perpetual Peace and Friendship between the Government of India and the Government of Bhutan signed at Darjeeling on 8 August 1949, Documents, Ministry of External Affairs (MEA), Government of India, URL: http://www.mea.gov.in/bilateraldocuments.htm?dtl/5242/Treaty+or+Perpetual+Peace+and+ Friendship (accessed on 12 August 2014).
12. Mathew Joseph C., "China-South Asia Strategic Engagements -2, Bhutan-China Relations", ISAS Working Paper, No.157, 23 August 2012, Institute of South Asian Studies (ISAS) National University of Singapore (NUS), Singapore, p.7,
13. *Ibid.*
14. John Bray, "Bhutan: The Dilemmas of a Small State," *The World Today* (London), Vol.49, No.11, November 1993, p. 215.
15. Author (anonymous), Chapter 5 titled "Bhutan's Perspective of Regional Cooperation", pp.155-156., URL: http://www.ide.go.jp/English/Publish/Download/Jrp/pdf/132_3.pdf (accessed on 12 August 2014).
16. *Ibid*, p.157.
17. Kapileshwar Labh, "Political Development of Bhutan: Emerging Trends", in Ramakant and R.C. Misra (eds.), *Bhutan: Society and Polity* (New Delhi: Indus Publishing Company, 1996), p. 215.

18. See Ashok Tuteja, "SAARC Summit Thimphu, April 28-29: Consensus on Climate Change, Trade", *The Tribune* (Chandigarh), 30 April 2010, URL: http://www.tribuneindia.com/2010/20100430/main2.htm (accessed on 13 August 2014).
19. See the Text of the 16th SAARC Summit Declaration (29 April 2010), Documents, Ministry of External Affairs (MEA), Government of India, URL: http://mea.gov.in/bilateraldocuments. htm?dtl/3886/16th+SAARC+Summit+Declaration+29+April+2010 (accessed on 13 August 2014)
20. *Ibid.*
21. Author (anonymous), Chapter 5 titled "Bhutan's Perspective of Regional Cooperation", p.161.
22. Christopher Snedden, "Some Thoughts about the South Asian 'Region'", *East Asia Forum*, URL: http://www.eastasiaforum.org/2010/06/12/some-thoughts-about-the-south-asian-region/ (accessed on 13 August 2014).

Non-Tariff Barriers to Indo-Pakistan Trade

— *Davinder Kumar Madaan**

Abstract

It is gainful to India and Pakistan for high volume of bilateral trade as both are neighbouring countries. India has a cost advantage over Pakistan in engineering goods, agriculture products, soyabean oil cake, tyres, textile machinery, plastics, transport equipments, tea, leather goods, etc. Pakistan can gain from the import of agricultural produce like rice, spices, tea and other edibles to meet the production shortfalls at competitive prices. India can also benefit from Pakistan by importing copper, edible fruits, sugar refined, portland cement, float glass, wool, oil seeds, etc. Prices of mutual trade items between the two countries are also competitive. An attempt has been made to compute mutual gains from trade between India and Pakistan by way of actual gains. In this context, the import prices of various commodities from each other and from rest of the world have been compared. It has been seen that the prices of various items which they have been importing from each other, are either competitive or lower than the world prices. The quality of imported commodities from each other is comparable with the quality of the commodities imported from the rest of the world as the item code at 6 digit level is same for import from the rest of world.

* Professor of Economics & Head, School of Social Sciences, Punjabi University, Patiala (India).

I

Introduction

India and Pakistan were highly dependent on each other for trade at the time of partition of Indian sub-continent. After partition, both the countries resorted to deliberate measures to minimise their trade dependence on each other. There was an embargo on bilateral trade during 1965-74. As a result, both the countries were forced to import many items from the world market at much higher prices. Right from the partition, Kashmir has been a bone of contention between the two countries even after four wars of 1948, 1965, 1971 and 1999. However, operationalisation of South Asian Free Trade Area (SAFTA) agreement in 2006 boosted the intra-trade ties between the two countries. In 1948-49, India's share in Pakistan's global imports and exports was 50.6 per cent and 23.6 per cent, respectively. However, in 2013-14, this share was 4.3 per cent and 1.6 per cent, respectively. There are great potential of mutual trade because of their geographical proximity, complementarity and competitiveness to each other.

During 2013, India's exports and imports with Pakistan were US$ 1.9 billion and US$ 0.4 billion, respectively. This official trade between India and Pakistan could have increased from US$ 2.3 billion to US$ 30.4 billion (13.5 times), if both had removed certain irritants in the way of trade. Hence, they realised less than eight per cent of the total bilateral trade potentials. Nearly 70 per cent of what Pakistan consumes is from import, but her imports from India are very less.

As tariff based barriers for trade cooperation have been declining in the globalisation era, Non-Tariff Barriers (NTBs) are being used to protect domestic industry by discouraging imports. These are quantitative restrictions, trade facilitation and customs procedures, technical barriers to trade, sanitary and phyto-sanitary measures, financial measures, visa restrictions, etc. NTBs are also putting restrictions on the bilateral trade potentials between India and Pakistan. Pakistan has the grievance that though India granted Most Favoured Nation (MFN) status to Pakistan in 1996, yet this gesture has not helped in increasing its exports due to strong NTBs on Indian side.

This paper is an attempt to discuss the NTBs to Indo-Pak trade, particularly Wagah land route, and suggests remedial measures. It estimates gains from mutual trade between India and Pakistan. The discussion has been organised into six sections. Section I, the preceding one, deals with the introduction. Section II pertains to trade cooperation between India and Pakistan. Section III deals with the bilateral trade from

Wagah land route. Section IV identifies NTBs to Indo-Pak trade via Wagah and identifies remedial measures. Section V discusses the mutual gains from trade and estimates the actual gains from each other during 2012. Section VI gives the conclusions and policy suggestions of the study.

II

Trade Cooperation between India and Pakistan:

The signing of bilateral trade agreement on 23 January 1975 led to the resumption of trade between India and Pakistan. In July 1982, Pakistan declared a list of 40 items, which can be importable from India. The mutual trade between them grew significantly in 1989, when Pakistan expanded this list of importable items from India to 571. This Positive List has been further enhanced to 1963 items as on 28th December 2011. On March 20, 2012, Pakistan switched over from this Positive List of 1963 items to Negative List of 1209 items that cannot be imported from India. Thus, more than 7500 items became importable from India. This was the very historic decision of Pakistan. However, the negative list was followed by a positive 3 list of 137 items that are importable from India through Attari-Wagah Land route. On 13th April 2012, the two countries opened an Integrated Check Post (ICP) at Attari-Wagah border in an area of 120 acres, costing Rs 150 crores. Further, on 20th January 2014, Pakistan's Cabinet approved the signing of a Memorandum of Understanding (MoU) for a deal to buy electricity from India for which an inter grid connection will be built between Amritsar and Lahore. Earlier, India offered to export electricity to the tune of 500 MW to Pakistan.

SAARC, which established on 8 December 1985, has played an important role in boosting the intra-trade ties between India and Pakistan. India and Pakistan are two major countries of SAARC. SAARC led to the establishment of South Asian Preferential Trading Arrangement (SAPTA) on 7 December 1995, and SAFTA on 1st July 2006 with the aim of reducing tariffs for intra-regional trade among the eight members (India, Pakistan, Sri Lanka, Afghanistan, Bangladesh, Bhutan, Maldives, and Nepal). Both the countries have preserved 614 and 936 sensitive items, respectively, for each other w.e.f. 1st Jan 2012. On 18th January 2014, it was agreed to bring down the sensitive list of items to 100 over a period of five years by Pakistan and in one year by India. There will be no tariff reduction on sensitive items of the members. Base rate tariff for sensitive lists would be reduced to 0-5 per cent by 1st Jan 2015 under SAFTA Phase II (SAARC Sect, 2013).

Composition of Trade and Tariff

Cotton, soyabean, p-xylene, polypropylene, woven fab, chickpeas, tomatoes, black tea, tyres for buses/lorries, cotton yarn, petro-oils, milk powder, and organic chemicals, were the major items of India's exports to Pakistan during 2013. During this period, Pakistan's tariff on import from India was as high as 25 per cent on milk powder, 15 per cent on reactive dyes, 12.6 per cent on woven fab, 12.5 per cent of tyres for buses/lorries, and 10 per cent on black tea. It was zero per cent on cotton, chickpeas, tomatoes, etc.

Similarly, the major items of India's imports from Pakistan were dates fresh/dried, portland cement, cotton, petroleum oils, sesamum seeds, terephthalic acid, gypsum, vinyl chloride, greasy wool, refined sugar, leather, copper, etc. during 2013. During this period, India's tariff was as high as 60 per cent on refined sugar, 30 per cent on sesamum seeds, 24 per cent on dates, 20.1 per cent on denim cotton fabrics, 10 per cent on sacks & bags, and 9 per cent on float glasses. It was zero per cent on portland cement and cotton, and 5 per cent on copper, petroleum oils, gypsum, greasy wool, etc.

III

Bilateral Trade from Land route:

India and Pakistan share land border of 2912 Kms. During 1948-65, both the countries used a number of land routes for bilateral trade, which included eight customs stations in Punjab province at Wagah, Takia Ghawindi, Khem Karan, Ganda Singhwala, Mughalpura Railway Station, Lahore Railway Station, Haripur Bund on River Chenab, and the Macleod Ganj Road Railway Station. Wagah-Attari land route was operational for trade during 1948-65. After the war of 1965, trade was stopped from this route. However, it resumed w.e.f. July 2005. Both the countries started truck movement at the Wagah Border w.e.f. 1st October 2007 for increasing bilateral trade. So-far, bilateral trade was through Mumbai-Karachi ports, which forced the Indian exporters to transport goods from Delhi to Mumbai Port and then to Karachi (2274 Kms). Its transaction costs were 2.7 times of those in the direct route between Delhi and Attari (478 Kms) (Taneja, 2007). Land route is cheaper, faster and safe as carrying cost through Attari border is least, and the transport time is shortest i.e. one hour only from Amritsar to Lahore with distance of 50 kms.

With the inauguration of ICP on 13 April 2012, the average number of trucks crossing the Wagah border per day increased from 51 in

2009-10 to 244 in 2013-14. Mutual trade via Wagah land route was about 25 per cent of the total trade in 2013-14. Table 1 depicts the position of India's trade with Pakistan via Wagah land route during 2009-14. It is clear from this table that the movement of number of trucks across Attari/Wagah Border increased from 18563 in 2009-10 to 89181 in 2013-14. The number of trucks that arrived from Wagah for India's imports from Pakistan during the 2013-14 stood at 43386, which was 127 per cent more than in 2011-12, when the old check-post was functional. However, the number of trucks that crossed over to Pakistan rose marginally from 38,917 in 2011-12 to 45795 in 2013-14. The items imported from Pakistan were cement, chemical, gypsum, dry dates, dry fruits, float glass, marble stone and sand, etc. The items that were exported to Pak were potatoes, tomatoes, onions, cotton, meat, ginger, garlic, green chillies, soyabeans, newsprint, polypropylene, carbon-dioxide in liquid form, etc.

Table 1: India's Trade with Pakistan via Attari/ Wagah Land Route during 2009-14

Trade Indicators/Year (April-March)	**2009-10**	**2010-11**	**2011-12**	**2012-13**	**2013-14**
Trucks Crossed to Pak via Wagah (Nos)	17000	32000	38917	41248	45795
Volume of Exports Via Wagah Route (US$ mn)	168	257	287	561	564
Total Exports to Pak (US$ mn)	1573	2040	1542	2065	2294
Share of India's Exports via Wagah in Total (per cent)	**10.7**	**12.6**	**18.6**	**27.2**	**24.6**
Trucks Arrived from Pak via Wagah (Nos)	1563	3598	19087	34366	43386
Volume of Imports Via Wagah Route (US$ mn)	83	99	201	322	107
Total Imports from Pak (US$ mn)	276	333	398	542	427
Share of India's Imports via Wagah in Total (per cent)	**30.2**	**29.8**	**50.7**	**59.3**	**25.1**
Balance of Trade via Wagah (US$ mn)	85	158	86	240	457
Balance of Total Trade (US$ mn)	1297	1707	1144	1523	1837
Total Trucks Movement at Wagah (Nos)	**18563**	**35598**	**58004**	**75614**	**89181**
Trade (Exp+Imp) Via Wagah Route (US$ mn)	252	356	489	883	671
Total Trade with Pak (US$ mn)	1849	2667	1939	2607	2721
Share of Trade via Wagah in Total Trade (per cent)	**13.6**	**13.3**	**25.2**	**33.9**	**24.7**
Annual Growth of Trade via Wagah with Pak (per cent)	-	**41.4**	**37.3**	**80.7**	**-24.0**
Annual Growth of Total Trade with Pak (per cent)	-	**44.2**	**-27.3**	**34.4**	**4.4**

Source: Govt. of India, Export Import Data Bank, Ministry of Commerce.

The volume of India's trade with Pakistan through Wagah route also increased from US$ 252 mn in 2009-10 to US$ 671 mn in 2013-14 as depicted in Table 1. It is worth mentioning that about one-fourth of India's trade with Pakistan was via Wagah land route during 2013-14. It means there are vast potential for increasing bilateral trade via Wagah border, and unfavourable balance of trade of Pakistan with India can also be neutralised. On 18 January 2014, the commerce ministers of the two countries decided to open Wagah-Attari land customs station on all 7 days of each week.

IV

NTBs to Bilateral Trade via Wagah

The bilateral trade potential could have not been exploited fully due to NTBs imposed by India and Pakistan. Some NTBs are as under:

1. Positive List through Wagah land route.

Pakistan has a Positive List that allows only 137 items for import through land route of Attari-Wagah border from India, but the potential is huge from Punjab and north India. These items include livestock, meat, vegetables, raw jute, cotton yarn, pineapple, black pepper, raw cane & beet sugar, oil cake, cement & clinker, pure terephthalic acid, polyethylene, polypropylene, newsprint, paddy harvesters, etc.

The items like newsprint, paddy harvesters, dryers, fruits & vegetable, cotton, etc., can benefit Indian Punjab. If Pakistan allows entire about 7500 items to be imported from India through Wagah land route instead of 137 at present, the growth of trade will be huge. It will open a new era for the industrial development of Indian Punjab. The industries like hosiery, textiles, carpets, blankets, shawls, engineering units, tractors, auto parts, metal and alloy, bicycles, foundries, sports, steel, etc. will flourish. The new Guru Gobind Singh Refinery in Bathinda could also export petroleum products to Pakistan from land route.

2. No Transit Agreement

In spite of WTO memberships, no transit agreement has been signed between India and Pakistan. As such, Pakistan is not giving access to India's exports to Afghanistan. Similarly India does not allow transit facilities to Pakistani goods through its territory to Bangladesh and Nepal. Transit agreement between the two countries can fetch hefty revenue to each other from movement of goods through their respective territories. The first Pakistan-Afghanistan Transit Trade Agreement signed on 29 May 1958, in Kabul, which allowed the transit of goods from India via Lahore. Pakistan also signed a transit trade agreement with Nepal in January 1962, which allowed the transit of goods via East Pakistan, now Bangladesh. It may be noted that Afghan-Pak Transit Trade Agreement (APTTA) has been established on 18 July, 2010. Under this agreement, Afghanistan's trucks have been permitted to carry their transit export cargo on designated routes to Pakistani seaports and Wagah border for destinations in India. However, Indian goods for Afghanistan were not allowed to transit through land route in Pakistan. Through APTTA, Afghanistan would have the opportunity to export to India. Recent India's import of onions from Afghanistan through this route has helped to bring down high price of this item in India.

Similarly, Pakistan and Afghanistan signed a number of agreements to facilitate land trade.

3. Lack of Land Trade Routes

India and Pakistan opened their land trade routes via Wagah/Attari in July 2005 and the cross-LOC trade via Chakan Da Bagh in Poonch district in J & K – Rawalakote in Pakistan Occupied Kashmir (POK), and via Salamabad in Uri – Chakoti, POK in October 2008. There is a need to open up more trade traffic through Indian Punjab via Hussainiwala (Ferojpur) - Ganda Singh Wala (Kasur); Patti/Bhikhiwind/Khalra-Lahore; Khemkaran-Kasur; Fazilka-Sahiwal; Fazilka-Amruka-Karachi; Dera Baba Nanak (Gurdaspur)-Kartarpur (Narowal); Munabao (Rajasthan)-Khokhrapar (Sindh), and other land routes in Gujarat and Kashmir. All these trade routes were operational on the eve of partition. The Wagah-Attari route continues to be operational. India notified 13 land routes for trading between India and Pakistan on 21 November 1994. The non-operational land routes are Patti-Bhikhiwind-Khalra (Punjab)-Lahore, Hussainiwala (Punjab)-Kasur, Barmer-Gadra Road-Munabao-Khokropar Railway Line (Rajasthan); and from Vadodra (Gujrat) - Assara Naka, Khavda, Jatti-Rajnadini-Lakhpat, Saltanpur Naka, and Suigam Naka. On 22 July 1976, both the countries launched the Samjhauta Express connecting Attari (Indian Punjab) with Lahore (Pakistani Punjab). This train service was disrupted from 1st January 2002 to 14 January 2004. Further, they also launched the Delhi-Lahore Bus on 19 February1999. At LOC, bus service launched between Srinagar and Muzaffarabad

(Pakistan) over 183 Km on 7 April 2005, and another bus service launched between Poonch (India) and Rawalkote (Pakistan) over 55 Km on 20 June 2006. Train service, 'Thar Express' between Munabao (Barmer district in Rajasthan) and Khokhrapar (Sindh) revived on 18 February 2006 after 41 years, but this route is yet to be re-opened for trade. However, both the countries are yet to start a train/bus service connecting Sialkot (Pakistan) with Jammu (India), and Kargil (India) with Skardu (Pakistan). From economic point of view, it is illogical to confine trade to ports only, when a large common land border is shared by both the countries. Land route is cheap, faster and safe. The Hussainiwala border is only 11 Kms from Ferozpore (Indian Punjab) and 9 Kms from Kasur, Pakistan. This route was the lifeline of traders dealing in dry fruits, clothes, vegetables and fruits till 1971. Besides, local cinema halls attracted a lot of Pakistani visitors. There is a high potential for cotton exports from Malwa region of Indian Punjab to Pakistan from this route. Apart from cotton, green chillies, ginger, potatos and onions can also be exported to Pakistan. Further, Amruaka (Pak) is just 7 Kms from Fazilka (Punjab) and thus distance of Ludhiana and Karachi from this railway route is just 900 Kms.

4. Trade via Third-Countries

It is estimated that the unofficial trade between India and Pakistan stands at more than US $ 5 bn annually. However, some estimates provided at various points in time range from US$ 250 mn to US$ 3 bn (Taneja, 2007 & Khan, 2013). 88 per cent of total informal trade has been routed through third countries like Afghanistan, Dubai, Hong Kong, Singapore, Colombo and Gulf States. Goods from Kolkata are being shipped to Karachi via Singapore and Colombo ports. Similarly, bicycles have been exported from Ludhiana, Indian Punjab to Karachi via Dubai instead of nearest Wagah border. An ordinary Indian bicycle worth Rs 2700 become more than double at Rs 6000 when routed through Dubai. Even the cost of a bicycle tyre, an item on Pakistan's positive list for direct trade with India, shoots up from Rs 250 to Rs 600 by the time it reaches across border. The third country tortuous route costs both India and Pakistan dearly in terms of foreign exchange outflows as well as third party trading commissions. For instance, on Mumbai-Dubai-Karachi route, transport costs could be 1.5 times the cost of transporting directly between Mumbai and Karachi. With the negative list regime, the goods in Pakistan will become importable through legal channels. It will reduce the cost of imported goods and increase the government's revenue.

5. Cross-border Infrastructure Constraints

No modern infrastructure facilities are available on Wagah/Attari border, particularly on the Pakistani side. Though ICP operationalised in April 2012, yet there is a weak transport and logistic infrastructure. No facility of container handling is available. There are several bottlenecks for transporting goods by the rail route. Goods that are transported by Samjhauta Express move at fixed timings on a biweekly basis. Further, there is no fixed timing for a goods train, which do not move across the border in the evening due to security reasons. There are limited number of parcel wagons (10) for every trip. The demand for wagons is much more than supply. This scarcity leads to high transaction cost, and bribes to the tune of US$ 2.5 per tonne in India. Pakistani traders pay a corresponding bribe of US$ 1.5 per tonne (Taneja, 2007). Further, no warehousing and cold storage facility, and limited scanners at border are also causing bottlenecks to trade. ICP needs to be equipped with full truck scanners, and adequate number of warehouses with concrete floors for storage of cement, gypsum, etc. The improved facilities for containerisation of rail cargo, rolling stock and wagon availability, etc. are to be implemented quickly. Pakistan should also upgrade its infrastructure facilities.

6. No MFN/NDMA Status to India

MFN status means a country agrees to treat another country equally with all the other countries in international trade. Pakistan's MFN status to India would enable Pakistani traders to import commodity from India by paying less duty than the existing slab, and hence would increase India's exports. Under the World Trade Organisation Agreement, India and Pakistan are under obligation to grant MFN status to each other. Though India has accorded MFN status to Pakistan in 1996, yet Pakistan has not reciprocated this gesture, and continues to restrict imports from India. In November 2011, Pakistan's cabinet decided to grant MFN status to India. However, it was backed out. On 18 January 2014, the meeting of Commerce Minister of Pakistan with his Indian counterpart on the margin of the 5th SAARC Business Leaders Conclave in New Delhi decided to dismantle the negative list of 1,209 items by Pakistan which automatically lead to Non-Discriminatory Market Access (NDMA), a nomenclature in lieu of the MFN status for India that is chosen by the Pakistan government to avoid political ramifications at home; and liberalisation of business visa regime. All these measures were to be implemented by the end of February 2014. However, Pakistan failed to operationalise these measures.

Due to the delay on the Pakistani side, Indian Commerce Minister cancelled his visit to Lahore on 'The India Show' organised by FICCI during February 14-16, 2014. On March 10, 2014, Pakistan's Commerce Minister mentioned that NDMA status would not be granted until India did not accommodate Pakistan's main exportable items like textile, cement, surgical instruments, and sports, which were in the sensitive list of India and imposed higher duties, as such Pakistan could not export their commodities to India (The Nation, 2014). It may be noted that 30 per cent of all items included on India's sensitive list against Pakistan are agricultural goods while 34 per cent are textile products. The removal of textile items from this list will only affect competition with large Indian firms. India's total imports of textile items were over US$3 bn, while those from Pakistan were only U$30 mn. It is estimated that Pakistan can increase its exports of textile items, particularly woven cotton fabrics including denim and lawn to U$365 mn – almost ten times the current level if a level playing field is provided (Taneja, et.al, 2011).

7. Dissimilar Customs Procedures

India and Pakistan have dissimilar customs procedures for trade. Following table shows that 9 documents for exports and 11 documents for imports are required in India instead of 8 documents for each export and import in Pakistan. Further, Cost of trade and time to import are also high in India as compared to Pakistan. However, time to export is less (16 days) in India as compared to Pakistan (21 days).

Documents, Time and Cost to Trade in 2013

Country	Documents (Nos) to		Time (Days) to		Cost (US$@Container) to	
	Export	Import	Export	Import	Export	Import
India	9	11	16	20	1170	1250
Pakistan	8	8	21	18	660	725

Source: World Bank. *Doing Business Report 2014*

In view of above facts, India and Pakistan should harmonise customs procedures, particularly at Wagah/Attari land border. Rules of origin certification should also be integrated.

8. Business Visa Restrictions

The major problems of granting business visa are related to city specific visas, police reporting on arrival and before departure, exit from the port of entry; limited length of stay, and delays in granting visas. Thought there should not be any compromise on national security issues, but genuine traders should not be victimised. More liberal business visas can increase huge bilateral trade.

The new Visa Agreement signed between India and Pakistan on 8th September, 2012, replaced 1974 agreement. It has been operationalised w.e.f. 14th December, 2012. Businessmen with income of Pak Rs 0.5 million or equivalent per annum, or annual turnover/gross sale of Pak Rs 3 million or equivalent are being given a one year Business Visa with five places, for upto four entries. Further, businessmen with an income of at least Pak Rs. five million or equivalent per annum or turnover of Pak Rs. 30 million or equivalent per annum will be given one year multiple entry visas, for upto ten places, with exemption from police reporting. The Wagah-Attari road travel option is automatically added to visa applications to facilitate visitors who miss their weekly flight from Delhi.

9. Lack of Financial facilities

Some Indian banks do not recognise Letter of Credit (L/Cs) from all Pakistani banks. Moreover, payments through Asian currency union are delayed. Further, lack of banking and foreign exchange facilities at border is also obstructing trade between India and Pakistan. In 2005, Governors of the Central Banks of India and Pakistan had signed an agreement to open branches of two Indian banks in Pakistan, and two Pakistani banks in India. But this agreement is yet to be implemented.

10. Communication Problems

Whenever there are disturbances at the Indo-Pak border, the mobile connections are blocked. It creates problems for businessmen of the two countries for mutual trade. Both countries are not allowing mobile roaming facility to businessmen. Therefore, the two countries should relax the restrictions on this connectivity.

IV

Gains from mutual trade to India and Pakistan:

India's gains for importing from Pakistan were worth US$ 20.6: million during 2012. One hundred six items in which India gained during this period were mainly lac, natural gums, resins & oleoresins; plates, sheets, film, foil & strip of plastics; sacks & bags of polymers of ethylene;

plants & parts of plants, beans, dried, shelled, salt; portland cement; shrimps & prawns, cane/beet sugar, light petroleum oils; medicaments; Sodium hydroxide (caustic soda), terephthalic acid & its salts; hydrogen peroxide; leather further prepared after tanning of bovine; solid lead & aluminium ores; spices; natural steatite; figs, fresh/dried; cuttle fish; white cement; almonds; cement clinkers; etc.

It may be noted that India had net actual gains worth US$ 371.6 mn for imports from Pakistan during 1995-2003. These gains were for importing sugar, raisins and sultanas, almonds, degresd wool, ayurvedic and unani herbs, petroleum and bitumen oil crude, poppy seeds, and naphthalene from Pakistan (Madaan, 2004). Further, India also gained US$ 2.63 mn from her trade with Pakistan during 1980-82 (Ghuman, 1986).

Similarly, actual gains to Pakistan for importing from India were worth US$ 101.3 million during 2012. The five hundred sixty items in which Pakistan gained during this period were mainly cotton, not carded or combed; coffee, tea, mate & spices; oil seeds and oleaginous fruits; vessels & other floating structures for breaking up; new pneumatic tyres of rubber for buses or lorries; oil-cake and other solid residues from soyabean oil; vaccines for human medicine; preparations of cereals, flour, starch or milk; medicaments for therapeutic or prophylactic uses; man-made staple fibres for spinning of viscose rayon; polyethylene having a specific gravity of 0.94 or more; polypropylene; reactive dyes and preparations based thereon; organic chemicals,quinoline/isoquinoline ring-system; water heaters, nonelectric distilling/rectifying plant; dairy produce; birds' eggs; natural honey; organic chemicals, unfused pyridine ring; slide fasteners; natural gums, resins, and oleoresins; maize; barley; meat & edible meat; sugars and sugar confectionery; edible vegetables; etc. It may be noted that Pakistan had net potential gains worth US$ 81.3 mn for importing nitrogenfunction compounds, universal, plates/sheets of iron-steel and polymerisation and co-poly products from India during 1998-2000. (Madaan, 2005).

Concluding Remarks

The preceding discussion concludes that there is enormous potential of trade between India and Pakistan. During post SAFTA period (2006-13), India and Pakistan realised less than 8 per cent of the total import potential of bilateral trade. In fact, trade relations between India and Pakistan have always been governed by political interests rather than by economic interests. However, SAFTA has helped the two countries to increase the volume of trade. The negative list regime will surely increase the trade and economic cooperation in a big way. It will reduce the cost of imported goods and increase the government revenue. In this way, the goods in Pakistan will become importable through legal channels and illegal trade via third country will diminish.

VI

Policy Suggestions

1. India and Pakistan should address the NTBs to exploit the huge potential of bilateral trade. It has been identified that positive list of Pakistan's imports from India via Wagah, infrastructure constraints at border, dissimilar custom procedures, no transit agreement, third country trade, lack of banking and foreign exchange facilities, visa restrictions, communication problems, etc. are posing hurdles to mutual trade.
2. Both India and Pakistan should resolve their political problem on Kashmir and exploit their vast mutual trade potential on the pattern of Indo-China model. Since war divides and trade unites, the time has come to gain from each other. Both have gained from mutual trade in the past. In 2012, the actual bilateral trade was less than 8 per cent of the potential trade, which can be expanded. The increase in bilateral trade can lead to peace between the two countries.
3. The opening of more land routes between India and Pakistan would give a big boost to trade and bring down freight cost. Like the opening of Attari-Wagah border where 25 per cent of the total bilateral trade took place in 2013-14, there is a need to open up more trade traffic through Hussainiwala, Khemkaran, Fazilka, Dera Baba Nanak routes in Punjab, and other land routes in Rajasthan, Gujarat and Kashmir. Earlier, all these trade routes were operational.
4. Pakistan should grant MFN/NDMA status to India in order to legalise the unofficial importable goods through third countries, which are more than US$ 5 billion per annum. It will reduce the cost of importable goods as well as Non-Tariff Barriers. Further, it will increase the customs revenue of Pakistan.
5. Promotion of trade relations, joint-ventures, joint marketing joint study groups on trade and other issues, strengthening of

SAARC, joint patrolling of LOC, frequent meetings of civil and political bureaucracy and political leadership, people to people contact, a liberal visa regime, etc., could be some formidable steps towards confidence building exercise between India and Pakistan.

****

References

Federation of Indian Chambers of Commerce and Industry–FICCI. 2004: *India-Pakistan Economic Relations – A Report.* New Delhi.

Govt. of India. 2014: *Export Import – Data Bank,* DGCI & S, Ministry of Commerce.

Govt. of Pakistan. 2014: *Federal Bureau of Statistics*, Islamabad.

Ghuman, Ranjit Singh, 1986: *Indo-Pakistan Trade Relations.* New Delhi: Deep & Deep Publications.

__________and Madaan, Davinder Kumar. 2006: Indo-Pakistan Trade Cooperation and SAARC, *Peace and Democracy in South Asia*, Sweden, 2(1&2).

Kumar, Ganesh A. and Saini, Gordhan Kumar. 2007: *Economic Co-operation in South Asia: The Dilemma of SAFTA and Beyond.* Working Paper. Mumbai: Indira Gandhi Institute of Development Research. October.

Madaan, Davinder Kumar. 1997: Pakistan and SAARC: Economic and Trade Development, In Grover, Varinder. (Eds). *Encyclopaedia of SAARC Nations-Pakistan. New Delhi:* Deep & Deep Publications.

__________ and Ghuman, Ranjit Singh. 2005: Trade Potentialities and Trade-off Between India and Pakistan, *The Indian Economic Journal,* Vol. 53. No. 3. October-December.

__________. 2007: Cotton Trade with Pakistan, *The Tribune*, Chandigarh, April 17.

__________. 2012: Huge Potential for Indo-Pak Trade Ties, *Daily Post, Chandigarh,* January 10.

__________. 2014: War divides, trade unites, *The Tribune*, Chandigarh, 1st February.

Mukherji, I.N. 1998: The South Asian Preferential Trading Arrangement: Identifying Products in India's Regional Trade, *Asia Pacific Development Journal*, 5 (1). June.

Rahman, M., Shadat W.B. and Das, N.C. 2006: Trade potential in SAFTA: An application of augmented gravity model. *Center for Policy Dialogue* (CPD), Paper 16, Pakistan.

SAARC Secretariat. 2014: *www.saarc_sec.org*

Taneja, Nisha. 2007: India's Exports to Pakistan: Transaction Cost Analysis.

Economic & Political Weekly. January.

Taneja, Nisha; Ray, Saon; Kaushal, Neetika; and Chowdhury, Devjit Roy. 2011:

"Enhancing Intra-SAARC Trade: Pruning India's Sensitive List under SAFTA," *ICRIER Working Paper 255*, New Delhi.

The Nation. 2014: 11 March, Pakistan.

United Nations. 2014: *Commodity Trade Statistics.*

******

Indo-Pak Disputes: Bumpy Road Ahead For SAARC

— *Emanual Nahar**

Abstract

The notion of Regional cooperation is a markable idea taken by the leaders of the member nations. The main rationale behind its establishment is to develop a congenial environment through summit diplomacy where all nations may interact peacefully with each other, cultivate sustainable peace and promote mutual economic well being, by harnessing available resources in the region through the peaceful process of economic integration. Nevertheless, after 31 years of establishment, no South Asian nations has been able to push the process of integration into full swing nor the organisation itself has become viable enough to promote peace, harmony and economic integration or prevent conflicts in the region. Indo-Pak bilateral disputes and conflicts accompanied by suspicion and mistrust have severely hampered the process of much needed regional cooperation in the South Asia.

Introduction: Concept of Regionalism

Regionalism in International Politics is assuming greater significance, both as a concept as well as a phenomenon. It is a multi-dimensional phenomenon viz: military, economic, cultural and ideological, hence its understanding requires comprehensive approach. Regionalism is an

* Dr Nahar is a Fellow & Professor in the Department of Political Science, USOL, Panjab University, Chandigarh.

effective instrument that emerged as an important part of the western strategy, wherein economic as well as military arrangements were worked out to fulfill the objectives of the concerned areas. Regionalism encompasses efforts by a group of nations to enhance their economic, political, social or cultural interactions including regional cooperation, market integration, development and regional integration.

There are various schools of thought regarding the preferred methods and approaches to international integration and regionalism. The Federal School of thought conceives of integration in legal and institutional terms and it stands for bringing together previously separate, autonomous or territorial units to constitute a new form of Union. For Federalism, the aim of the Union is to integrate different entities but not to assimilate them. It is about finding the balance between self rule and shared rule, about being a unified entity and maintaining diversity and difference. This is one of the greatest appeals of Federalism; it formally acknowledges these differences which are so vital to political system and society based on pluralism. Federalism in the context of the EU is the application of federal principles to the process of European integration where the term integration refers to the sense of a coming together of previously separate or independent parts to form a new whole.

Secondly, Functional School of Thought proposed to build a structure based on functions and common interest and needs shared by states which linked authority with increasing weight of scientific knowledge, aided by technology and expertise. According to David Mitrany, the creator of functionalism in Internatioal Relations, functional approach provides the states the opportunity to successfully cooperate in non-political context. Such a developmental cooperation would lead to process called autonomous development towards multiplication, expansion and deepening of functional international organisations. Functionalism proposed to build a form of authority based in functions and needs, which linked authority with needs, scientific knowledge, expertise and technology, i.e, it provided a supraterritorial concept of authority.

Neo-Functionalism is a theory of regional integration, building on the work of Ernst B. Haas, and also Leon Lindberg, both American political scientists. Neo-functionalists focused their attention in the process of integration among states, i.e. regional integration. Initially, states integrate in limited functional or economic areas. Thereafter, partially integrated states experience increasing momentum for further rounds of integration in related areas. According to this school of thought, economic integration (functionalism) generates a political dynamic that leads to further integration. Closer economic ties will further strengthen political cordination in order to work effectively and eventually lead to political integration as well – a process called 'spillover'. According to neo-functionalists, there are two kinds of spillover: functional and political. Functional spillover is the interconnection of various *economic* sectors or strategic areas, and the integration in one policy-area spilling over into others. Political spillover is the creation of supranational governance models as the European Union. All the above mentioned schools of thought are based on European experience, and have made notable contributions in the process of Regional Integration of European Nation-States, for enhançing their development in various aspects. The modern age is an age of International co-operation and inter-dependence of the states. No state, however, powerful, can afford to live or act in isolation. To avoid anarchostic situations and develop international cooperation in varoius fields, regional organisations came into being. Regional organistaions emerged because of the urge to solve regional problems in a cooperative and common framework. The Modern regional organisations which came into existence after World War-II can be divided into three parts: (i) Regional Defence organisations such as NATO, CENTO and WARSAW pact. (ii) Hybrid Organisations such as OAS, OAU and the Arab League etc. But this study is not concerned with these two type of organisations, infact the the primary concern of this study is the third type of organisations, i.e. (iii) The Functional Organiations.

Functional Regional Organisations are in a sense, International Organisations as they incorporate international membership and encompass geopolitical entities. However, their membership is characterised by boundaries and demarcations characteristic to a defined and unique geography, such as continents, or geopolitics, such as Economic Blocks. They have been established to foster political-economic cooperation and integration or dialogue amongst states within a restrictive geographical or geopolitical boundary. Regional integration agreements have led to major developments in international relations between and among many countries, specifically significant increases in international trade and investment and in the formation of regional trading blocs. Regional integration arrangements are mainly the outcome of necessity felt by nation-states to integrate their economies in order to achieve rapid economic development, decrease conflict, and build mutual trusts between the integrated units. This paper examines the working of regional arrangement within South Asia, i.e. SAARC and performance of SAARC, under the light of Indo-Pak disputed Issues.

II

SAARC is an organisation of South Asian Nations comprising the Governments of Bangladesh, India, Pakistan, Sri Lanka, Bhutan, Nepal, Maldives and Afghanistan. The first concrete proposal for establishing a framework for regional cooperation on the basis of functional approach in South Asia was made by the late President of Bangladesh, Zia-ur Rahman, on May 2, 1980. SAARC emphasises on closer integration of neighbouring economies as a first step in creating a larger regional market for trade and investment. Though Economic growth of the South Asian Region was mentioned in its charter as its aim and objective, cooperation in the economic field, in practical terms, was taken up much later by the member States.

From 1985 to 2015, 18 Summits have been at various places. All the members expressed a seriousness over growing linkages between drug trafficking and international arms trade and terrorist activities. The head of states or governments recalled the adoption of the 1996 UN Declaration on measure to eliminate international terrorism. SAARC has undertaken several initiatives to tackle these problems. The Kathmandu Summit (2002) declaration unanimously accepted that terrorism in all its forms as a challenge to all nations. But there were differences of opinion between the countries during this summit especially between India and Pakistan that made it difficult to arrive at a consensus. Terrorism is a major issue which hurdle strengthen the Cooperation within SAARC. It has been seen in the past, terrorist have threatened to derail peace process between India and Pakistan as happened in the case of Parliament attack in December 2001 and later the after Mumbai blasts. India strongly held that Pakistan based Kashmiri militant, groups Jaish-e-Mohammad and Lashkar-e-Taiyeba are responsible for these attacks and pressurised on Pakistan to ban these groups and take appropriate action, including extradition to India.

There are so many problems which create obstacles in the way of working of SAARC and hamper the process of regional co-operation within its arrangement and purview. Bilateral issues are a setback to the SAARC development Process. When the SAARC Summits were put off due to Political reasons Honorary SAARC summits have played an important role in developing contacts among leaders of the SAARC States. It also provided opportunities to the leaders for informal bilateral contacts and consultations on the sidelines of the summits. The summits have been postponed without really considering. It created adverse impact on the institution of SAARC. For example SAARC Summit of 1989 was postponed because of the presence of Indian peacekeeping forces in Sri Lanka (Lama, July 2001). The Sri Lankan Prime Minister Rana Singhe Premadasa said that he would not attend the SAARC meeting unless Indian forces were withdrawn from his country. After Colombo Summit 1998 which was to be held in November 1999 it was postponed because of the clashes between India and Pakistan, on grounds of a military coup in Pakistan. In 1992, the Dhaka Summit was cancelled in the aftermath of the Babri Masjid demolition due to threats issued to the then Indian Prime Minister Narsimha Rao by fundamentalist forces, clearly demonstrating that an internal matter of a country has the capacity to derail SAARC.

The thirteenth Summit of SAARC was to held in January 2005. It was postponed due to the tragedy of Tsunami and then refixed on February 2005. It was again postponed. New Delhi denied to be part of the Summit and blamed security environment in Bangladesh was not suitable for the Summit. It is deep-rooted distrust between India and Bangladesh on Political dispute that has created barriers before a fruitful dialogue.

Economic cooperation with in the SAARC started in 1993, when the first regional agreement on economic cooperation formed, called the South Asian Preferential Trade Agreement (SAPTA) was signed at the seventh summit in Dhaka which came into force on 7th December 1995. The SAARC preferential tariff concessions aimed to achieve a Free Trade Agreement (FTA) decided to liberalise their economies in trade. It proved to be unsuccessful and did not do much to integrate the region economically. In 2004 the Preferential Trade Agreement was replaced by South-Asian Free Trade Agreement (SAFTA) that finally came into effect in 2006. According to this Agreement, SAARC states are to reduce or eliminate tariff. Pakistan India and Sri Lanka will cut tariffs up to 5 per cent within 7 years of the start of agreement. The SAARC countries will also maximise their lists of items that are given preference for intra SAARC trade. All countries can however, "Maintain a list of sensitive products" fir which they will not have to reduce tariffs. The share of intra SAARC trade in global trade of SAARC countries at 5.5 per cent in 2008, which is far below compared with 58 per cent in NAFTA,

54 per cent in European Union, 25 per cent in ASEAN. During the course of the 13th SAARC summit at Dhaka, Dr Manmohan Singh correctly stated that; Regional economic co-operation in South Asia has fallen for short of our expectations and the dreams of our founding fathers. It remains far behind the more successful examples in both Asia and other regions of the world.

Though the SAARC countries have agreed upon free trade areas, tariff concessions need to be structured in such a way that it facilitates the flow of products. However, in the past tariff concessions which have been given by various countries of South Asia are on those products which are not tradable items between the countries, or are on the negative list. Also Pakistan has been reluctant to restore normal trading relations with India Kashmir-Issue being the major dispute until Gen. Zia President Pakistan reportedly said: 'I do not want to see the emergence of Indian lobby in Pakistan. SAARC is still a long away from fulfilling its potential of being a powerful regional bloc. A clear distinctions needs to be made between bilateral and multilateral relations on the issue of free trade. This is one of the reasons why products are largely smuggled and rerouted through third countries. Both the countries have similar socio-economic needs which can be fulfilled through mutual cooperation. Bilateral investment is the most effective trial to create mutual stake of India and Pak which would help in defusing tension and subsequently resolving all such issues, which create obstacle in the way of economic growth of the entire region. Strong economic relations will serve as a catalyst role towards the peace-building process.

The problems in the working of SAARC arise due to differences in perception of member-nations regarding the nature, role and structure of this organisation. Such differences are the result of different vintage points determined by respective national interests of the member-nations. Pakistan's approach towards SAARC has been mainly political and it has shown least interest in regional economic interactions. Nepal's major demand from SAARC is to develop South Asia as a Zone of Peace. Sri Lanka wants to tackle its domestic problems through cooperation of this South -Asian Organisation, whereas Bangladesh's primary concern is the management of river–waters. SAARC summits have been reflection of such differences. It was, in-fact, Kathmandu Summit, where the things began to change in the right direction, a step towards regional cooperation. However still prevailing differences in perception of member-nations especially regarding institutional framework of SAARC, different economic structures of member-nations, vast disparities in the working of respective Political Systems and the resultant differences in attitude and interests, does not provide favourable ground for regional cooperation.

SAARC is failure to take up bilateral issues and have been attributed as one of the major cause for the failure of regional Co-operation in South Asia. The heads of SAARC nations have stressed that important political issues affecting bilateral ties need to be taken up SAARC to be successful in south Asia. However, the inclusion of bilateral issues has many advantages and sometimes leads to mistrust and suspicion among the nations. Resolving bilateral issues can be achieved through bilateral negotiations rather than diluting the SAARC platform to find solution to such disputes. The SAARC charter prohibits the discussion of bilateral issues. Some Pakistan analysts have accused India of being the main culprit and feel that hampered SAARC. However, from India's point of view most of the problems it has with its neighbours are bilateral in nature and do not concern with other member states.

III

Bilateral disputes and conflicts between India and Pakistan create major hindrances in the successful working of SAARC. Indo-Pak relations has been mainly a story of conflicts and discord, mutual distrust and suspicion. Even though the two South Asian nations share historic, cultural, geographic, and economic links, their relationship has been plagued by hostility and suspicion and strained by a number of historical and political issues Legacy being a major determining factor of the both countries and conditioned their bilateral relations.

Kashmir issue is the root cause of all tensions between India and Pakistan. The question arises that how India will take the Kashmir issue? India says that Kashmir is not the "Core Issue" and the issue is more about the problem in Kashmir rather than the problem of Kashmir, It does not recognise Kashmir as a dispute territories therefore discussing the loyalty of its accession to the Indian Union does not arise at all, whereas for Pakistan, the disputed territory of Kashmir is the core issue. It is no doubt that Kashmir has been the focal point of discord between India and Pakistan Since the partition of the country. Even the three wars 1965, 71 and Kargil War between them could not solve this problem.

Jammu and Kashmir region has resulted in frequent fighting along the line of control (LOC) which both countries accepted in 1972 Simla agreement. Both nations have maintained troops along the line. But the occupation of the Siachen area by Indian and Pakistan troops in April 1984, this portion was termed as the Actual Ground position line (AGPL).

The 60-Kilometre long Sir Creek lies on the boundary between Pakistan and India in the marshes of Rann of Kutch and flows into the Arabian Sea. It was not included in the 1968 Tribunal Award on the Indo-Pakistan western boundary, because both sides had agreed to exclude the area from the deliberation of the tribunal. The Sir Creek area is rich in fish and is a breeding ground for prawns. Any change in the land boundary will greatly affect the External, Economic Zone (EEZ). The dispute is over the interpretation of the boundary line dividing the Creek. India's wants boundaries to be demarcated from the centre of the Creek while Pakistan wants the bank of the Creek as international boundary. Kashmir is important for Pakistan because all of its rivers flow from Kashmir and water is vital for Pakistani side as the latter is facing a major water shortage. In 1960, India and Pakistan signed the Indus Water treaty which divided the use of rivers and canals between the two countries. Pakistan obtained exclusive rights for the three western rivers, Indus:- Jhelum and Chenab. India retained rights to the three eastern rivers Ravi, Beas and Sutlej.

Baglihar Dam is a Dam Project on the Chenab River in the Doda district of Jammu and Kashmir. Pakistan feels that India is violating the Indus treaty by constructing this dam on the river Chenab and also feels that the construction of spiliway-gated structure will deprive it of upto 7000 cusecs of water daily and will have an adverse impact on its irrigation system. India has clearly stated that the construction of Baglihar project is not the violation of Indus water treaty. The Indian side has said, that all water which has been withheld will be released after being used for power generation. The Wular Barrage is a project started by India in 1984 at the Wular Lake downstream from the Jhelum river. It consists of a dam with a navigating lock of permit navigation during the lean winter, 8 months. In 1987 work was stopped following a protest by Pakistan that this was a violation of the Indus Water Treaty of 1960 in that it was meant for water storage. Indus stand is that it is meant to enhance navigation, which is permissible under the treaty. Various rounds of talks have been held so far but an agreement has remained elusive.

The two largest states of the region: India and Pakistan were born as twins, but rival twins, through a baptism of blood and fire. Tensions between India and Pakistan, in particular, become high pitched from time to time.

The alleged Cross- border terrorism in Jammu and Kashmir become another serious problem between India and Pakistan. At his press conference on July 2001, President of Pakistan, General Musharfa, justified the Kargil aggression and asserted that Pakistan's support to 'Jehadis' in Kashmir was like India's arming the 'Mukti Bahini' (Ghuman 2006 : 295).

The issue of terrorism has been on the agenda of SAARC since the first summit held in 1985. With the passage of time, the issue of terrorism have taken a more complex character and there is clear realisation among the member countries of SAARC that there is no other alternative to have coordinated strategies to respond effectively to curb terrorism. From the very beginning, SAARC took terrorism issue and approved that the standing committee should set up a study group to examine the problem of terrorism. During the summits all the members agreed to fight against terrorism and also recognised to importance of the principle laid down in UN Resolution 1373. Even the heads of state expressed happiness at the signing of SAARC Regional convention on suppression of terrorism and considered it a historic step towards the prevention of terrorism from the region. Most of the SAARC members have suspicion and mistrust towards India which has weakened India's position in South Asia and left the space for China. India needs to give a re-look in its policies with SAARC countries. An Analysis of socio-economic agenda within the purview of SAARC reveals that the organisation has achieved limited success.

III

In spite the tensions or irritants between Indo-Pak relations SAARC is the best hope to improve the regional co-operation in South Asia. A number of initiatives have been taken by the two states under the auspices of SAARC for the economic growth, cultural development and collaboration in social, technical and scientific fields. The enhanced cooperation has generated CBMs and leads the composite dialogue which is turn into non economic benefits for the two states and a steady and positive improvement in their bilateral relations. A major effort of SAARC was to bring India and Pakistan closer to negotiate over Kashmir dispute at the January 2004 Summit meeting, and the first time leaders of both nations adopted a positive posture towards each other. In the same meeting, they also pledged to resume the state level talks on Kashmir issue. The member states signed the Additional Protocol on 'Suppression of Terrorism,' which was also ratified in 2005. In spite of severe bitterness and misgivings between New Delhi and Islamabad, both expressed their willingness to minimise the gap in various SAARC Summits, which had jolted the rhythm of the bilateral dialogue process.

Multi-track diplomacy is also an important aspect of emerging scenario of cooperation. Track-1 diplomacy is limited to the official level talks between two countries and it is used for conflict resolution. Track-II diplomacy comes in the purview of CBMs. Such diplomacy was started between India and Pakistan in the 1970s. But it was limited up to quasi or semi-government level. Therefore, in recent years, there has been more thrust on people to people contacts which is called multi track diplomacy and it includes educationalists, businessman, sportsmen, art groups, partitioned families etc. Multi track diplomacy is bringing desirable fruits for peace and co-operation in the region.

Conclusion

The SAARC members entered in the field of economic co-operation through SAPTA. After some time which was replaced by SAFTA, while SAFTA was seen as the route to opening up trade, it was always needed to address the problems of trade asymmetry in the region. The SAARC process moved slowly to address these issues, bilateralism become a preferred option to stimulate the intra-regional trade. India has already entered into bilateral free trade arrangements with Nepal, Bhutan and Sri Lanka. The mutual trade between India and Pakistan has not flourished much due to the hostile and hated political relations. Intra regional trade among the SAARC members stand to benefit will in the bargain but the track record of intra-regional trade within SAARC countries has been dismal or marginal. It can be seen if we compare the percentage of intra-regional growth between the member states of SAARC. It grew from 3.2 per cent in 1980s to only 5.5 per cent in 2008 which is far below when compared with 58 per cent in NAFTA, 54 per cent IN EU and 25 per cent in ASEAN (Mehta 2012). Kashmir is a major bone of contention between India and Pakistan. In fact, this problem always becomes an insurmountable hurdle whenever any effort is made to normalise and strengthen mutual ties in trade and strong economic relations. From the many years, Pakistan is not in favour to give MFN status to India due to the Kashmir issue. In the absence of MFN status a large number of Indian export items to Pakistan have been routed through a third nation. An unofficial trade between both nations is increasing day by day which is not beneficial. If this unofficial trade is regulated by official channels both the countries can earn a lot of income through custom duty. The trade between India and Pakistan takes place mostly through Bombay-Karachi route but at the eve of partition most of the trade was carried through via Wagah- Attari border. The distance between Amritsar and Lahore is just about 50 km. Bombay-Karachi involves huge transport and trans-shipment costs. On the other side, land routes (Wagah-Attari, Lahore-Amritsar) can give a boost to border trade. Though the SAARC states have agreed upon free trade areas (FTA) and extend tariff concession but it needs to be structured in such a way to facilitate the free flow of goods and products. There has been a tremendous progress over the past few years, trade between India and Pakistan was just over US $2.5 billion in 2013 that could easily grow to US $10 billion. No doubt SAFTA has opened up the new ways of economic co-operation among the member states.

To develop SAARC into a successful-working regional model, emphasis should be laid on removing fear, suspicion, distrust among the member-nations. Such negative approch of members and severly hamper the process of steady and continous cooperation. Study of the speeches of member-nations at various SAARC Summits clearly reflect that they are alive to the needs and advantages of regional cooperation, and willing to acccept the new international economic realities. SAARC can prove to be a highly beneficial organisation for South Asian Nations, if all the members work together on one platform. Considering the vast natural and human potential of South Asian Nations, economic coopereation among them could develop South Asian region as competitive International market. For This, it is essential that they understand present geopolitical realities and do not allow their political conflicts come in the way of regional economic cooperation. It will further depend upon the prudence and wisdom of the membernationns in taking advantage of cooperative environment. For resolving their bilateral disputes to create a climate of regional peace and stability, and thereby making SAARC – a successful regional Organisation.

Notes and References

- Aditya, Anand (2006), 'Contours of Conflict, Co-operative Regimes and Critical Mass: A Study of the South Asian Region' in Dr Kulwant Kaur and Baljit Singh Mann (ed.) *"South Asia: Dynamics of Politics, Economy and Security"*, Knowledge World Publications, New Delhi.
- Ajoy Ghosh, (2003), *Indo-Pak Conflict: Threat to South Asian Security*, Reference Press, New Delhi.

- Baljit Singh, (2005), 'Regional Co-operation in South Asia: Problems and Prospects', *'South Asian Survey'*, Vol. 12, No.2, Sage Publications, New Delhi. See also A.S. Narang (2006) "Indo-Pak Relations and SAARC: Retrospect and Prospect", in Kulwant Kaur and Baljit Singh (eds.), South Asia—*Dynamics of Politics, Economy and Security,* Published by knowledge world, New Delhi, pp. 99-112.
- Emanual Nahar & Sheveta Sehgal (2013), *SAARC, in contemporary World: Issues and Concerns*, Swastik Publications, New Delhi.
- Jitendra Narayan, (2006), 'Indo-Pak Relations a Snake Ladder Game' in Dr (Mrs) Annupurna Nautiyal (ed.) "India's *Foreign Policy in the New Era",* Gyan Publishing House, New Delhi.
- Kishore C. Dash, (2008), *Regionalism in South Asia*, Routledge Publications, London and New York.
- Mahendra, P Lama, (2001), 'SAARC: The Future Ahead', *World Focus*, Vol. XXII, No. 7, (July), pp. 14-17.
- Mohan Chakraborty, (2008), 'Pakistan and SAARC : A quest for Pragmatism in the New World Order, *World Focus*, Vol. XXIX, No. 5, (May), pp. 188-192
- N.S. Gehlot and Anu Satsangi (2004), *Indo-Pak Relations: Twist and Turns from Partition to Agra Summit and Beyond*, Deep and Deep Publications, New Delhi.
- Parmod Kumar Mishra, (1997), *South Asia Conflicts and Cooperation*, Kalinga Publications, Delhi.
- Partha S. Ghosh, (1995), *Co-operation and Conflict in South Asia*, Manohar Publications, New Delhi.
- Rajen Harshe, (1999), 'South Asian Regional Cooperation: Problems and Prospects', *Economic and Political Weekly*, Vol. 34, No. 19, pp. 1100-1105.
- Saroj Pathak, (2006), 'India and SAARC: Challenges and Opportunities in Annupurna Nautiyal (ed.), "*Challenges to India's Foreign Policy in the New Era",* Gyan Publishing House Pattanaik, Smruti S (2004), 'Indo-Pak Relations and the SAARC Summits', *Strategic Analysis*, Vol. 28, July-Sept, pp. 427-439., New Delhi.
- Surendra Chopra, (1988), *Post Simla Indo-Pak Relations Confrontation to De-escalation*, Deep and Deep Publications, New Delhi.
- Sushil, K. Pillai, (2003), 'Border Conflicts and Regional Disputes' in Monique Mekencamp, Paul Van Tongreen and Hans Van de Venn, *Searching for peace in Central and South Asia : An Overview of Conflict Prevention and Peace building Activities'*, Lynne Rienner Publishers Colorado, USA.

India's Security Concerns: Nuclear Proliferation in South Asia

— *Kuldeep Singh**

Abstract

To begin with, proliferation issues in South Asia must be understood in context of vertical and horizontal proliferation. Vertical proliferation takes place as nuclear states modernise their nuclear arsenals with more reliable delivery systems and warheads. Countries including the United States, China, India, and Pakistan, are in the process of modernising their arsenals through actions such as proposals for "a reliable replacement warhead" (as in the case of the United States). In the context of South Asia, nuclear modernisation is mainly a function of prevailing threat perceptions arising from security dilemmas. Modernisation of arsenals includes the development and testing of longer-range missiles-such as the tests of the Agni-IV by India, and the Shaheen-II by Pakistan.

Introduction

Foreign policy of a nation is primarily determined by the national interests who are diverse and dynamic. The security concept became comprehensive in the new world order. It included various threats such as terrorism/international terrorism, environmental degradation, ethno nationalism, energy security, human security, translational organised crimes and maritime security. These non traditional threats are a great challenge to peace and security and can best be tackled by collective global efforts but still the traditional security threat that safeguarding

* Dr Kuldip Singh, (Fellow P U) Associate Professor, PG dept of Political Science, GNN College, Doraha, Punjab.

one's sovereignty and territorial integrity can not be ignored. Nations are spending ever increasing amount to enhance their military strength and technological breakthrough to seek superiority in war. Hence, amongst all national interests who have their significances in themselves, security concerns are paramount significant for a nation because these relates to the very existence of a nation. Though, we shall discuss India's Security Concerns: nuclear proliferation in South Asia which mainly pertains to security threats of nuclear proliferation from Pakistan yet we can not do justice to the study without the study of impacts and interests of super powers like China, USA, Russia etc. in South Asia.

Like India have diverse national interests in south Asia. Some times we have commonality of interests even with our opponents like Pakistan. When we confined ourselves up to SAARC countries we have numerous commonalities of interests. When India adopts foreign policy of Gujral doctrine India has nothing hostile interests against its neighbouring SAARC nations and India have to play a role of Big Brother without following the principles of reciprocity.

Both India and Pakistan have been trying to get the membership of nuclear club and trying hard to get the status of recognised nuclear power by the super powers. We have the common stand on NPT and CTBT. Both have common interests if India successfully gets the gas pipe line supply from Iran via Pakistan. Pakistan is eager to get electricity from India. Sino-Indian differences are considerable on issues relating to the non-proliferation system, Asian security, regional stability in Southern Asia, and security in the maritime commons, space, and cyberspace. The two rising powers broadly agree on matters relating to the international economic system, energy security, and the environment. Both India and China have number of border disputes and claims and counter claims on certain areas. China has been abetting and aiding left-wing Maoists extremists in India to weaken its internal cohesion and to use them in case of conflict with India. China in Tibet has been constructing a dam on Brahamputra River which will restrict the flow of water to Indian Territory. During 2012, there was an attempt made by the BRICS nations to reform the current system of representation inside the International Monetary Fund (IMF) during the last G20 meeting in Los Cabos (Mexico) in June.

China and India tend to agree on the importance of state sovereignty and the need to reform global governance institutions to reflect the new balance of power. They also share a strong commitment to the open economic order that has allowed both powers to flourish in the global market place. But the two diverge on many details of the international system, such as the future viability of the Non-Proliferation Treaty and the role of state-owned enterprises in fostering globalisation.

Both China and India want a stable Asia-Pacific that will allow them to sustain their economic prosperity, but they perceive threats very differently and have divergent priorities. Importantly, India seeks a resolute American presence in the region to hedge against possible Chinese excesses, while China sees the United States as significantly complicating its pursuit of its regional goals and worries about American containment attempts.

China and India rely heavily on open sea lines of communication, and as a result, they both support the current maritime security regime. However, their interpretations as to its provisions have occasionally diverged. In space, China enjoys significant advantages over India and has emphasised the military dimensions of its program, while India has only recently begun developing space-based military technology. Both countries are just beginning to wrestle with the difficult task of forming cyber security policies, but they have already acted to limit objectionable or illegal activities online. In striking the balance between online freedom and social stability, India has encountered a higher degree of disgrace in the public sphere than its counterpart.

Chinese and Indian approaches to both energy and the environment broadly converge. Because India and China face a rising domestic demand for energy, they heavily rely on foreign suppliers of energy resources. This has prompted both governments to seek more efficient power sources and to secure their presence in overseas energy markets. On environmental policy, the two countries focus on primarily local and short-term concerns that must be balanced with the need for economic growth.

India has diverse and dynamic interests with USA who has been playing a vital role in the region. India and US have commonality of interests when both consider international terrorism is the greatest challenge to world peace even both are working together to fight out the threat of terrorism. Both are closely working together to check the enhancing dominance of China in south Asia. U S is also watching closely the Sino-Pak friendship ties. The friendship of China and Pakistan has been working against India when Pakistan transferred some areas like Aksai Chin, Shakasgan valley of occupied Kashmir to China. China helped a lot in providing nuclear and missile technology to Pakistan. Earlier

USA had the close friendship with Pakistan even supplied the strategic arms supply to Pakistan before Pressler Amendment. But presently U.S. has tilted towards India when signed civil nuclear agreement 123 in 2007. Even he refused to sign the same treaty with Pakistan. U.S. is annoyed with Pak on terrorism and concealment of Osama Bin Laden in Pakistan. U.S. annoyed with Pak because of supply of nuclear technology to North Korea and Iran. We do feel a combined nexus between U.S. China and Pak when India puts its claim for the permanent seat in Security Council. The three have close nexus when we get some military and technological aid from Russia. Pakistan has strong intention to make Muslim nuclear bomb to terrorise Israel. U.S. and India have close ties with Israel and Pakistan has close ties with Arabs. In the prevailing era of imbalance of powers tilted towards US which are termed sometimes uni-polar/ unipolar with multi centrality world, India, Russia and China jointly clandestinely trying to create balance of powers again. Hence the diverse and dynamic national interests of India, Pakistan, China, Russia creates a complex atmosphere in South Asia which pose a serious security concerns for South Asia in general and India in particular.

Two recent reports—Global Trends 2030: Alternative Worlds by the US National Intelligence Council, and US Strategy for a Post-Western World: Envisioning 2030 by the Atlantic Council—give a clear indication that 20 years after the end of the Cold War, the world is under a new form of global governance. Although Washington remains the only superpower in the world, US hegemony has declined globally. New centres of political power have emerged in new economic centres which are gradually developing in Asia and Latin America.

Today, Asia could return to have a leading role, especially thanks to the rise of China and India at a regional and global level. This has already resulted in a paradigm shift in the US foreign policy which is more focused on the Asia-Pacific region. China is emerging as a leading global power and represents the most important country in the world in manufacturing, production and commerce. As an emerging economy, India, too, is set to become an important centre in the new emerging multi-polar world order.

Horizontal proliferation is the spread of nuclear weapons technology from nuclear states to other entities, including aspiring nuclear weapon states, as well as non-state actors such as terrorist groups. Horizontal proliferation generally involves a significant role for WMD supply networks that may or may not have a connection to official entities in a nuclear state. In the South Asian context, this variant of proliferation is especially pertinent, given the history of the A.Q. Khan network and its assistance to states such as North Korea and Iran. In addition, horizontal proliferation includes second-tier proliferation, where developing countries trade and barter nuclear technology with each other. While vertical and horizontal proliferations are variants of the proliferation dynamic, it is entirely possible that a nuclear state (such as Pakistan) could make use of non-state networks in the pursuit of nuclear modernisation.

Genesis

South Asia is one of the most populated regions of the world, with India and Pakistan alone accounting for about 1.35 billion people. Both countries have been bitter rivals since partition of the sub-continent in 1947 that led to the creation of independent Pakistan and independence for India. The two countries have fought two wars over Kashmir (1947, 1965), one over East Pakistan/Bangladesh (1971), one limited war (Kargil, 1999) and the ongoing insurgency in Kashmir (since 1989). The 2001-2002 crises further highlighted the dangers of terrorist violence provoking a conventional conflict that could lead to a nuclear crisis. Kashmir, which lies at the heart of the dispute, is more than a simple territorial problem. The province has a Muslim majority, and for India it is a symbol of its secular credentials as well as a repudiation of the partition, which was based on religion. For Pakistan, Kashmir is crucial because it is seen as an unfinished agenda of partition, which was supposed to provide a homeland for the sub-continent's Muslim community. Thus, Kashmir is an 'integral part of both countries' perceived self-identities.

Since 2001-2002 crises, Islamabad and New Delhi have conducted several rounds of peace talks aimed at bringing a lasting settlement to the Kashmir issue. This peace process has involved several confidence-building measures such as strengthening of transport links between the two countries. The two sides also signed a crucial agreement on reducing the risk of nuclear accidents in February 2007. Nevertheless, the key dispute, Kashmir, is nowhere near resolution. This implies that both New Delhi and Islamabad are more inclined toward strengthening existing military capabilities, both conventional and non-conventional, to prevent an unfavourable scenario in a future standoff.

Furthermore, the Siachen glacier is also a region of military significance. The glacier, to the north of Kashmir, commands a strategic overlook of the small border between Pakistan and China and can potentially be used as a point of attack on India from northwest Kashmir.

The glacier became a battle ground between the two armies in April 1984 and despite repeated talks, there has been no movement toward demilitarisation. The complex rivalry between India and Pakistan involves territorial disputes based on notions of national identity as well as terrorist violence.

The China Impact

The role of China in South Asian security issues as well as in future conflict scenarios is crucial when considering two realities

(a) the historical animosity between India and China, and

(b) the long standing 'all-weather' political and military alliance between Pakistan and China.

Indian analysts often cite transfer of nuclear and missile technology from China to Pakistan as evidence of an encircled threat to India like 'string of pearls'.[1] Through nuclear and missile technology transfers to Pakistan, Beijing restricts India to the South Asian strategic framework, and this constrains New Delhi's stated desire to seek a more global presence. From the Chinese political establishment's perspective, the concern is over India's defence expansion, its desire and movement toward a stronger regional and global role, and its increasing strategic connections with as US.[2]

At the same time, the present threat perceptions between India and China are not the same as between India and Pakistan, which are more immediate and based on a 'hot' territorial dispute and state-sponsored terrorism. Nevertheless, analysts in India have long pointed to Chinese military modernisation as a coercive threat to India. This modernisation includes missile development, such as the current deployment of the DF-21 and DF-3 missiles in Qinghai and Yunnan provinces.[3] Furthermore, there is some suspicion among Indian analysts that though Beijing's stated policy is that of minimum deterrence, the stationing of missiles such as DF-3 and DF-21 reflects a posture of nuclear coercion, and under some conditions, does not preclude a first strike against its neighbours.[4] It is also possible that since 1998, Beijing may have deployed nuclear weapons on the Tibetan plateau in response to a perceived Indian conventional military advantage and the May 1998 nuclear tests. Thus, despite growing trade between the two sides, there is some degree of unease in India over China's long-term intentions, more so in light of predictions of increased competition between the two countries for global energy resources. The concern in India is that if bilateral relations take a negative turn at some point in the future, China's current military modernisation will give China a significant advantage.

Impact of Non-state Actors

As aforementioned, nuclear weapons development and enhancement in South Asia are intricately related to long-standing rivalries between the concerned states. However, instability does not just stem from the risk of nuclear warfare between states in the region. Non-state actors also play a significant role in the nuclear security framework, aside from their role in facilitating nuclear proliferation. First, terrorist groups (such as Jaish-e-Mohammed and Lashkar-e-Toiba) that are connected to the Pakistani religious-political establishment can provoke tensions between India and Pakistan through mass casualty attacks. This was amply demonstrated following the December 2001 attack on the Indian Parliament by Jaish-e-Mohammed militants, which led to a ten-month stand-off between the two armies. A second danger is through a Kargil-style episode in which militants, in cooperation with official Pakistani agencies and the military, occupy territory in Kashmir. As the July 2007 siege of the Lal Masjid (Red Mosque) complex in the heart of Islamabad showed, militant groups are steadily expanding their geographical area of influence, adversely affecting the stability of Pakistan. Although the nuclear weapon complex is under military control, there might be pockets within the military that are sympathetic to fundamentalist groups. At the very least, political and religious instability in Pakistan creates uncertainty in the minds of policymakers within and outside the region.

Finally, fears have been heightened since 9/11 over the possibility of nuclear weapons technology transfers from Pakistan to terrorist networks, especially after it was revealed that some senior Pakistani nuclear scientists met with the Al-Qaeda leadership prior to 9/11. A related concern in the aftermath of 9/11 is that a fundamentalist Islamic group with Taliban/Al Qaeda links could take over Pakistan and with it, possession of the country's nuclear arsenal. Thus, Indian (as well as U.S.) threat perceptions include not just bilateral nuclear stability issues between India and Pakistan, but also the consequences of nuclear technology and materials falling into the hands of militant groups.

In general, the complex nuclear weapons scenario in South Asia is shaped by two main factors. First, the intense nature of the dispute between India and Pakistan strikes at the very core of their nationhood. It involves territorial disputes and terrorist violence, and is further complicated by the desire of some terrorist groups to acquire non-conventional technology. Second, South Asia is part of a broader nuclear weapons context that includes China and the United States. Military developments by either Washington or Beijing, which are perceived as a direct threat, also impact military policies (both conventional and non-conventional) in South Asia. At the same time, the continued strategic military collaboration between China and Pakistan (such as the joint development of the JF-17 fighter plane) is a factor that motivates India to continue nuclear and conventional modernisation. Furthermore, while the territorial disputes between India and China are relatively dormant, there is no final resolution. As developments in 2006-2007 demonstrated, there is still a considerable gap between the two sides on the territorial issue.[5] Due to this combination of factors, there are no clear incentives for either party to drastically reorient its nuclear policy.

Nuclear Policies in South Asia

Keeping the various security disputes and attitudes in mind, the next step is to consider the nuclear doctrines and policies of protagonists in the region. Both India and Pakistan strive for a minimum deterrent. The objective of India's nuclear strategy is credible minimum deterrence (CMD), meaning a secure and reliable second-strike capability after absorbing an adversary's first strike. The main potential targets of this projected deterrence capability are Pakistan and China. Pakistan's nuclear doctrine also seeks a credible deterrent, against India, and according to one senior nuclear weapons planner, its weapons are aimed solely at India. In particular it seeks to deter New Delhi from launching a conventional military attack such as an offensive for limited war objectives, including destruction of terrorist training camps, as well as attacks on nuclear facilities.

For both India and Pakistan, key components of their attitudes in nuclear defence demonstrate the incompatibility between their mutual nuclear postures. India's offer of a nofirst use pact has been rejected by Pakistan as nuclear weapons are an integral element of its (Islamabad's) defence doctrine. On the other hand, Islamabad has offered New Delhi a nowar pact, which ostensibly would reduce the prospect of full-scale conventional war and the risk of nuclear crises. However, such a proposal does not touch upon the proxy war waged by the Kashmiri militants and therefore has been rejected by New Delhi.[6]

Thus, both India and Pakistan strive for a secure second-strike capability as an integral element of their credible minimum deterrent doctrines. Since, neither side has constructed systems that are deemed completely satisfactory and reliable, nuclear modernisation continues. For India, this means a survivable delivery mechanism that can conceivably strike major cities in China. At present the longest range deployed missile is believed to be the Agni-IV with a range of 3,500-4,000 km, and can reach parts of western China.

This implies that for the foreseeable future, the Indian scientific-military establishment will reinforce their commitment to adequate delivery systems, especially the Agni-III and the nuclear sub-marine project (the Advanced Technology Vessel or ATV) that could carry a sea-based deterrent in the form of a sub-marine-launched cruise missile (the Sagarika-currently under development). Russia had agreed to lease two nuclear submarines to India under a package deal for the retrofit of the Admiral Gorshkov aircraft carrier which has already handed over to India in December 2013. India is about to receive Nepra sub-marine.

As stated earlier, Pakistan's deployed missile systems can reach most parts of India. These deployed missiles include the Ghaznavi (Hatf-3, range 290 km), Shaheen-I (Hatf-4, range 600-800 km), and the Ghauri-I (Hatf-5, range 1,500 km). Development is also taking place on the Shaheen-II (Hatf-6, range 2,000-3,000 km), which was successfully tested in February 2007. These missile developments illustrate Pakistan's desire for a more secure deterrent, once the range issue had been dealt with. In addition, Pakistan is also seeking a more secure second-strike capability through the acquisition of the Agosta 90B class submarine in late 2007. This vessel, the second to be added to Pakistan's navy, can carry the nuclear capable Harpoon cruise missiles.

Both countries have also achieved considerable progress in manufacturing another delivery system-cruise missile. India, in partnership with Russia, has developed the BrahMos, while Pakistan has the Babur. These missiles are meant to have land, sea, and air versions, and at least in the case of the BrahMos, will also have a variant for export. In the near future, Indian defence planners hope to introduce land attack cruise missiles with the capacity to carry a nuclear warhead over 1,500 km.[7] In addition, sub-marine and air force versions of the BrahMos are due to be tested in 2007. The missile is also being installed on ships and IL-38D maritime reconnaissance aircraft to give "strategic relevance" to the Indian Navy. Similarly, Pakistan has successfully tested its nuclear capable Babur (Hatf VII) cruise missile (range 700 km) in March 2007.[8]

In sum, in order to strengthen their nuclear delivery capabilities both India and Pakistan are seeking to perfect their missile arsenals, both ballistic and cruise. The dynamic nature of the pursuit of more reliable deterrence capabilities is also affected by strategic developments involving extra-regional actors, especially China and the United States.

Conclusion

Hence India has a very serious security concerns in South Asia vis-a-vis Pakistan, China and militant organisations (such as Jaish-e-Mohammed and Lashkar-e-Toiba). The security concerns are multi dimensional. The India has traditional enmity with Pakistan and China. Both Pakistan and China have close military and economic ties. China has provided nuclear and missile technology to Pakistan. Both Pakistan and China pose a serious security threats for India. China being a super power, having veto power in UN, having advanced nuclear and missile capability, economically strengthen, technologically and industrially advanced than India pose a real threat to India. But the biggest threat is militant organisations having the nuclear capability without any responsibility and no danger to existence poses a vital security threat to India because militants do not have any limitation like nations. Perhaps India without the close relations with US, Japan, Tiwan, Philpine, etc. cannot be in a position respond to the serious security threats posed by Pakistan, China and militant organisations.

References

1. See, Raja Menon, "China's proliferation and India's security," Seminar, June 2006.
2. Jing-dong Yuan, "The Dragon and the Elephant: Chinese-Indian Relations in the 21st Century," The Washington Quarterly, summer 2007, 30:3, p. 135.
3. "Promoting Strategic and Missile Stability in Southern Asia," IPCS Special Report 17, New Delhi, April 2006, p.12, www.ipcs.org.
4. Gurmeet Kanwal, "China's War Concepts," Air Power Journal, Vol. 3, No. 3, July-September 2006, pp. 68-69.
5. John W. Garver, "The Security Dilemma in Sino-Indian Relations," India Review, October 2002, Vol. 1, No. 4, pp. 3-4.
6. "India rejects 'no-war' pact plea," The Hindu, January 25, 2002, www.hinduonnet.com.
7. Rajat Pandit, "India-made BrahMos to Hit Global Arms Market," The Times of India, January 3, 2007, http://timesofindia.indiatimes.com.
8. "Pakistan military test fires missile," USA Today, March 22, 2007, www.usatoday.com.

Theorising India's Role in SAARC

— ***Pushpinder Kaur****

Abstract

This paper examines India's role in South Asian Association for Regional Cooperation (SAARC) by taking into three different stages that the SAARC has passed through so far. India being a natural leader of South Asian region played determining role when the SAARC was at the formative stage. New Delhi was successful to change menu as well as the operating principle of this regional body. However, its role was reactive after the inception of SAARC as India was not very enthusiastic about its prospects. Inspite of this fact that bilateral issues were not within domain of SAARC but still the small members including Pakistan used it to raise bilateral issues. India's perception towards SAARC changed in the late 1990s due to its aspiration to be an emerging power. Its attempt to be the leader of South Asian region generated critical mass for the progress of SAARC. Notwithstanding that Indo-Pakistan hostility has been continuing to undermine prospects of SAARC.

Introduction

India's Prime Minister, Narender Modi's diplomatic initiative to invite leaders of the SAARC countries on his swearing in ceremony in New Delhi on 26 May 2014, has once again not only underlined the significance of South Asian region but also the necessity of SAARC as a vibrant regional organisation in its foreign policy calculations. Either the head of state or the head of government from all the members of SAARC attended

* Assistant Professor, University Institute of Legal Studies, Panjab University, Chandigarh.

his swearing in ceremony except Bangladesh which was represented by its Foreign Minister. The SAARC countries reciprocated this move with same enthusiasm. Have this diplomatic initiative of India and response of the SAARC members thereof, created an enabling environment for India to play its due role in the SAARC and thereby make it as an effective instrument of regional cooperation in South Asia? In order to know that what kind of role India will play in the SAARC and how it would be appreciated by the other member of SAARC, it is essential to understand, the role played by New Delhi in SAARC in the past and how it was received by the other members? India's role in SAARC can be better understood by dividing it into three broader contexts like formative stage (1981-1985); initial stage (1985-1990) and subsequential stage (since 1991).

I Formative Stage

India's role in SAARC can be traced back to the late 1970s, when the idea of regional cooperation in South Asia was floated by the General Zia-ur-Rehman then President of Bangladesh. Initially, he gave the idea of regional cooperation in the domain of high politics as Bangladesh felt insecure because of New Delhi's assertive role in the region ranging from the dismemberment of Pakistan in 1971 to annexation of Sikkim in 1975 apart from latter's increasing involvement in Tamil issue of Sri Lanka. However, it was India's strategic compulsion to assert as a regional power particularly after its debacle in 1962 was with People's Republic of China and Pakistan's attack on India in 1965. Further, in order to ensure its security vis-a-vis Beijing and to augment its capability, India also demonstrated its technical nuclear capability at Pokhran in May 1974. All these development sent the wrong signal to small South Asian nations that India is behaving as a regional bully. It is that small nation psyche which led to the inception of the idea of regional cooperation in the region. Interestingly, the idea of SAARC was neither conceived by New Delhi nor Islamabad, rather it was the initiative of Dhaka which set the ball rolling. Bangladesh's India of regional cooperation in arena of high politics in South Asia was not appreciated by India.

India's initial reaction to the proposal for the creation of SAARC was reticence and caution based on the apprehension that the exercise could be a banding together of India's smaller neighbour to generate limits on India's political, diplomatic, economic and security options[1]. Although, New Delhi was not enthusiastic about the regional cooperation in the region but it played its due role to make sure that the SAARC could not jeopardise its national interest. At New Delhi's instance the menu of SAARC was changed from high politics (security & strategic matters) to low politics (economic and cultural domain). While participating in the deliberation from 1981 to 1985, India argued that high politics in the South Asian region has more potential to enlarge the constituency of conflict than that of cooperation. Issue pertaining to low politics ranging from economic to cultural issues have more potential to expand the constituency of cooperation from bilateral to multilateral. Another change ensured by New Delhi in the SAARC charter was that the operational principal of SAARC should not be majority but unanimity. Besides this, it also ensured that the bilateral issues shall not figure on the agenda of SAARC. These changes were substantial in nature: the former was in substance and latter were in methodology. At the formative stage, India insisted for these changes as it was aware of this fact that the SAARC is the product of insecurity syndrome of small nations vis-a-vis New Delhi and they can gang-up against it in the future. To bring small nations around on these changes, India also made tactical moves and even threatened them to establish SAARC without its membership, knowing well that without New Delhi's membership, the regional cooperation would not make any sense. The assertive role played by India at the formative stage was shaped by India's potential to be the natural leader not only of South Asian region but that of SAARC because of its size, capabilities and power potential in comparison to other members. Despite the substantial changes in the SAARC charter, India's perception about SAARC was not positive because of the various reasons. First, India thought that it is the design of west to marginalise it in the South Asian region. Second, the negative mind-set of the small South Asian nations led to the articulation of the idea of SAARC. Their mind-set was that at bilateral level they cannot handle New Delhi effectively as the latter is more capable than them. Third, India was not comfortable with regional approach in its neighbourhood-as advocated by SAARC. New Delhi's preferred bilateral approach towards small neighbours was giving the former a place of advantage vis-a-vis the latter. Fourth, India was not enthusiastic about SAARC because New Delhi was aware that it would be used as a platform by its neighbours to raise their bilateral disputes with India. Fifth, Indian policy makers were of the firm belief that New Delhi is unlikely to accrue substantial economic benefits from any SAARC arrangement[2]. Sixth, concern of Indian policy makers was that a regional organisation might impinge on her freedom of action in foreign affairs.

It can be inferred from the aforesaid account that New Delhi was not much enthusiastic about the outcome of SAARC as a regional body but it had played the determining and assertive role when the SAARC charter was deliberated and approved. However, India was not hopeful of any positive outcome from the working of SAARC as a regional organisation in South Asia given the regional scenario at that time but by playing assertive role at the formative stage, it did not allow the incorporation of any provision in the SAARC charter which could have jeopardised its national interest at the later stage.

II Initial Stage

After the inception of SAARC in 1985, India was neither enthusiastic about its leading role in SAARC nor New Delhi was seen as its natural leader by the other South Asian states. The small nations' psyche behind the idea of regional cooperation in South Asia was to create regional structure in the form of regional organisation and thereby to deal with New Delhi effectively at the multi-lateral level as they felt crippled to handle it at the bilateral level because of the power asymmetry in the region. Having huge power potential and capabilities, India was expected to play leading role in SAARC, which it could not play due to various three reasons. First of all, Islamabad contested New Delhi's leadership in regional organisation as the former did not want the SAARC to become an instrument in the hands of latter. Pakistan was driven by the fear psychosis that India's leadership in SAARC would further consolidate latter's already established hegemony in South Asia. Further, Islamabad was under the impression that SAARC was an Indian design to establish its hold on the South Asian region. For Pakistan SAARC was a zero-sum game as India being a leading South Asian nation would gain at the cost of small nation. Therefore, Islamabad contested New Delhi's leadership in SAARC. Second, the lack of consensus amongst other small members about India's leading role in SAARC because of their fear of India's hegemonic design and unsolicited interference in their domestic affairs. Small members did not contest but they were quite sceptical about India's leadership of SAARC. Third, India's failure to address this fear and thereby build trust amongst small members that its predominance in SAARC would not be detrimental to their interests. However, India was the biggest country in every sense of the term but its role in shaping the discourse of regionalism in South Asia was minimal. India was a reluctant player although it was a regional power in economic, political and strategic terms. New Delhi remained in dilemma over whether it should take the lead in SAARC or not. Indian policy makers and senior bureaucrats argued that India deliberately played a lowkey policy towards South Asian regional cooperation, particularly at a time when the idea of regional cooperation was being mooted by Bangladesh and New Delhi had been reluctant to increase the momentum of cooperation within the region, even after the initiation of the regional organisation[3]. India's policy towards SAARC was reactive rather than pro-active during the first decade of its inception. Indo-Pakistan rivalry further proved detrimental to the progress of SAARC and its structure did not allow it to become a functional entity apart from the other couple of factors.

India's ability to prevent foreign funding of SAARC is indicative of a capacity to forestall its use as an instrument of big power control. This makes the foreign participation in SAARC more problematic[4]. The differing political and economic interests of the SAARC members make for two contending approaches to regionalism. One implicitly functionalist view, which India advocates, sees SAARC as a vehicle for regional peace and security through advancing socio-economic development and cultural harmony in the region[5]. Pakistan and Sri Lanka show greater interest in arms control measures as do other smaller states. These differences reflect national perceptions of regional interests[6]. There has always been an underlying concern that SAARC was only a cover for the neighbours to conspire against India. SAARC has, therefore, been a procession of summits and declarations that were intended to be implemented, but rather to play to domestic and sometimes international galleries[7].

III Sub-Sequential Stage

In the 1990s, India's foreign policy had witnessed a major change in which it has been aspiring to be on the high table at the global level. However, the aspiration for global leadership role requires India to play leadership at the regional level. In order to be a regional leader, New Delhi articulated Gujral Doctrine as policy posture to improve its relations with small neighbours. Main thrust of India's changed policy perspective was that New Delhi did not expect reciprocity from its small neighbours. Gujral Doctrine was the policy posture wherein India tried to be the leader of South Asian region. India's changing mind-set was reflected in this policy of positive unilateralism towards its small neighbours wherein New Delhi did not expect reciprocity from them. India signed bilateral Free Trade Agreements (FTAs) with Bhutan, Bangladesh, Nepal and Sri Lanka which are favourable to them. This policy of positive discrimination was adopted by India to win the trust of its small neighbours that can facilitate the growth of South Asian regionalism[8]. This policy was a political investment made by New Delhi to reap the long term benefits not only in economic terms but also in political and strategic domain. It was also argued in the mainstream literature that globalised India realised that success of its liberalised economy depends upon its ability to increase exports to new markets elsewhere therefore it cannot ignore South Asia where it enjoys comparative advantage in almost every economic sector[9]. Apart from comparative, India always enjoys locational advantage as it constitutes the hub of the South Asian region and its neighbours are located on its periphery and physical connectivity infrastructure is already in place because before independence Pakistan and Bangladesh were part of India. India, Pakistan and Bangladesh approximately constitute more than 94 per cent of South Asia in terms of landmass and population.

India became proactive in SAARC in the late 1990s, as it realised that if SAARC would continue to be a defunct organisation, it would drive the small South Asian states to come close to the external players like China which would be a major setback to its South Asian policy because New Delhi has always been remained against the outside interference in South Asian affairs. Its consistent position on South Asia has been to keep it sanitised from external intervention as New Delhi identifies its security scenario with the entire South Asian region. External intervention in South Asia jeopardises its regional security scenario. Of late New Delhi felt the need of regional cooperation to keep Beijing's involvement minimum in the region.

To put life in SAARC, India articulated Gujral Doctrine that enabled India not only to settle water disputes with Nepal and Bangladesh but also to sign bilateral Free Trade Agreements (FTAs) with Nepal, Bhutan and Sri Lanka. Pakistan condemned Gujral doctrine by arguing that it is an Indian attempt to isolate Pakistan in the region. It was also argued that this doctrine promotes sub-regionalism and undermines regional cooperation in South Asia. But this was not the case because sub-regionalism and bilateralism are also the more meaningful tools to promote regionalism in a region of which South Asia is no exception.

Since India-Pakistan conflict had remained a major hurdle in the progress of SAARC, New Delhi also tried to improve its relations with Islamabad. In 1997, India and Pakistan agreed to initiate composite dialogue to solve their outstanding disputes. The process of composite dialogue was started in early 1998, which got derailed because of the nuclearisation of South Asia in May 1998. In February 1999, Atal Behari Vajpayee, then Prime Minister of India inaugurated a bus service between Amritsar and Lahore when he himself boarded the bus to Lahore. The composite dialogue between the two neighbours was revived again in the form of peace process which was set in motion between them in November 2003. New Delhi was convinced that the success of peace process would generate enough critical mass for the progress of SAARC.

The core objective of India's policy towards SAARC is to integrate South Asian states into a common market, create a web of regional interdependence and preserve India's strategic primacy. However, the SAARC region cannot be allowed to become the highest ambition to be pursued by India but if New Delhi cannot carry its neighbours along, its weight will not be fully felt in other parts of Asia[10]. In the era of globalisation, all South Asian states sought to integrate with global market, therefore they could no longer avoid cooperating with each other at the regional level. Until the 1990s, regional cooperation was either politically willed or resisted, whereas in the 1990s, it was driven by larger economic considerations and became inevitable. India now had the opportunity to integrate the regional market under its leadership[11]. Further, the access to Indian market has become imperative for small states in the region to ensure their economic growth. For instance, Sri Lanka signed Free Trade Agreement (FTA) with India in 1998 and is now eager to integrate itself with India in general and neighbouring southern states in particular through Comprehensive Economic Partnership Agreement and a land bridge. Bangladesh has already negotiated Free Trade Agreement with India and Bhutan has already elevated its income levels by responding to India's energy needs through the harnessing of water resources[12].

India as being a largest economy of South Asian region needs to take a lead and make sure that benefit of regional cooperation are equitably and in a time-bound transparent framework shared and felt by all the SAARC countries[13]. India's relatively better developed infrastructure, capabilities and experience in all these areas could be tapped usefully for the common good of the region and India's world class facilities/expertise used to enhance regional capabilities. Regional cooperation and a coordinated mechanism for dealing with natural and man-made disasters should also become an area of priority. The South Asian University and a regional integrated tourism circuit, for example, would go long way in promoting value addition and incremental opportunities to all countries[14].

India's neighbours generally feel more comfortable in a regional design that incorporates bilateral priorities and concerns. A regional approach is also in accordance with the ethos of the emerging global order and will be effective to bring about a regional integration in economic and strategic terms. This is an argument for strengthening, not weakening, SAARC[15]. However, India's efforts to promote regionalism in South Asia through the aegis of SAARC continue to be marred by the primacy of contentious politics among the nations of the region particularly between India and Pakistan[16]. If the leadership of India and Pakistan can set aside their history of conflict and animosity, then SAARC could well 'reinvest' itself as the South Asian equivalent of the European Union[17]. SAARC needs to rediscover the basis of the cooperative enterprise in the South Asian region, and incorporate security studies as integral to its concerns[18]. India has been a key promoter of Afghanistan's integration with South Asia. India's push for Afghanistan's inclusion in SAARC was primarily directed at seeking economic and regional integration of these two regions[19]. India tends to pose her hegemonic nature towards the smaller South Asian neighbours by utilising the power asymmetry among the SAARC members which places India an advantageous position amongst them. This hegemonic position provides India the scope to emphasise on bilateral initiatives rather than multilateral platforms. These attitudes by India resemble to one of the core arguments of neo-realism that the exercise of the dominant postures by the big powers over the smaller ones is constant reality of the anarchic international structure[20]. Consequently, power unevenness between India and the other SAARC members generates the environment of suspicion on the dominance of one over the others. Neighbouring states have always been doubtful about India's foreign policy postures within region, whether it is a bilateral or a multilateral initiative[21]. However, India tried to address fear of small states in the region through the Gujral Doctrine but New Delhi needs to think out of the box to construct the South Asia as a shared space in the vocabulary of international politics. India need not look at SAARC as a regional economic grouping in which it should get immediate and proportionate returns. Rather, India should look at it as a political investment. It must look at the grouping as a constituency it needs to consolidate for its candidature as one of the poles in a potentially multi-polar world[22].

Conclusion

To sum-up, it can be argued that New Delhi has played significant role in SAARC since its formative stage. Although, India was not initially receptive of the idea of regional cooperation in South Asia but slowly and gradually New Delhi changed its perception towards the SAARC proposal. India played decisive role when the SAARC was at the formative stage and did not allow SAARC to become detrimental to its national interest as the regional environment was hostile and the mindset led to the articulation of the idea of SAARC was anti India. India played decisive role in the deliberations when the process to establish SAARC was set in motion. However, India was a reluctant partner in SAARC deliberation but its role was determinant at the formative stage. After the inception of SAARC, India played reactive role because New Delhi's preferred mode to connect with its neighbours was bilateral instead of multilateral approach. Of course, India's role in SAARC was conditioned by structural constraints of this region, perceptions of small states and its own inhibitions. New Delhi was a reactive nation as far as SAARC was concerned almost for one decade since its inception. Due to change in the regional and global scenario and India's foreign policy priorities thereof, New Delhi's attitude towards SAARC changed considerably in late 1990s. India's aspiration to be an emerging power at the global level requires New Delhi to play leading role and to ensure peace in the South Asian region. India articulated Gujral doctrine as its foreign policy posture to play leading role in the South Asian region that enabled it to solve water disputes with Nepal and Bangladesh and free trade agreements with Nepal, Bhutan and Sri Lanka. India's role changed from reactive to proactive in SAARC in late 1990s. However, Indo-Pakistan bitterness continues to hamper the growth of regional cooperation in general and progress of SAARC in particular. New Delhi needs to think out of the box to construct South Asia as shared economic, cultural and strategic space.

References

1. J. N. Dixit, "Prospects of South Asian Cooperation in the Transformed World", *South Asian Survey*, Vol. 10, No. 1, 2003, p. 49.
2. Kishore C. Dass, *Regionalism in South Asia: Negotiating Cooperation, Institutional Structures*, New York: Routeledge, 2008, p. 199.
3. Lok Raj Baral, "Cooperation with Realism: The Future of South Asian Regionalism", *South Asian Survey*, Vol. 13, No. 2, 2006, p. 270.

4. Ross Mallick, *Development, Ethnicity and Human Rights in South Asia*, New Delhi: Sage Publications, 1998, p. 23.
5 *Ibid.*
6 *Ibid.*
7. Eric Gonsalves, "Regional Cooperation in South Asia", *South Asian Survey*, Vol. 13, No. 2, 2006, p. 205.
8. Kishore C. Dass, n. 2, p. 200.
9. *Ibid.*
10. S. D. Muni and C. Raja Mohan, "Emerging Asia: India's Options", *International Studies*, Vol. 41, No. 3, 2004, p. 319.
11. *Ibid.* p. 320
12. *Ibid.*
13. Amar Nath Ram, "SAARC in a Globalised Era-Imperatives and Opportunities", *India Quarterly*, Vol. 65, No. 4, 2009, p. 444.
14. *Ibid.* p. 445.
15. S. D. Muni, "Problem Areas in India's Neighbourhood Policy", *South Asian Survey*, Vol. 10, No. 2, 2003, p. 188.
16. Suman Sharma, "India and SAARC in the Post-Cold War Phase", *World Focus*, November-December 2011, p. 883.
17. Amarjit S. Narang, "Indo-Pakistan Relations and SAARC: Retrospect and Prospect", Kulwant Kaur & Baljit Singh Mann, eds., *South Asia: Dynamics of Politics, Economy & Security,* New Delhi: Knowledge World, 2006, p. 111.
18. A. P. Rana, "New Directions' in the Study of SAARC: Evaluating the Bases of Regional Cooperation in South Asia", *South Asian Survey*, Vol. 10, No. 1, 2003, p. 26.
19. Shanthie Mariet D' Souza, "Afghanistan in South Asia: Regional Cooperation or Competition", *South Asian Survey*, Vol. 16, No. 1, 2009, p. 34.
20. Noor Mohammad Sarkar, "Why SAARC is Less-Effective? A Neo-realist Explanation of India's Role in SAARC", www.academia.edu/3814473/Why_SAARC_is_Less-Effective_A_Neo-realist_Explanation_of_Indias_Role_in_SAARC accessed on 24/09/2014 at 3:30PM.
21. Arvind Gupta, "South Asia in India's National Security Strategy", Krishnappa Venkatshamy and Princy George, eds., *Grand Strategy for India: 2020 and Beyond*, New Delhi: Pentagon Press, 2012, p, 186.
22. Bhupinder Brar, "SAARC If Functionalism has Failed, Will Realism Work", *South Asian Survey*, Vol. 10, No. 1, 2003, p. 40.

Strengthening SAARC: India-Sri Lanka Experience

— *Gurnam Chand**

Abstract

With globalisation gaining momentum, regional organisations are gaining importance day by day. The economic and social welfare of a country is greatly advanced if it interacts as a part of a regional block rather than individually. The emergence of a number of regional blocks in Asia, Africa and America are evidence of this reality. SAARC is dedicated to economic, technological, social, and cultural development emphasising collective self-reliance. It is the biggest regional grouping in terms of human resources. To make SAARC vibrant, a qualitative change is required among SAARC members to improve the form and content of bilateral relations among members. It will help to create better understanding among members to appreciate the nuances of collective cooperation. In this context, growth of India-Sri Lanka relations during the last two and half decades is an interesting example of building win-win relationship.

Introduction

The setting up of the South Asian Association for Regional Cooperation (SAARC) marked the beginning of regional cooperation in South Asia. SAARC was established in December 1985 at a summit of seven countries of South Asian region namely Bhutan, Bangladesh, India,

* The writer Dr Gurnam Chand, Associate Professor and Head Department of Political Science, M. R. Govt. College, Fazilka, Punjab.

Maldives, Nepal, Pakistan and Sri Lanka held at Dhaka. Initiatives for SAARC was taken in 1977 by the then President Zia-Ur-Rehman of Bangladesh.[1] With the entry of Afghanistan the membership of SAARC now stands at eight. There is widespread feeling of pessimism among South Asian countries at the halting progress made by the SAARC since its inception in 1985. SAARC is the world largest regional grouping of 1.47 billion people; it has not been able to assert its collective strength like Association of South East Asian Nations (ASEAN) or the European Union (EU).[2] It has also not been able to advance in a manner it was expected to.

The emerging economic strength of some of the SAARC members in the context of the new global order has opened the eyes of many external associates to be its partners. The attainment of maturity of SAARC is reflected from the fact that it has expanded itself by admitting Afghanistan as eighth member state besides granting 'observer status' to china Japan, south Korea, Iran, USA and European Union.[3]

The foreign secretaries of the seven countries met for the first time in Colombo in April 1981. The Committee of the whole, which met in Colombo in August 1985, identified five broad areas for regional cooperation. New areas of cooperation were added in the following years. Some of the primary objectives of SAARC are to promote the welfare of the people of South Asia and to improve their quality of life; to accelerate economic growth, social progress and cultural development in the region; to promote and strengthen collective self-reliance among the countries of South Asia; to promote active collaboration and mutual assistance in the economic, social, cultural, technical and scientific fields.[4]

Although it has been stressed repeatedly since the inception of SAARC, that mutual political disputes should not be dragged into the area of regional cooperation. If SAARC wishes to be a viable and dynamic organisation, it cannot avoid tackling political and security matters which affects all the countries; just as ASEAN and other regional organisations have been doing.

India and Sri Lanka attitude and perception towards SAARC

Developments in the domestic and external sphere of SAARC countries, during the last two and half decades, have undergone significant transformation. As a result it has led to reorientations and readjustments in the attitude and perceptions of these countries towards SAARC. The eight members nations are of different sizes have diverse political systems, economic disparities, different security perceptions, preponderance of India in South Asia, suspicion and mistrust of SAARC members among themselves. Yet despite the disparities and different attitude and perceptions, member countries have made significant progress in 17th SAARC summits towards finding common ground for economic, social and cultural cooperation.

Initially, India's perception towards SAARC was negative, as India feared that small countries will gang up against her. Later on India's attitude towards SAARC has become positive. Of course India has taken care of her national interest but without defining it in competitive paradigm. Due to dominant position of India other countries are not cooperating. SAARC can be successful if India hegemony is converted to influence.[5]

Inaugurating the meeting of Foreign Ministers of SAARC at New Delhi on 1st August, 1983, late Mrs Indra Gandhi said that India earnestly wanted positive response of SAARC nations towards regional cooperation. She made it clear that SAARC had no military objectives and that so far as India is concerned; she stood for friendly relations among the neighbours and non interference in the affairs of others.[6]

Both India and Sri Lanka believe in regional cooperation as one of the best means for promoting their bilateral as well as regional interests. Both have utilising the Colombo Plan for securing their respective socio-economic interests and both are cooperating to make SAARC a successful regional association.

In view of the regional problems mentioned earlier, it is extremely important to find out attitude and perceptions of both the countries. In this paper, however, we will confine ourselves to studying attitude and perceptions of Sri Lanka.

The fifth SAARC annual summit was to be held in Colombo (Sri Lanka) in 1989, but could not be held due to existence of sharp differences between India and Sri Lanka on the ethnic conflict of Tamils in Sri Lanka. The sixth SAARC summit was held on 21st December, 1991 at Colombo. The seven leaders agreed to liberalise trade through step by step approach. They also decided to closely examine the Sri Lanka's proposal to establish a SAARC Preferential Trade Agreement (SAPTA) by 1997. SAPTA contains provisions for favourable treatment to be given to the least developed countries in SAARC region. It was expected that discussions would soon begin to replace SAPTA by a SAFTA (South Asia Free Trade Area).[7]

In October 1992, the Sri Lankan President Ranasinghe Premdasa visited New Delhi as the SAARC Chairman; Indian Prime Minister P. V. Narasimha Rao signaled that Sri Lanka ire over suspected India's role in SAARC summit in Colombo in 1991 had become thing of the past. In a joint communiqué issue after the visit, India and Sri Lanka gave a call for upgradation and cooperation among SAARC countries for combating and preventing terrorism through regular official level consultations and exchange of information on a need to know basis.

In December 1992, Sri Lankan Prime Minister did not support the attempt on the part of Pakistan to raise the Babri Masjid demolition issue in the SAARC meeting. Sri Lanka did not support the Pakistani attempt to raise Indo-Pak relations (Kashmir issue and nuclear proliferation issue) at the SAARC meeting. The mature view of Sri Lanka to disallow Pakistani attempt reflected a healthy sign for the growth of India-Sri Lanka relations.

The tenth SAARC summit was held in 29-31 July, 1998 at Colombo. The summit was held in the background of nuclear tests conducted by India and Pakistan in May 1998. To boost the trade and commerce among SAARC nations, this summit decided to set up a committee of experts. Former Prime Minister Atal Behari Vajpayee and the Pakistan former Prime Minister Nawaz Sharif tried to identify the regional problems that needed to be resolved. The summit expressed the concern at the lack of progress in the direction of custom free South Asia. However, emphasis was laid on the need to work for greater regional trading.[8]

The fifteenth SAARC summit was held in Colombo in August, 2008. The summit reaffirmed members countries commitment to the principles and objectives enshrined in the SAARC Charter. India and Sri Lanka recognised that SAARC has been making steady and incremental progress over the years. The summit recognised the need for SAARC to further strengthen its focus on developing and implementing regional and sub-regional projects in the agreed area on priority basis. Member's countries were convinced that the process of regional cooperation must be truly people-centered, so that SAARC continues to strengthen in keeping with expectations as a robust partnership for growth for the peoples of South Asia.[9]

SAARC countries were of the view that if bilateral issue not taken will lead to economic integration, but that has not happened. So, time has come for SAARC countries to engage in bilateral issues. To make SAARC vibrant; a qualitative change is required among SAARC members to improve the form and content of bilateral relations among members. It will help create better understanding among members to appreciate the nuances of collective cooperation. In this context, growth of India-Sri Lanka during the last two and half decade is an interesting example of building win-win relationship. Both the countries have not been letting any opportunity to go waste which can help them to increase the scope and speed of India-Sri Lanka cooperation at the bilateral as well as at the SAARC levels. The leaders of the two countries have been using every occasion to achieve the objective through personal meetings as well as the exchange of delegates.

India-Sri Lanka Political Experience (Intervention to Non-intervention Policy)

Both India and Sri Lanka are third world countries and both happen to be the members of the non-aligned movement. They also share a common colonial past. As such, both of them have certain common interests to pursue in the international arena, especially vis-a-vis the developed countries. It was in the pursuit of these interests that they became members of the SAARC. The cooperation envisaged in the idea of SAARC, however, cannot nourish unless the South Asian countries, including India and Sri Lanka, have a mature relationship both at the bilateral and the multilateral levels.

India-Sri Lanka relations are based on a deep and abiding friendship on shared historical experience and common civilisation and cultural values sustained by geographical proximity and ethnic affinity.[10] Sri Lanka President Mahinda Rajapaksa has aptly described India-Sri Lanka relations as of 'relative.' In recent years, the relationship has been marked by close contacts at the highest political level, growing trade and investment, cooperation in the field of development, education, culture and defence as well as broad understanding on major issue of international interest. India supported the right of the Government of Sri Lanka to act against the Liberation Tigers of Tamil Eelam, helping bring the three-decade armed conflict between the Sri Lankan forces and the LTTE to an end in May 2009. At the same time, India conveyed at the highest levels its deep concern at the plight of the Tamils. India's clear, sincere and abiding commitment to the unity, sovereignty and territorial integrity of Sri Lanka and its supports for a peaceful, negotiated settlement for the Sri Lanka Tamilian issue that put animosity behind and sowed the seeds for eliminating all irritants in the political relations between the two countries. The Institutional framework for the relationship is provided by frequent contacts at the political level. The strong ethnic, cultural, linguistic and religious links between the two countries have resulted in the development of close relationship at the people to people level.[11] There have been shifts and changes in the pattern of relationship marked by mutual differences, irritants, co-operation and friendship. Both the countries have developed adequate strength to withstand the stresses and strains is a notable feature of their bilateral relationship.

At the core of India foreign policy is a reiteration of the Indian government's commitment to protect Sri Lanka's unity, sovereignty and Territorial integrity.[12] India has changed its policy towards Sri Lanka from intervention to non-intervention. India's pragmatic policy of non-intervention in the internal affairs of Sri Lanka and Sri Lanka's commitment towards India's security concern created a credible atmosphere and consequently brought a new era in relations between two countries. India's new policy has contributed to remove the cultivated fear complex of Sri Lanka. The leadership and the people in Sri Lanka have changed their mindset and thinking about India; for the first time, India is considered as an asset rather than a threat to the Sri Lanka's security.[13]

Until 1980's India-Sri Lanka relations remained for the greater part friendly and cordial. The negotiated settlement of the citizenship and maritime boundary issues stood as classic examples of the results that could be achieved through mutual goodwill and understanding. However, with the aggravation of the ethnic conflict and the consequent Indian involvement in the ethnic conflict, there grew an adversarial relationship between the two countries. The escalation of ethnic conflict in Sri Lanka and possibility of involvement of external powers in the ethnic conflict and its perception in India and Sri Lanka compelled India and Sri Lanka to come to an agreement on 29th July 1987. Subsequently Indian Peace Keeping Force was sent to Sri Lanka to oversee the implementation of the accord. India proactive politico-military intervention proved ultimately failure.

A key reason for India-Sri Lanka relations to improve dramatically since the mid 1990's was the change of governments in both the countries (as power moves from the hand of the United National Party to the Sri Lanka Freedom Party after 17 years). Following the General Election in India the Congress party led by Rajiv Gandhi was replaced in New Delhi by the National Front Government headed by Vishwanath Pratap Singh. V.P. Singh declared his Sri Lankan policy by saying, *"In the first place, it was mistake to have sent our troops* there. The whole affair had started on a wrong note. Our position was clear: we favour a *phased withdrawal of the IPKF from Sri Lanka."*[14]

The Sri Lanka policy of V. P. Singh Government became clear when the External Affairs Minister I.K. Gujral gave the statement that, India no longer wanted to intervene in Sri Lanka militarily. The Sri Lankan Government should deal with its Tamil problem as an internal affair in which India would not take any interest. He also said that the Indian Territory would not be allowed for subversive activities against Lanka under any circumstances.

The V. P. Singh Government was succeeded by the Chandrashekhar Government. Its tenure was short lived and by February-March 1991. It was clear that India would be going in for another general election. During the rule of V.P. Singh and later that of Chandraskehkar, India-Sri Lanka relations had been of low key nature.[15] After the assassination of Rajiv Gandhi on May 21, 1991 entire Indian perspective on the LTTE changed. On 14 May 1992 the LTTE was formally banned in India.

In the General election of 1991, the Congress Party came back in power and P. V. Narasimha Rao became the Prime Minister of India. After assuming power Rao declared his Sri Lankan policy. He said that, India would not desire to take any active part in resolving the problems of Sri Lanka. These problems would have to be solved by Sri Lankans themselves, regardless of whether they are Sinhalese or Tamils, "At the bilateral level, India showed more interest in developing of framework for a working relationship with Sri Lanka, rather than identifying itself with Sri Lankan Tamil cause."

The Government of India and the Government of Tamil Nadu would ensure to the extent possible, that the LTTE did not have base or sanctuaries in India. India remained opposed to any secessionist or terrorist group operating from its territory against any of its neighbours.[16] An Agreement was signed between India and Sri Lanka in July 1991 to establish an Indo-Sri Lanka Joint Commission. Its sub-commissions included those on trade, investment and finance, science and technology.

President Premasdasa visited India in October 1992 and discussed the bilateral relations of two countries.

Chandrika Bandaranaike Kumaratunga became the Prime Minister of Sri Lanka. She headed a coalition of political parties, People's Alliance. She attempted to resolve the ethnic conflict through peaceful means and involved in direct talks with LTTE. After being elected, President Chandrika Kumaratunga paid a significant visi to India in March 1995 and laid the base for close relation with India. President Chandrika Kumaratunga again visited in May 1995 for the SAARC Summit.

The Narasimha Rao Government lost power in 1996 and H.D. Deve Gowda became the new Prime Minister of India. I. K. Gujral once again assumed the office of External Affairs Minister. President Kumaratunga sent her Foreign Minister Lakshman Kadirgamar to India on a goodwill visit in 1996. India and Sri Lanka focused their attention on economic cooperation. Later on I. K. Gujral became the Prime Minister in late 1997. He clearly understood the importance of maintaining friendly relations with the neighbours. He introduced 'Gujral Doctrine.'

After the midterm elections in 1998, Bhartiya Janta Party along with its alliance (National Democratic Alliance) came in to power at the Centre. As soon as Atal Bihari Vajpayee became the new Prime Minister of India, the Sri Lanka representative was among the first to reach India. India reassured Sri Lanka that it respected the sovereignty and integrity of Sri Lanka and it had no intention to intervene in its internal affairs.[17]

The fourth session of the India-Sri Lanka Joint Commission took place in New Delhi on December 18, 1998. The Indian Prime Minister Atal Bihari Vajpayee visited Sri Lanka to attend the 10th SAARC Summit. He said that India would be willing to conclude bilateral Free Trade Agreements with the member countries. By the end of December 1998, President Kumaratunga's visit to India resulted in the conclusion of the historic Indo-Sri Lanka Free Trade Agreement. The Sri Lankan President said,

> *"The agreement would not only cement close relations between India and Sri Lanka but also serve as a pacemaker for regional cooperation in South Asia."*[18]

In May 2000, when the conflict intensified between the LTTE and the security forces over Elephant Pass and refugees started streaming to India, the Indian government approached the issue cautiously. When Sri Lanka requested for troops or arms also after the Elephant Pass fell to the

LTTE on April 2000 and the security forces were trapped in Jaffna, India declined to oblige.

Like previous governments, the administration of President Mahinda Rajapaksa devotes the highest priority to India-Sri Lanka relationship. President was of the view that the India-Sri Lanka Agreement of 29th July1987 provided the best prospects for a solution. While there were those who were critical at the time of signing of the Agreement, over the years people have come to appreciate the fact that the 13th Amendment to the constitution, which enacts the provisions of the Accord, provide space for a meeting of minds of those from all sides holding moderate opinion. There is also an appreciation of the role played by the IPKF.

In 2006, the government launched military campaign to root out the LTTE. After a 30 month long military campaign, Sri Lankan armed forces have ultimately military defeated the LTTE and freed the nation from three decades of terror in May 2009.[19] There is consensus within an outside Sri Lanka that with the LTTE out of the way, a golden opportunity has presented itself before the government to work towards a just, honourable and durable political settlement of the ethnic conflict. [20] The government has promised a political package to address the grievances of the Tamil community and resettle the displaced persons in the north. President Mahinda Rajapakse also noted at victory rally in Colombo on 3 June 2009, "The war is over. Now is the time to win the hearts and minds of Tamils". India's constant refrain, over the years has been that Sri Lanka to come up with a political solution, including devolution of powers to the minorities to solve the Tamilian issue.

In the post-LTTE period without reconciliation the internal situation in Sri Lanka would continued to be restive.[21] On the re-election of President Mahinda Rajapaksa in January 26, 2010, Prime Minister Manmohan Singh reiterated, "*We have time tested ties of* friendship and co-operation. I look forward to working closely with you to further strength *our close and multidimensional bilateral relations in the coming years.*"Affirming a strong relationship with India, Sri Lanka President Mahinda Rajapaksa stated, "*All countries are* friends of Sri Lanka but India is Sri Lanka's relation (relative)."[22]

India-Sri Lanka Economic Integration Experience (ISLFTA)

As most of the SAARC countries are underdeveloped, economic integration is much needed for the development of this region. The process of economic integration in South Asia gained momentum with the implementation of SAPTA in 1995 under the broader frame work of SAARC. SAPTA contains provisions for favourable treatment to be given to the least developed countries in SAARC region. SAPTA was established in the hope that by the first decade of 21st century a South Asian Free Trade Area would become a reality. Although SAARC countries agreed SAPTA to SAFTA but proper implementation of SAFTA had not been achieved till date. SAARC countries have not facilitated trade within SAARC countries. They are doing trade via third countries. There is enough space for the SAARC countries for economic co-operation.

When SAARC is compared with regional organistion such as EU and ASEAN, it is left behind them. Intra regional trade amongst the members of SAARC is approximately 5 per cent, whereas, it is more than fifty per cent among the members of EU and more than twenty-five per cent amongst the members of ASEAN. India trade with SAARC countries is very little.[23] Even though SAFTA is an ambitious agreement to achieve its fundamental goal of trade liberalisation, it is being criticised because its coverage has been limited to trade in goods. Due to existence of bilateral FTAs between member's countries, which benefit bilaterally, the common interests are being sacrificed.

India-Sri Lanka economic integration has transformed and developed rapidly in all aspects in the past two and half decades. India's foreign policy decision to offer Sri Lanka favourable terms in trade has yielded greater economic partnership. The political stability in Sri Lanka and commitment of the leadership provide the business communities of two countries to work on new ideas and explore the opportunities for trade, commerce and investment. Bilateral trade between two countries has increased tenfold and it is hoped it would touch US $8 billion by 2015.

In the post, 1990 consistent efforts have been made by India and Sri Lanka to upgrade bilateral economic relations. India and Sri Lanka have established a dense bilateral network of institutions and mechanisms so as to ensure sustained cooperation irrespective of domestic politics and changes in the external environment of the two countries. An Agreement was signed between India and Sri Lanka in July 1991 to establish an Indo-Sri Lanka Joint Commission. A large legal frame work is provided by India-Sri Lanka Free Trade Agreement on 28th December, 1998 with an overall objective to promote trade and economic relations between the two countries and to promote Foreign Direct Investment (FDI). It entered into force from first March, 2000.[24] Other legal frame works are: a Double Taxation Avoidance Agreement (DTAA), a Bilateral Investment Protection and Promotion Agreement (BIPPA), and agreements/ MoU on Air Services, Small Development Projects, and Co-operations in small scale industries tourism, Information Technology, agricultural, Education, roads, highways, science and Technology.

Aside from the legal framework, it has an institutional framework in the form of the India-Sri Lanka joint commission, a dispute settlement mechanism and frequent contacts at the political level, including at the highest levels, President, Prime Minister and Foreign Ministers of both the countries are engaged in bilateral discussion covering the entire gamut of the bilateral relationship. There is regular institutionalised dialogue at all levels of government including Foreign Secretary- led consultations, commerce secretary level talks between customs authorities, fisheries officials, the Navy/Coast Guards etc. Both the nations realised that restrictions on trade between the two are detrimental to their economic growth and prosperity. They also realised that relaxation of the restrictions, abolition of tariffs and lifting restrictions on free movement of manufactured goods and services minimise the illegal trade between the two countries. [25]

The FTA which was signed at the highest political level marked an important milestone in India-Sri Lanka relations and trade relations in particular, as it concretised and paved the way for closer economic integration. It is expected to bring about enhanced trade between the two countries as well as to expanded and diversified cooperation in a range of economic spheres, including investments. The agreement provides for duty preference access for the goods manufactured in two countries. Both the countries have listed products for immediate duty free entry into each other's territories. India has agreed to phase out its tariffs on a large number of items within a period of three years. Sri Lanka will likewise do so in eight years.[26] Both the countries have drawn up negative lists in respect of which there are no duty concessions. Both the countries intend to reduce the items in the Negative List through periodic consultations. The agreement sets out the rules of origin criteria for eligibility for preferential access. Product having domestic value addition of 35 per cent will qualify for preferential market access. Sri Lanka's exports with a domestic value addition content of 25 per cent will also qualify for entry into the Indian market if they have a minimum10 per cent Indian content.

The India-Sri Lanka FTA has led to significant upturn in overall bilateral trade. In 2011, the overall trade turnover was US$ 4919 million while it was US$ 3020 million in 2010. This is almost an eight fold increase from US$ 658 million in 2000, when FTA came into effect.[27] The overall trade turnover has grown five times since the entry into force of the FTA. India is now the largest trade partner of Sri Lanka. Sri Lanka has also emerged as India's largest trade partner in South Asia. India is now the largest exporter to Sri Lanka. Sri Lankan exports have grown faster than Indian exports to Sri Lanka, growing tenfold as against a fivefold increase in Indian exports since the signing of the FTA.[28] FTA has facilitated two way trades between India and Sri Lanka. India was the second largest exporter to Sri Lanka before the FTA and is now the largest exporter to Sri Lanka. But, more important, India became the third largest export destination for Sri Lankan products (rising from 16th rank) as a result of FTA. Bilateral trade in 2012-13 amounted to US$ 4.63 billion.

Sri Lankan exports to India are mainly non-traditional items such as vanaspati, copper and marble that have benefited from the FTA. An indicator of relative benefits of the FTA to the two countries is that more than 90 per cent of Sri Lankan exports gain from FTA concessions as against only 45 per cent of Indian exports to Sri Lanka receiving the same benefits.

In terms of investments, India maintained its position as one the leading investors in Sri Lanka. According to latest figures from the Board of Investment of Sri Lanka, India is among the top four overall investors in Sri Lanka with cumulative investments over US $800 million. Investments from India picked up rapidly after the signing of the FTA.[29] India was the second largest foreign direct investor in Sri Lanka in 2011, with an investment of US$ 147 million. In 2012, India emerged as the fourth largest overall investor in Sri Lanka with investment about US$ 160 million.[30]

Although there is economic cooperation between India and Sri Lanka and it is growing over the years and FTA is a significant step forward but a lot more needs to be done in the near future. There is a scope for improvement. The Governments of India and Sri Lanka also felt that more action was required to unleash the full potential of our bilateral economic relations. Accordingly, in June 2003, the two governments decided to set up a Joint Study Group to explore possibilities of starting negotiations for a Comprehensive Economic Partnership Agreement. Both countries after thirteen rounds of negotiations jointly announced in July

2008 that CEPA agreement was fully negotiated and ready for signature. CEPA is expected to build on momentum generated by the FTA. CEPA seeks to extend bilateral opening beyond trade in goods, to include services, investment and overall economic co-operation. It will address some of the issues that have come up in the implementation and operation of the FTA as well. It will impart renewed impetus and synergy to bilateral economic relations. CEPA aims at creating a more facilitating environment for Sri Lankan exports and seeks to remove some of the perceived impediments to exports from Sri Lanka.

Both sides had decided to sign the CEPA during the 15th SAARC summit held in Colombo but due to reservations expressed by Government of Sri Lanka. During the 8th session of India-Sri Lanka Joint Commission held in January, 2013 at New Delhi, both countries have agreed to hold intensive consultations towards forging a special economic partnership for comprehensive and sustained economic cooperation.

To conclude, during last two and half decade, leadership in both the countries gave a new life and showed interest in India-Sri Lanka relations. Leadership in both the countries concentrated on reviving areas of common interest, which has been ignored so far due to ethnic conflict. Instead of focusing on conflict intervention, India has pushed economic integration as its main policy objective in the bilateral relations. 'Gujral Doctrine of India Foreign Policy', which aimed at strengthening relations with neighbouring countries played a significant role in improving the relations between two countries. Atal Bihari Vajpayee and Chandrika Kumaratunge signed the historic FTA. Ranil Wickremesinghe which was known for its west-oriented policy, supported close relations with India. The relations have become stronger during the tenure of Prime Minister Manmohan Singh and President Mahinda Rajapakse. The maturity of relations between both the countries is evident from Sri Lanka's strong support to India for permanent seat in the United Nations Security Council. The year 1998 saw the biggest boost in economic relations when both the countries signed FTA. After signing of the FTA, both the countries have not been letting any opportunity to go waste which can help them to increase the scope and speed of India-Sri Lanka cooperation at the bilateral as well as at the SAARC levels. FTA has resulted in rapid expansion of trade volume, growth in investments, better connectivity, and a more intensive economic and development cooperation between both the countries. FTA has helped narrow the trade gap between the two countries in favour of Sri Lanka, while attracting more Indian investments into the country. FTA between India and Sri Lanka, which was an early experiment in South Asia, provides useful lesson's for other South Asian economies in term of progress in strengthening trade and economic linkage. This study concludes that economic relationship between India and Sri Lanka are at the highest level of cordiality. Study gives projections that India and Sri Lanka will develop development partnership in the coming years. Economic relations can go a long way in building and cementing stable and peaceful political relations. The main task of the government of both the countries is to maintain the same pattern of relation by providing a continuity in co-operation and strengthening their mutual understanding in order to take their relations to the new level of excellence and to develop model relationship which can be emulated by other SAARC countries .

References

1. India while advocating regional cooperation did not make any proposal for institutional cooperation because it anticipated resistance from its neighbours, particularly Pakistan. The disparity in size, demography, resources and levels of development between India and all its immediate neighbours led to this approach. There was perception that, in view of the perennial tensions between India and Pakistan, and the distance that characterised India's relations with Bangladesh and Sri Lanka, Zia-ur-Rahman's proposal would be purely cosmetic exercise. There was also apprehension that the forum, if created would be a regional platform for 'India bashing.'
2. Compare to other regional organisations, SAARC has not been able to advance in a manner it was expected to. The EEC as well EU has not only led to the economic integration of twenty five member states but also enabled its members to transcend their political sovereignty and national identity in order to promote the notion of European Community as a political and cultural entity. ASEAN has become a vibrant regional organisation which has promoted intra-regional trade and also tried to construct common strategic space in Southeast Asian region.
3. The inclusion of china as an observer is seen by most SAARC member states as a counter balance to India. To take China 'Observer Status' positively, SAARC countries can engage China in Trade.
4. Davinder Kumar Madan,"SAARC: Origin and Development," in Verinder Grover (ed.), India Government and Politics, Deep and deep, New Delhi. pp. 634-670
5. When in EC mutual distrust has been converted to mutual trust, EC became successful in trade. In NAFTA despite political differences, they have achieved economic integration. Originally ASEAN was a security

organisation and recently has taken economic agenda. So SAARC countries should learn from these organisations.

6. Indra Gandhi, Inagural address at the South Asian Regional Co-operation meeting of Foreign Ministers at New Delhi on August 1, 1983 in Verinder Grover (ed.), India Government and Politics, Deep and deep, New Delhi. pp. 615-618.
7. Colombo declaration issued on 21 December, 1991, SAARC Secretariat, Kathmandu, http://www.saarc- sec.org, accessed on 15 January, 2014.
8. Declaration of the Tenth SAARC summit Colombo, 31 July,1988, SAARC Secretariat, Kathmandu, http://www.saarc-sec.org, accessed on 15 January, 2014.
9. Fifteenth SAARC Summit Colombo, 2-3 August, 2008, SAARC Secretariat, Kathmandu, http://www.saarc-sec.org, accessed on 15 January, 2014.
10. S. Muthiah (2003), *The Indo-Lankan: Their 200 Year Saga,* Colombo, Indian Heritag Foundation, p. 1.
11. R. Hariharan, Revisiting India's Sri Lanka Policy Options, *www.asthabharti.org published in Dialogue,* Vol. 10, No. 5, July-September 2009.
12. Every joint statement issued by the government of India and Sri Lanka since the mid-1990 has made a reference and reassurance to protect Sri Lanka's sovereignty. See *http:/www/meaindia .nic.in.*
13. P. Sahadevan (2004), "India-Sri Lanka: A Changing Relationship", *Dialogue,* New Delhi, Vol. 5, No. 3, January-March, p. *153.*
14. Farzana Begum, *Dynamics of Indian Diplomacy and Foreign Affairs,* Swastik Publications, Delhi, p. 62.
15. J. N. Dixit, *Assignment Colombo* (1997), Konarak Publication, New Delhi, p. 295.
16. *Ibid.*, p. 298.
17. Avtar Singh Bhasin (2001), India-Sri Lanka Relations-Section-IX, Nineties-The Decade of Hope and Despair, in India-Sri Lanka Relations and Sri Lanka's Ethnic Conflict-Documents-Vol. V, Indian Research Press, New Delhi, pp. 2591-99.
18. Dushni Werakoon (2001), "Indo-Sri Lanka Free Trade Agreement," *Economic and Political Weekly*, Mumbai, Vol.36, No. 6, 24 February-2 March, 2001, p. 627.
19. Army Chief lieutenant General Sarath Fonseka Said in an address over national television.
20. S. D. Muni (2009), "What Next in Sri Lanka after LTTE Defeat?" *The Tribune,* Chandigarh, May 4.

21. There is Little doubt that President Mahinda Rajapaksa, after the decimation of the LTTE in May 2009 has moved at snail's pace to devolve powers to the Tamil minority promised under the 13th Amendment. During the civil war, Rajapaksa had even talked of a '13th Amendment plus' or more powers to the Tamils. But after the Sri Lankan Army victory, Sinhala triumphalism dominates and now the ruling party talks of '13th Amendment minus' and even scrapping the amendment together.
22. http://www. thehindu.com., accessed on 18 July, 2013.
23. There are great potential of mutual trade between India and Pakistan because of their geographical proximity, complementarity and competitiveness to each other. During 2012, the official trade between India and Pakistan could have increased from US$ 2.1 billion to US$ 29.8 billion, if both removed certain irritants in the trade. In 1948-49, India's share in Pakistan global imports was 50.6 per cent, which went down to 4.6 per cent in 2012-13. Non-Tariff Barriers are putting restrictions on the bilateral trade potentials between India and Pakistan.
24. Ministry of External Affairs, (BSM Division: Sri Lanka), "Brief on India Sri Lanka Relations." See, http//meaindia. nic.in/foreign relations/Sri Lanka. Pdf.
25. Frazana Begum , *op.cit. p*.172.
26. S. S. Upadhyay (2007), *India and Sri Lanka: Economic and Political Relations,* ABD Publishers, Jaipur, p. 151.
27. High Commission of India, Colombo, "Bilateral Trade between India and Sri Lanka," http://www.hcicolombo.org-I mht, accessed on 12 January, 2014.
28. High Commissioner of India, Colombo, "Bilateral Commercial Relations," http://www.hcicolombo.org., accessed on 17, April 2011.
29. High Commissioner of India, Colombo, "Investment and Development Cooperation between India and Sri Lanka," http://www.hcicolombo.org-4 mht
30. High Commissioner of India, Colombo, "Investment and Development Cooperation between India and Sri Lanka," http://www.hcicolombo.org, accessed on 12 January, 2014.

Curbing Transnational Terrorism in South Asia: A Regional Concern

— ***Kanwar Deep Singh****

Abstract

As a turbulent and complex region with multi-ethnic societies with divisions along linguistic, regional, communal, and religious lines, South Asian nations have been engaged in brutal fighting within and across borders, critically obstructing the region's growth and development potential. This paper argues that most states in South Asia started cooperating with each other when they realised that terrorism posed a threat to their very existence and the survival of their governments. However, this cooperation is missing in those cases where governments still think that terror can be harnessed for strategic benefits. The cross-border dimension of many of the internal, often interrelated, security crisis that seriously affect South Asian states and inter-state relations highlights the importance of developing an effective, broad-based regional response to the threat. This paper aims to analyse the trends of transnational terrorism in South Asia and to assess the regional approach to counter it.

Introduction

Issue of modern terrorism has been a complex one arising due to ideological, political, ethnic and religious objectives in various countries across the globe. The dawn of the 21st century has witnessed the rise of a most serious crisis in the form of global terrorism. Irrespective of their position, power, influence and progress, all nations across the globe have experienced the disastrous impact of terrorism. Some terrorist campaigns are short-lived while others extend their lifespan challenging the writ and freedom of the state authorities. In the backdrop of the growing and altering non-conventional and conventional threat perception, and the era of globalised world leading to easier access to technology, today terrorism has emerged as the most challenging security threat that South Asian Nations are dealing with.[1]

International terrorism is not a new phenomenon to the world or to South Asia in particular. The 11th September incident has only demonstrated another facet of international terrorism – the tremendous potency of technology and innovation – besides the globalisation of economies, which have come to transcend national boundaries. Multi-national corporations and non-state players now have a worldwide reach. These have compromised the authority of the state. Non-state players and black money as well as narcotics trade have acquired power, making some of the terrorist groups financially viable and independent. The revolution in information technology and communication also enables instant transmission of ideas and information at a global level, by the terrorist outfits who can now exploit 'cyber' terrorism as well as the deadly and sophisticated Precision-Guided Missiles (PGMs), and other weapons of mass destruction. The rise of religious fundamentalism has introduced a new ideology which sanctifies '*Jehad*' (holy war) and '*Fidayeen*' (suicide) attacks.[2] This exploits the situation of 'backwardness' and economic disparity of the frustrated youth of society.

Transnational Nature of Terrorism in South Asia

Today, South Asia generally evokes the image of a region that is plagued by violent religious extremism where groups like the *Taliban, Al-Qaeda* and *Lashkar-e- Tayyeba* (*LeT*) are active. This is also known to be a region where Maoists groups are running riot in large part of its territory. Groups like the LTTE who pursued their separatist agenda could only be wiped out with great effort. South Asia has hogged the limelight because of their activities.

The phenomenon of terror has over shadowed the fact that a number of South Asian economies are growing at a fast pace and have the potential to grow even faster if not hampered by frequent acts of terror. Terrorism has plagued the region for the last several decades. However, counter-terrorism came on to the global agenda after 9/11. Though the US has managed to thwart terror after that, South Asia has not been equally lucky. Most South Asian nations are still facing the problem of terrorism, and if anything, the problem has only intensified in several cases. India, Pakistan and Afghanistan were among the nations most impacted by terrorism in 2011, according to a New Global Study, which said the terror strikes worldwide had increased fourfold since the start of the Iraq war in 2003.[3] According to Global Terrorism Index (GTI) Pakistan, India and Afghanistan accounted for 12 per cent, 11 per cent and 10 per cent of global terrorist incidents respectively from 2002 to 2009.[4] Nevertheless, some positive developments have also been noticed on this front which have placed South Asia at a crucial juncture where further cooperation can help the region overcome this problem. Terrorism has defied an agreed definition. But after 9/11 there seems to be a rowing opinion that this should not be allowed to come in the way of fighting a phenomenon, which is harmful to everyone. The United Nations Resolution 1390 (2002) adopted by the Security Council at its 4452nd meeting, on 16, January 2002, reaffirmed that acts of international terror constitute a threat to international peace and security.[5] The causes of terrorism vary from country to country. In the South Asian region, the terror groups can be placed in three categories:

- ***Terrorism arising out of religious fundamentalism***
- ***Left-wing extremism***
- ***Terrorism resulting from the desire for secessionism.***

The threat of terrorism is no longer confined to a particular region or state, but it has become globalised and operates in a network system. With globalisation and advancement in technologies, terrorism has also spread in the veins of all nations and India is no exception. Before 11 September 2001, terrorism was perceived as a local affair. It was condemned but not seriously dealt with by the international community. However, the massive blow of 9/11 came as a wake-up call to the international community and shattered the earlier complacency. Today terrorism is no longer considered an internal affair of one state, but one that has an international connotation. Each act of terror, no matter where, is often linked to, or supported by terrorists somewhere else.

Terrorist outfits originating in one country can operate as part of a transnational or international network, and thus can have transnational or international consequences. For example, it is the fact that individuals from various nationalities were operating in Terrorist Groups in Jammu and Kashmir in 90's[6]. In terms of the Afghanistan-Pakistan border region, *Al-Qaeda* forces and the *Afghan Taliban* that fled from Afghanistan are active in parts of Pakistan, and Al-Qaeda is believed to have connections with indigenous Pakistani terrorist groups that engage in 'anti-Western' attacks and separatist militancy in Indian Kashmir. These terrorist groups also have connections to the *Haqqani* group, *Lashkar-e-Toiba and Jaiish –E – Mohammed.* In Bangladesh some forms of terrorist activity exists due to foreign terrorist groups of the region which are also connected to local groups. Afghanistan, there has been evidence of Bangladesh-born militants being recruited and trained by the *Taliban.*[7] With regard to the transnational nature of terrorism in Sri Lanka conducted by the LTTE, the Indian state of Tamil Nadu was known to harbour LTTE cadres and support its operations in Sri Lanka. The LTTE was also suspected of having links with terror groups in Pakistan.

The nature of support differs from country to country which support these groups. Pakistan for instance has been known to provide safe haven, training, funding and weapons for anti-India *Jihadi* groups which operate in Jammu & Kashmir. It is imperative to differentiate between countries on the degree of complicity from their governments in activities. Though the Governments of Myanmar, Bhutan and Bangladesh are not directly involved or have not been proved in aiding and abetting anti-India groups, these governments have remained as silent spectators and allowed their territory to be used for anti-India activities either by design or by compulsion. However, Myanmar, Bhutan and Bangladesh have offered positive cooperation with India, a fact that establishes the good intentions of these countries.[8] This is in sharp contrast with Pakistan, where any kind of cooperation has been too little and too late. Hence, the nature of support is a discerning factor in judging the level of complicity of the respective governments. In a way, the nature or form of support can be used to establish the intent of the supporting country. ***Based on the level of support that the states provide, states can be bifurcated into those which actively support terrorism in India and states which act only as sanctuaries to terror groups. Pakistan falls under the former while states like Bangladesh, Bhutan and Myanmar fall under the latter.***[9]

India: A Case of Multiple Threats

India suffers from both cross-border and homegrown religious extremism, as well as ethnic and left-wing insurgency. Many terrorist and insurgent groups operate across borders and are either based in other countries or cooperate with groups in other countries. Although there is no evidence of an official Al-Qaeda presence in India, many incidents since 2006 bear the marks of ideological inspiration from Al-Qaeda. Extremist groups that are based in Pakistan or Bangladesh and operate regularly in India, principally in Jammu and Kashmir, include Lashkar-e- Toiba, Jaish-e-Mohammed, Hizb-ul-Mujahideen, Harkat-ul-Mujahideen, *Al-Badr, Harkat-ul Jehad-al-Islami, and Jamatul Mujahideen.*[10] Some observers have reported a nexus between Indian Maoists and Liberation Tigers of Tamil Eelam (LTTE) and among Maoists, the Pakistani ISI, and Islamic or Kashmiri groups. There have also been suggestions of operational coordination between Nepali Maoists and their Indian counterparts. The present Maoist (Naxalite) movement in India is based largely in tribal areas in 170 districts in 12 states.[11]

Concomitant with India's growth in economy, population and strength, the country witnessed increasingly frequent internal conflicts. Though, India faced insurgency issues in the North East in Nagaland in the early 1950s, its tryst with contemporary terrorism dates back to 1980s when the movement for *Khalistan* began. It was a religiously motivated separatist movement which wanted a separate state for the Sikhs called "*Khalistan*".[12] This period, which saw the birth of modern terrorism in India, gradually started to evolve in other parts of India like Jammu and Kashmir, the seven sister states of the North-East and the central and eastern parts of India. Most of these movements sought independence from India while some sought to destabilise and bleed the Indian government. The area of operations in most cases was restricted to India as the people behind such movements fought only against the Indian state. ***In spite of their strongly domestic profile, external support structures in India's immediate neighborhood were one of the primary factors which helped these groups to sustain and intensify their campaign fueling several instances of internal strife in India. The external support for terrorists comes from Pakistan, Bhutan, Myanmar and Bangladesh. India shares land borders with all these countries. Of these, Pakistan has been the most active and vehemently supporter of anti-India groups with even elements from the Government-owned Intelligence wing actively involved in aiding and abetting these groups. It is known to have supported Sikh militancy in the 1980's in India and gradually created support structures for Islamic militancy in the northern state of Jammu and Kashmir. It is now documented that it is also supporting some groups in the North Eastern region of India.*** Bangladesh, Myanmar and Bhutan have also known to have provided or provide safe haven to North Eastern Insurgent groups.[13]

Indian Government has banned 36 terrorist outfits operating in India, under section 35 of Unlawful Activities (Prevention) Act, 1957. Out of 36 organisations, seven are transnational terror groups. Of the seven transnational groups, two groups: *Al-Qaeda and LTTE* are truly global names.[14] The other five groups in India are *Lashkar-e-Taiba (LeT), Harkat-ul -Mujahideen, Al-Badr, Jamat-ul-Mujahid and Hizbul Mujahideen (*HM). The other groups included ULFA, SIMI and lesser known entities such as *Hynniewtrep National Liberation Council* of Meghalaya, *Kanglei Yaol Kanba Lup* of Manipur and *Akhil Bharat Nepali Ekta Samaj*, which though virtually unheard of are considered deadly enough by the Government to be designated as *Terrorist Organisations.*[15]

In South Asia, terrorism has long been a factor influencing interstate relations. With the proximity of states, terrorism quickly becomes transnational in nature. Therefore, it is imperative to understand that in a world which is getting smaller and more interconnected each day through technological developments and intricate international trade, economic, political, and social relations, the epidemic of terrorism breeding in one country, invariably affects the peace and stability of another. States in SAARC have extremist and terrorist organisations broadly subscribing to either Maoist, separatist or extremist religious ideology with cross-border linkages. ***Terrorism has further jeopardised the sovereignty and integrity of the States in the region, and posed a threat to friendly and good neighbourly relations impacting on the evolution and effectiveness of the SAARC.***[16]

Countering Terrorism: Cooperation in SAARC

The last decade of twentieth century was the heyday of the terrorism in South Asia. If it was LTTE in Sri Lanka, then Maoists were fighting the monarchy in Nepal. Similarly terror groups were increasing their presence and activities in India, Bhutan, Bangladesh, Myanmar, Pakistan and Afghanistan. A turning point in counter-terrorism however came because of an event that took place outside the region. This event was 9/11 which made international community realise that if terrorist groups are allowed to flourish in South Asia then they would not allow the rest of the world to live in peace.[17] The attack on the twin towers not only brought the West into South Asia but it also prompted them to encourage India and Pakistan to cooperate under SAARC and work for peace and progress. The developments at the Islamabad SAARC summit could be taken as starting point in this context. Effort was made to consolidate this development in subsequent SAARC summits. Though these efforts could not significantly bridge the gulf between India and Pakistan they did motivate other nations to cooperate on terror. Most of these countries were themselves under terrorist threat. Besides, international opinion had decisively turned against terrorism. There is a growing realisation throughout the world that transnational terrorism and organised crime cannot be controlled without bilateral or regional cooperation. National leadership in the South Asia region recognises the need for such cooperation, but is unable to translate the principle into action owing to historical bilateral suspicions.

Since its inception, concern over terrorism and the need for greater regional cooperation has prominently figured in the SAARC agenda. Starting from the signing of the SAARC Regional Convention on Suppression of Terrorism in Kathmandu on 4 November 1987 that came into force on 22 August 1988, strong consensus existed among the states for regional counterterrorism cooperation.[18] Numerous commitments have since reiterated the political commitment to counterterrorism at the regional level. ***A SAARC Terrorist Offences Monitoring Desk (STOMD)*** was established in 1995 in Colombo to support the implementation of the convention by collecting, assessing and disseminating information on terrorist offences, tactics, strategies and methods. An Additional Protocol to the SAARC Regional Convention on Suppression of Terrorism was signed in 2002 but which came into force in January 2006[19]. In actual practice, however, no effective coordination is occurring because of a **"trust deficit"** among SAARC member countries. The only progress made through the SAARC mechanism has been an increase in the frequency of meetings of the police chiefs, who now get together twice a year. On the bilateral side, the much hyped ***Joint Anti-Terror Mechanism (JATM)***[20] announced by the prime minister of India and president of Pakistan (Havana Agreement, September 2006) also seems to have gone nowhere. The Bangladeshi newspaper The Daily Star reported on May 10, 2006 that SAARC police chiefs felt that SDOMD (SAARC Drug Offences Monitoring Desk) was not actively working, and they wanted to set up a ***SAARCPOL***[21] along the lines of ***EUROPOL.*** It is not clear whether the ***SDOMD*** is able to bring coordinated action against drug trafficking in the region. According to the US State Department's International Narcotics Control Strategy Report for 2007, only India and Pakistan regularly share information through SDOMD. In August 2007, the Home

Secretaries of India and Bangladesh decided to revive the ***Joint Working Group (JWG)*** to exchange actionable information to check terrorism and render mutual cooperation.

The Fourteenth SAARC Summit in New Delhi in April 2007 decided to implement existing conventions on terrorism and enhance cooperation among member states in tackling organised crime. The Home Ministers' meeting in Delhi in October 2007 resolved to take "proactive and sustained" measures to implement the SAARC Regional Convention on Suppression of Terrorism and Additional Protocol.[22] Members also agreed to accelerate implementation of the Draft Convention on mutual legal assistance in criminal matters and to upgrade the existing mechanism for cooperation and exchange of information. Finally a Convention on Mutual Legal Assistance in Criminal Matters was signed in August 2008. However, these commitments have, resulted in limited concrete action.

One of the major initiatives in the region was made in the South Asian Association for Regional Cooperation (SAARC) Summit in 1987, when for the first time a Regional Convention for the Suppression of Terrorism was agreed upon by member states. However, in spite of the possess of over two decades, SAARC has not made any serious effort to implement the provisions of the convention. At the 15th SAARC summit held in Colombo in 2008[23], leaders again took a pledge to fight terrorism collectively, but in reality SAARC has not made any progress forward on this matter. Perhaps a lot could be attributed to the political complexities of the region, with special reference to Kashmir. However, it has been argued that most member states except Pakistan have joined hands with India in the suppression of terrorism.

Since India is at the centre of SAARC and is the only country which shares borders with every other member country, counter terror cooperation in South Asia often boils down to cooperation between India and other SAARC nations. Now the discourse on counterterrorism has gone beyond establishing the existence of terror groups and their camps in countries. If the action against terror groups by Bhutan and Bangladesh proved their existence, 26/11 and arrest of Ajmal Amir Kasab along with access to David Coleman Headley has conclusively proved that terror groups have been operating from Pakistan[24]. Finally, the statement made by Musharraf that Pakistan created militant groups to wage war in Kashmir can now be taken as an official admission. Today, South Asians are assessing counter-terror cooperation in South Asia faced with three questions—whether to cooperate, how to cooperate or not to cooperate. As terrorism and its operations and destructive outcomes are translational in nature in South Asian region, it would be an impracticable and momentary measure for the different states to battle against it individually. So, on the positive side , some South Asian states have adopted bilateral efforts to overcome activity by terrorist groups. One inspiring and unprecedented example of neighbourly cooperation and understanding is when Bangladesh managed to abandon number of terrorist camps operating in Bangladeshi territory and handed over the leadership and cadres of the terrorist groups to Indian authorities. Following improvement in relations, India and Myanmar conducted joint military operations—***Operation Goldenbird***[25] (May 1995) and ***Operation Leech*** (1996) against the terrorist and insurgent activities. Bhutan and India took joint military action against insurgent groups under the code name ***Operation All Clear***[26] in the year 2003.

Pakistan and Afghanistan

The situation in Pakistan and Afghanistan requires combined analyses as the Taliban's sway over both countries increases. For successful counter-terror cooperation in South Asia, it is imperative that India and Pakistan also cooperate. Unfortunately, this cooperation is not as forthcoming as has been the case between India and other countries. Pakistan presently seems to be going through a churning process. A weak democratic government is pitted against a traditionally strong army, which has its own world view. In recent times, Islamist groups like *Tahriq-e-Taliban* have also become important players. Thus a three cornered struggle for dominance appears to be underway in Pakistan. The country is a state of flux, which has not given these players enough time for a major rethink of existing policies. On the other hand, the objective of gaining strategic depth by having greater say over the affairs of Afghanistan has further muddled the whole situation.[27] A clear Pakistani approach towards counter-terrorism is not likely to emerge till a strong democratic government takes root in the country. The situation in Afghanistan and Pakistan has emerged as a big headache not only for South Asia but also for the rest of the world. This is why major Western powers also in Afghanistan under ISAF and NATO[28] do not seem to be getting a grip on the problem and the worsening crisis in the West has made them look for quickest exit route.

Historical mistrust, short-term foreign policy objectives, lack of capacity at the national and regional level, fragile political systems, and technical limitations have variously been held responsible for crippling regional efforts to curb this transnational terrorist activities. South Asian nations breed terrorism due to their deficiencies in governance and political ethos reflected in corruption, opportunism, nepotism, and ineptitude. Their capacities for justice administration and implementation of law continue to deteriorate. SAARC countries have not kept pace with the growth of population, and communal ill-will is created with the uneven processes of modernisation rapid transformation, and issues such as the displacement of civilians and the psychological and emotional trauma of the victims of terror and violence.[29]

Conclusion

South Asia has made some progress in counter-terror cooperation. Now terror groups in most South Asian countries are not seen as assets. On the other hand, most of these countries have realised that presence of such groups within their territories makes the security situation volatile and poses a threat to them. This has prompted action against several terrorist and insurgent groups. As desire to eliminate these forces has emerged, many countries are refusing to see insurgents as freedom fighters, leading to clear-cut action against them. This has dramatically changed the security situation in a large part of South Asia. This opportunity if properly utilised may lead to an economic boom in many of these countries. Sri Lanka, Bangladesh and Bhutan seem to be the major beneficiaries of this. The countries which are hamstrung are those who have not been decisive in their approach towards terrorism.

Pakistan and Afghanistan seem to be internally in major turmoil. The continued crisis has often raised questions about their survival. Though these countries have managed to keep their geographical territory intact, the development process seems to have suffered, giving further opportunity to extremist and terrorist forces. A strong SAARC could have attempted to solve the crisis in Afghanistan and Pakistan region. But as SAARC itself struggles it has given allowed external powers to come in and make attempts to control the situation. If the countries of the region have a genuine desire to cooperate on counter-terrorism, then this cooperation should not be kept hostage to legal regimes. In any case, the interpretation of the law depends on people who are supposed to follow it. So even if some agreement is reached and the member countries are not willing to cooperate then they would achieve little. On the other hand, if the countries are sincere about fighting terrorism then they would find ways to cooperate. South Asia has to decide whether it wants to overpower terror or will it allow terror to overpower it.

Terrorism in the South Asian region has become increasingly more transnational and merciless in nature with the effects of globalisation and developments in technology – threatening the security of all nations of South-Asia. ***Counterterrorism strategies have to be an international effort due to the transnational nature of terrorism in the matters of networking, funding, armaments and weapons, and political and religious support. Thus, terrorism is a regional concern and it can only be effectively eradicated with regional measures and cooperation. Terrorism can only be contained through concerted, sustained international effort and understanding.***

References

1. Sandra Distredi, *Indian Foreign and Security Policy in South Asia,* New York, Routledge, 2013, pp. 144-147.
2. N.K. Gupta, "Terrorism in Kashmir: A threat to India's Secular Polity," Kulwant Kaur (ed.) *Global Terrorism Issues, Dimensions and Options,* New Delhi: Kanishka Publishers, 2005, pp. 177-180.
3. The Indian Express, December 4, 2012.
4. *Ibid.*
5. Anand Kumar, "Assessing Counter-terror Cooperation in South Asia", Anand Kumar (ed.), *The Terror Challenge in South Asia and Prospect of Regional Cooperation*, Published by Pentagon Security International, New Delhi, pp.118-123.
6. K. Warikoo, "Religious Extremism and Terrorism In Kashmir", Mahavir Singh (ed.), International Terrorism and Religious Extremism, New Delhi: Anamika Publishers & Distributors (P) Ltd., 2004, pp. 254-255.
7. Hasan-Askari Rizvi, "Islamabad's New Approach to Kashmir", Waheguru Pal Singh Sidhu and *et. al.* (ed.), Kashmir New Voices, New Approaches, New Delhi: Viva Books Pvt. Ltd., 2007, pp. 141-142.
8. Archana Upadhay, *India's Fragile Borderland's : The Dynamics of Terrorism in North-East India*, I.B. Tauris Publications, London, 2009, pp. 123-126.
9. Candra Bhushana, *Terrorism and Separatism in the North-East India,* Delhi, Kalpaz Publication 2004, pp 33-37.
10. N.S. Jamwal, "Terrorist Modus Operandi In Jammu and Kashmir", *Strategic Analysis*, Vol. 27 No. 3, Jul-Sep 2003, pp. 384-386.

11. K. Santhanam *et.al.*, Jihadis in Jammu and Kashmir-A Potrait Gallery, New Delhi, Sage Publications, 2003, pp. 224-226.
12. K. Bhushan and G. Katyal, *Attack on Parliament Challenges Before the Nation,* New Delhi: A.P.H. Publishing Corporation, 2002, pp. 49-50.
13. Kamaroopi, "The North-East: Insurgency and Development" *Economic and Political Weekly,* July 27, 2002.
14. K. Santhanam *et.al.*, Jihadis in Jammu and Kashmir-A Potrait Gallery, New Delhi, Sage Publications, 2003, pp. 224-226.
15. Candra Bhushana, *Terrorism and Separatism in the North-East India,* Delhi, Kalpaz Publication 2004, pp 33-37.
16. P.M. Kamth, "Challenges to India's Foreign Policy in the new Era: Need for a Holistic Approach", Annupurna Nautiyal (ed.) *Challenges to India's Foreign Policy in the New Era*, New Delhi, Gyan Publishing House, 2006, pp. 36-40.
17. Harish Kapur, *Diplomatic Journey-Emerging India,* New Delhi, Manas Publications, pp. 24-31.
18. Tridib Chakroborti, (2010), 'Charting out the SAARC Destiny: Perambulating its way Forward' *World Focus*, Vol. XXXI, No. 7, Delhi: (July), pp. 247-251.
19. Chanchal Kumar (March 2012), 'Indo-Pak Relations and SAARC: Building Bridges', *World Focus*, and Vol. XXXIII, and No. 3, (March), pp. 41-45.
20. Ashwani Kumar, "International terrorism and India", V. D. Chopra (ed*), India's Foreign Policy in the 21st century*, Delhi, Kalpaz Publications, 2006, pp. 69-73.
21. *Ibid.*
22. Saswati Chanda and Alok Kumar Gupta, "Pakistan-Bangladesh Nexus in Abetting Insurgency in India's Northeast," in Dipankar Sengupta and Sudhir Kumar Singh's (ed.) "Insurgency in North-East India: The Role of Bangladesh", Authors Press, New Delhi, 2004, p. 279.
23. J.N.Dixit, "Emerging International Security Environment: Indian Perceptions with focus on South Asian and Central Asian Predicaments." K. S. Santhanam and Ramakant Dwinedi (ed.), *India and Central Asia Advancing the Common Interest,* New Delhi, Aramaya Publishes, 2004, pp. 16-22.
24. Rajen Harshe, "India-Pakistan Conflict over Kashmir: Peace through Development Cooperation", South Asian Survey, Vol. 12 No.1, January 2005, pp. 54-55.
25. Pradip Saikia, "Northeast India as a Factor in India's Diplomatic Engagement with Myanmar: Issues and Challenges," Strategic Analysis, New Delhi, Vol. 33, No 6, November 2009, pp. 880-881.

26. Samay Ram, *Tackling Insurgency and Terrorism*, New Delhi: Manas Publications, 2004, pp. 133-134.
27. Rizwan Zeb, "Pakistan And Jihadi Groups in the Kashmir Conflict", W.P. Singh Sidhu et. al., *Kashmir-New Voices, New Approaches,* New Delhi: Viva Books Private Limited, 2007, pp. 70-71.
28. Saswati Chanda and Alok Kumar Gupta, "Pakistan-Bangladesh Nexus in Abetting Insurgency in India's Northeast," in Dipankar Sengupta and Sudhir Kumar Singh (ed*). Insurgency in North-East India: The Role of Bangladesh,* Authors Press, New Delhi, 2004, pp. 279-281.
29. J.N.Dixit, "Emerging International Security Environment: Indian Perceptions with focus on South Asian and Central Asian Predicaments." K.S. Santhanam and Ramakant Dwinedi (ed.), *India and Central Asia Advancing the Common Interest,* New Delhi, Aramaya Publishes, 2004, pp. 16-22.

Climate Change and SAARC: The Politics of Regional Cooperation

— *Dr Rajnish Saryal**

Abstract

The term climate change is commonly used to explain global warming of the world due to the rise of average global temperature. The ever growing use of fossil fuels for energy requirements of modern industries across the world is primarily responsible for climate change. The energy requirements of industries are slated to increase in future considering the level at which the GDP of some of the developing countries is growing. At the present time, the share in the emission of GHGs of developing countries particularly China, India, Brazil and South Africa has been increasing tremendously. This has resulted in concerted efforts on the part of developed countries particularly the United States and the European Union to place the developing countries at par with the developed countries in the climate change negotiations. India being a developing country has been arguing that the 'per capita emission' and 'historical responsibility' should be the starting points of any negotiation on climate change. However, such demands unless supported by likeminded actors could not be realised in the climate change negotiations. The South Asian Association for Regional Cooperation (SAARC), a supranational organisation of the South Asian Region, showcases a great potential for such collective bargaining in the climate change discourse. The South

* Assistant Professor in Political Science, Panjab University Regional Centre, Ludhiana.

Asian region that comprises of seven developing countries is one of the highly vulnerable regions of the world due to its unique topographical, climatic and costal conditions. The climate change has further aggravated this situation particularly by making costal countries more vulnerable in the event of sea rise due to global warming. The present research intends to explain the potential role of SAARC to articulate a common agenda on climate change of SAARC members. The paper further seeks to unravel the capacity of SAARC as a negotiating agent in the collective bargaining on post Kyoto regime vis-à-vis European Union.

The International Environmental Politics emerged as a new field of study in International Relation in the 1970s. The developed countries in the post industrialised phase felt the burns of environmental degradation caused by their unbridled economic growth through energy intensive industrialisation. Severe environmental problems of global reach like ozone depletion and global warming, etc. did change the old parameters of national security which correspond with national jurisdiction. With the rise of these new problems, the existence of life on earth came into question. This resulted in creating a kind of phobia in the world which led the peoples across borders to recognise these as common problems. This recognition was authenticated by the conclave of world's two biggest environmental summits namely United Nations Conference on Human Environment (UNCHE) and United Nations Conference on Environment and Development (UNCED).

The global environmental issue like climate change indeed has gone up to the agenda of nation states during the last two decades. This has generated interest among the scholars of International Relations (IR hereafter) theory to reexamine the mainstream theories of IR to answer questions raised by climate change, as for example, does the traditional parameters of national security really need redefinition in the wake of climate change posing global threat? The climate change as a global problem questions the earlier division of international politics into high politics and low politics. This division is eroding particularly in the wake of climate change negotiations as it requires direct communication between all the stake holders right from the top to the bottom level. The local, regional and international stake holders are equally relevant in any international deliberation on climate change. It is the area where conflict as well as cooperation is the most likely outcome of any international discourse. Therefore, the two dominant traditions of International Relations theory – Realism and Liberalism - later termed as neorealism and neoliberalism, have given birth to an academic debate while explaining the nature of the issue of climate change and the challenges, threat it is posing to the nation states and its possible solutions.

In the light of this background, the present paper seeks to unravel the debate of neo realism and neo liberalism on the issue of climate change and establishes that non-state actors and particularly supranational actors find support both from the neorealist and neoliberal school of thought. However, the significance of the role of supranational actors in climate change negotiations under the United Nations Framework Convention on Climate Change (UNFCCC hereafter) or for that matter in any other international deliberation varies from one theoretical perspective to another. The paper further evaluates the role of South Asian Association for Regional Cooperation (SAARC hereafter), a supranational organisation of South Asian states in the international climate change negotiations. Through the analysis of SAARC role in the climate change negotiations, I have tried to put forward the relative capabilities and weakness of regional organisations like SAARC where climate change has posed more or less same threats to the security of its member states. For this purpose I have divided this paper into three parts. Section I explains the position of neorealism and neoliberal institutionalism on the issue of climate change. The section II maps historical progress made by SAARC in formulating a collective bargaining position of its member states to deal with the binding provision of climate change regime. The last section, embark upon a critical appraisal of SAARC as a negotiating agent in the climate change negotiations under UNFCCC and its relative position vis-à-vis European Union.

I

International climate change negotiations started systematically with the establishment of UNFCCC. The First Inter-governmental Panel on Climate Change (IPCC)[1] Assessment Report that was completed in 1990 played an important role in establishing the Intergovernmental Negotiating Committee for UNFCCC by the UN General Assembly. The text of the Convention was adopted at the United Nations Headquarters, New York on the 9 May 1992. It was open for signature at Rio de Janeiro from 4 to 14 June 1992, and thereafter at the United Nations Headquarters, New York, from 20 June 1992 to 19 June 1993.

It entered into force in 1994.[2] Those States that have not signed the Convention may accede to it at any time.

The Convention on Climate Change provides the overall policy framework for addressing the issue of climate change. It sets an overall framework for intergovernmental efforts to tackle the challenge posed by climate change. It recognises that the climate system is a shared resource and its stability is at stake owing to the increased emission of carbon dioxide and other GHG emissions from industrial other undertakings. The supreme body of the Convention is the Conference of the Parties (COP hereafter). It is the highest decisionmaking authority of the convention. It is an association of all the countries that are Parties to the Convention.

The COP is responsible for keeping international efforts to address climate change on track. It reviews the implementation of the Convention and examines the commitments of parties in light of the Convention's objective, new scientific findings and experience gained in implementing climate change policies. The COP meets every year, unless the parties decide otherwise. This is the overall international framework under which negotiations on climate change are moving forward. In 1997, the Kyoto Protocol was adopted by COP-3 after intensive and tense negotiations. Most industrialised nations and some central European economies in transition (all defined as Annex B countries) agreed to legally binding reductions in greenhouse gas emissions of an average of 6 to 8 per cent below 1990 levels between the years 2008-2012.[3] The signing of Kyoto Protocol indicated the convergence of interests of different states over common issue. The concern of the students of International Relation theories is to theorise this convergence of interests of various states on a single issue. The theorisation, in fact, provides a systematic framework for the better understanding of international events. Moreover, climate change with its global ramification constitutes a fine case for the IR theories to explain the nature of contemporary world politics.

All the world events that constitute the scope of International Politics stands defined to large extent by the two dominant traditions of IR. These are – realism and liberalism which later evolved into neorealism and neoliberalism. The analysis of past international events reveals that the realist theory sometime outdone the liberal approach to IR. The realist approach has been the dominant paradigm of world politics during the inter war and cold war periods. The proponents of this tradition unreservedly explained the high politics of that period. However, during the last two-three decades particularly, this theory has encountered certain anomalies with the rise of environmental problem of global reach like climate change. The practitioners of this paradigm[4], however, still believe that these issues are merely a kind of new puzzles which will be solved in the due course of time. These issues are considered by the realists as a new agenda on the priority list of states. As Porter and Brown point out that global environmental problem became an issue of 'high politics' in the 1980s, largely through the end of superpower competition and the collapse of the cold war.[5] Two points are implied here – one, the movement from low politics to high politics is objective and external. It simply means that these issues are conceived as a given, as just one more issue on the agenda of the states. Two – issues in international relations are worthy of attention only when they are of any consequence to state actors.[6]

In response to the rise of global environmental politics, the realist international relations theory has, thus, continued to privilege the state. Accounts of the global environmental politics focus on the activities of the states and put questions from the perspectives of the states.[7] The problem of environmentalism, in this view arises from the difficulty of regulating independent political actors in the context of an anarchical international system. States are the key players in this system as they are engaged in zerosum, relative-gain power games and are also requires defending their interests against each other's. In the wake of the emergence of phenomenon like environmental cooperation, regime building and institutionalising of world politics, the neorealist – a new version of classical realism still reckons that such an action depends on the interest of hegemonic power and this hegemonic power tends to play a relative-gain power game with zero-sum output.

Although the power of states has remained a central reality of international relations, neo-liberals new version of liberalism mainly focused on those factors which help in the generation of cooperation among states on issues of global importance. In this respect, the contribution of neo-liberal institutionalism, an important strand of neoliberalism, has particularly been noteworthy. The basic assumptions of neoliberal institutionalism are: One, the neo-liberal institutional theorists characterise states as key actors in deciding the course of International politics. Being key actors in International politics, they apply rational behaviour in almost all areas of international discourse. The rationality of states find expression in gain maximising behaviour in a situation of tough competition where they aspire for absolute gain through cooperation rather than relative gain in an issue area. Two, the neo-liberal institutional theorists, however, do not consider states to be the only significant actors in the international politics. This painted an altogether different picture of the state from that of the realist and neo-realist perspective which describe states to be more conscious of the gains by the other states. Three, the neo-liberal institutionalism, however, believes that cooperation among states is a non-predictable phenomenon and there is always a possibility of cheating and non-compliance on the part of states to the rules, regulations and norms evolved by institutions. However, despite these problems "states shift **loyalty** and resources to institutions if these are seen mutually beneficial and if they provide states with increasing opportunity to secure their international interests."[8]

The analysis of above listed assumptions shows the commonality that neorealism and neoliberal institutionalism share on number of issues. One, that both neorealism and neoliberal institutionalism agree on the point that international system is anarchic. Two, that states are the key actors in the international system. However, neoliberal institutionalists maintain that although states are important actors in the anarchic international system, they are not the only actors. The non-state actors such as NGOs, institutions and other also play a crucial role in determining the outcome of international system by facilitating cooperation among states. The underlying difference between neorealism and neoliberal institutionalism lies in the very conception of state rationality and motivation. Neorealism claims that states with all possible powers at their disposal strive to make relative gains over others in all competitive as well as cooperative enterprises. Whereas, the neoliberal institutionalism maintains that states do not worry about the gains of others and in fact, they cooperate with each other primarily to maximise their absolute gain. Thus, the neoliberal institutionalism believes in the non-zero sum game where all the parties conceptualise some sort of positive outcome in every cooperative enterprise.

Matthew Paterson argues that in the international political discourse states behaviour is not always governed by power politics. The economic measures of welfare rather than power interests constitute the agenda of modern states. States do not always worry about the likely outcome of all International deliberation. The **'chances of states'** invasion as a result of any such deliberative outcome are not conceded to be serious since the margin of their survival is not small. Moreover, the absolute gain maximising behaviour of states guides them not to win each play of the game in the relative terms.[9]

Thus, making a point from what Paterson explained the nature of modern states, it is clear that states are not always engaged in maximising their relative-power. There are some areas where mutual cooperation is always considered a rational choice by states. The economic, environment and the like are some areas where cooperation has become an endemic feature of international relation. Therefore, it is generally argued that the neo-liberal institutionalism provides a good framework to study these issues in a more comprehensive way.

Now, what transpires out of this debate is the fact that both neoliberal institutionalism and neorealism agree that there emerges complex web of rules, principles, institutions, nonstate actors and supranational actors that may provide a congenial atmosphere to the negotiation process of climate change. However, it remains debatable as to what outcome one could perceive from this negotiation process. In order to understand this phenomenon I have taken up the case of SARRC to find out whether the neorealist explanation of world politics is applicable on SAARC in the case of climate change negotiations or the neoliberal institutionalism assertion that states find it mutually beneficial to shift their loyalties to institutions such as SAARC (as a negotiating agent in climate change negotiations) as far as articulation of common agenda on climate change is concerned.

II

South Asia region of the world is spread from the arctic temperatures of the Himalayas to the arid areas of south-eastern Pakistan and western India to the intense tropical humidity of Bangladesh, southern India, the Maldives, and Sri Lanka. There is a great variation in the climate of this vast region. The proximity of this region to the sea coast and the seasonal monsoonal impact despite high variation in altitude are responsible for this variety of climate.[10] The climate change is posing a serious threat to this region due to its unique geography (add reference). The problem is further aggravated owing to the high density of population and acute poverty of the people inhabited in this region. Mahbub-ul Haq in his report on *Human Development in South Asia* describe South Asia as 'most deprived region of the world' in terms of poverty, illiteracy and human deprivation.[11] The South Asian Association for Regional Cooperation (SAARC) now comprises eight states of South Asian region was established in 1985 with a view to collectively fights the above mentioned common problems of this region. The Charter of the SAARC explains the socio-economic welfare and cultural development of the South Asian people as the principal objectives of SAARC. The Charter puts specific emphasis on the achievement of the goal of collective collaboration in the economic, social, cultural, technical and scientific fields.[12]

Climate change appeared on the agenda of SAARC off late. All the states of this region have already experienced the burn of climate change with more or less same intensity. The IPCC in its fourth report predicted that climate change is expected to increase the frequency and intensity of current climate related hazards/extreme weather/hydrometeorological events, greater monsoon variability in the world.[13] The first assessment report of Indian Network of Climate Change Assessment (INCCA) in 2010 has also confirmed that climate change is expected to have severe impact on the hydrological cycle, Glaciers/mountainous area, water resource (drought, flood, drinking water, forest & ecosystems, sea level / coastal area/losses of coastal wetlands and mangroves), food security, health and other related areas of South Asian region.[14]

The climate change, thus, poses a serious threat to the very existence of South Asia. SAARC being the only supranational organisation of South Asia is generally projected to take up the case of South Asia in the climate change negotiations under UNFCCC. Till now, the climate change negotiations under UNFCCC were largely conditioned/determined by the *north-south* dichotomy between developed and developing countries. The developing countries (G-77) including the SAARC nations comprised the *south* somehow constituted a loose position in the climate change negotiations under UNFCCC on common issues that concern all the developing nations. The *south* has by and large failed to secure the desired outcome in the climate change bargaining with the *north*. There are many reasons that explain the failure of *south* for not being able to convince/ pressurise the *north* to concede the demands of *south* in the climate change negotiations. Adil Najam has done an elaborate study in that area.[15]

Recently, SAARC has been projected as a more suitable platform for addressing the climate change related problems of the region as well as articulating a common SAARC position in the international climate change negotiation under UNFCCC. Such a projection is much anticipated to the severe and immediate common threat that the region is facing and the common apprehensions and reservations of all the member states of

SAARC in the international negotiation on climate change. Apprehension of betrayal by the *north* in the climate change negotiation has historical roots. The failure of *south* on account of achieving New International Economic Order (NIEO) served as a breeding ground for these apprehensions, although, there is a remarkable difference between the negotiation processes of NIEO and climate change. The demand for NIEO was made by the developing countries whereas it was the developed countries that made the first call on climate change. The developing countries set in motion with some reservations for the climate change negotiations. They want 'historical responsibility', 'polluter pay principle', 'collective but differential responsibility', 'per capita emission', 'technology transfer', 'climate change fund', should be made the first and guiding principles of climate change negotiations.

The SAARC regional discourse on climate change that first consolidated itself in the shape of ushering a new era of enhanced cooperation among SAARC members in the area of joint research on Green house effect and its impact on the South Asian Region got critical global dimension only in July 1998 in the tenth SAARC summit. In this summit the heads of the States or Governments of SAARC expressed their satisfaction on the common position taken by SAARC members prior to the adoption of Kyoto protocol on climate change in the third Conference of Parties of UNFCCC. In the Summit Declaration the SAARC members also "...urged all industrial countries to ratify the protocol and to undertake urgent and effective steps to implement the commitments undertaken by them to reduce their emission of greenhouse gases."[16] In 1998 again the fourth UN Conference of Parties held in Buenos Aires witnessed the same euphoria among the SAARC members. Prior to the meeting of COP-4, the SAARC Environment Ministers met in Colombo on October 30 and November 1, 1998 and agreed to urge Annex-1 countries to expedite the signing of Kyoto protocol for its ratification.[17]

At the regional level, the SAARC leaders declared year 2007 as the Year of Green South Asia. In the Fourteenth SAARC Summit April 2007 the member states expressed their deep concerns over melting of glaciers owing to the average increase of global temperature and the consequent rise of sea level. They called for a high level cooperation among the member states of SAARC to assess and manage the risks and impact of climate change on this region.[18] A well-articulated position of SAARC on climate change in respect of regional as well as global negotiation process emerged after the Dhaka Declaration on Climate Change and the adoption of 'SAARC Action Plan on Climate Change' in the SAARC Environment Ministers meeting in Dhaka 3, July 2008.[19] In the Declaration, the Environment Ministers of SAARC after recognising the seriousness of the issue of climate change and acknowledging the progress made in the COP-13 held in Bali, Indonesia in December 2007 (adoption of the decisions commonly called the *Bali Road Map including the Bali Action Plan* with its four building blocks – Mitigation, Adaptation, Technology Transfer, and Finance and Investment), resolved to cooperate for capacity building of member states to call upon Annex-I countries to fulfil their commitments as per UNFCCC for providing additional resources to developing countries to fight climate change.[20] The SAARC Action Plan on Climate Change identify one of its objectives as – "To support the global negotiation process of the UNFCCC such as the Bali Action Plan, through a common understanding or elaboration of the various negotiating issues to effectively reflect the concerns of SAARC Member States."[21] The Action Plan advocated the need of capacity building of member states for the international climate change negotiations. In the fifteenth SAARC Summit, the member states again reiterate the same pledge. For the international negotiations to become meaningful the member states "endorsed the convergence of per capita emissions of developing and developed countries on an equitable basis for tackling climate change. They were of the view that any effort at addressing climate change should take into account historical responsibility, per capita emissions and respective country capabilities."[22]

The sixteenth SAARC summit held in Thimphu during 28-29, April 2010 was primarily dedicated to the theme of climate change. The Heads of the States or Government of SAARC member states adopted the Thimphu Statement on Climate Change which chalk-out the various national and regional initiatives in a more focused manner to strengthen the regional cooperation to address the issue of climate change. The Thimphu summit further established the Inter-governmental Expert Group on climate change to "monitor, review progress and make recommendations to facilitate the implementation of Thimphu statement."[23] The Ministers of Foreign Affairs of SAARC nations also signed SAARC Convention on Cooperation on Environment in the sixteenth SAARC summit to facilitate high level cooperation in area of environment and sustainable development.

Over the period of time the SAARC' presence has become conspicuous in the interregional and global environmental negotiations.

SAARC has signed Memorandum of Understanding with various interstate organisation like South Asia Cooperative Environment Programme (SACEP) in July 2004; UNEP in June 2008 and United Nation International Strategy for Disaster Reduction (UNISDR) in September 2008. SAARC took a well-articulated position on the issue of climate change in the fifteenth Conference of Parties (COP-15) held in Copenhagen, Denmark, 7-18, December 2009. In the common SAARC statement on climate change presented to COP-15 by the Democratic Socialist Republic of Sri Lanka the "SAARC reiterates that, in view of the historically high level of GHG emission, to which South Asia made insignificant contribution, adherence to the principle of common by differentiated responsibility is critical in combating climate change in accordance with the principles and provisions of the convention and its Kyoto protocol."[24]

Further it declared "Given the vulnerability, inadequate means and limited capacities, we are of the firm view that developed countries must commit to ambitious and binding GHG emission reduction targets. The long term cooperative action of parties must include equitable sharing of atmospheric space, provision of adequate of financial resources for adaption, NAMAs, NAPAs, capacity building, and technology development and transfer for combating climate change as per the convention."[25] This position is quite reminiscent of the position earlier taken by the south on the demand for New International Economic Order.

In the sixteenth Conference of Parties (COP-16) Cancun, Mexico, November 29-December 10, 2010, the then Chair of SAARC (Bhutan) reiterated the same SAARC position taken during the COP-15. The SAARC highlighted the need of greater efforts on the part of developed countries to ensure rapid social and economic development of developing countries to achieve Millennium Development Goals within the time frame. In the COP-16 SAARC was granted the observer status in the UNFCCC. This is for the first time that SAARC categorically explained its position on the various issues involved in the negotiation process of climate change. The SAARC exhorted the international community to the following commitments:

(i) Provide adequate, new and additional resources easily accessible to address the full incremental cost of tackling climate change, under the authority of the Conference of the Parties (COP)/ Conference the Meeting of the Parties (CMP), that do not divert funds for development;

(ii) Allocate at least 1.5 per cent of the GDP of Annex-I countries to meet the adaptation needs of all developing countries;

(iii) Urgently adopt operational guidelines for facilitating flows of short-term funds for undertaking climate change activities. Similar guidelines need to be developed for subsequent funds in due course;

(iv) Ensure balanced and separate financing for both adaptation and mitigation;

(v) Ensure access to adaptation finance for all developing countries that are vulnerable to adverse effects of climate change, with special focus on LDCs and SIDS;

(vi) Ensure effective access to and funding assistance for the transfer of climatefriendly technologies;

(vii) Set up technology innovation centres and networks in SAARC region and globally to promote development and transfer of technologies addressing adaptation and mitigation issues;

(viii) Establish an International Centre for Adaptation, Research and Training in SAARC region, as a medium for sharing experience in adaptation;

(ix) Provide adequate and full support for conservation of forests as an integral part of the REDD Plus mechanism;

(x) Deep and legally binding greenhouse gas emission reduction commitments by all developed countries with effective timeframes as recommended by the IPCC; and

(xi) Immediate action by all nations on the basis of the Bali Action Plan.[26]

After the sixteenth SAARC summit no headway was made in highlighting the South Asian concerns in the international negotiation on climate change. In the seventeen SAARC summit 10-11, November 2011, however, climate change find place only as an appendage in the security concerns of South Asia highlighted by the chairperson of the Summit.

III

SAARC presents a complex case for the students of International Political Theory. Its response to climate change is more rhetorical than real despite the fact that the whole region is being severely affected by the adverse effects of climate change. SAARC the only interstate organisation of South Asia could not consolidate its status of observer with the UNFCCC. The answer for this clumsy approach may be found in the theoretical explanation of international politics. The neorealist narratives of the role of hegemon in regional grouping and articulation of its common agenda, for example, may be used to analyse the case of SAARC. Hegemon plays this role by exploiting her economic and military hegemonic position in a given region. Economically, the hegemon may grants superfluous economic aids or concession to states of a given region to modify their behavior in a particular direction or the hegemon may use force or threat of use of force to dictate terms to other states of the given region. This is how USA had led the various interstate military organisations during the cold war. SAARC which is an organisation of eight states does not fit in this neorealist analysis. All the member states of SAARC are developing states. India being the largest state – geographically, demographically, economically and militarily is also a developing state and is yet to realise the standards of developed states. Therefore, India cannot play the role of a hegemon since yielding the economic concession to the member states of SAARC may dear to the economic development of India. Moreover, the presence of clandestine nuclear weapon in the South Asian region evades the prospects of hegemonic military status of India in the region. India, thus cannot lead from the front in the climate change negotiations particularly in respect of articulating a common and assertive negotiating stance of SAARC member states despite the fact that climate change is considered a security threat to the whole South Asian region because the security threats posed by climate change do not recognise the national borders.

The neoliberal institutional theory, however, provided an altogether different explanation of regional and international cooperation in given issue area. The supporters of this theory argue that states generally shift their loyalties to institutions if they find them mutually beneficial to all. Neo-liberal institutionalists, therefore, put emphasis upon the need of formation of various kinds of international institutions, organisations and NGOs with a view to find solutions to the global environmental problems. It has been argued by advocates of this approach that in the international environmental politics a wide range and large number of non-state actors – including companies, local authorities, financial institutions, social groups, and individuals – are typically at least as important as states as actors in these processes.

As against the established notion that states are legal party in any diplomatic deliberation, the supranational organisation such as the European Union and other non-state actors have played an important role in the international environmental politics. The EU has been a party to many international environmental agreement and treaties. In other words, the neo-liberal institutionalists account of international environmental politics contest the statecentric biases of realist explanations. Keohane, Hass and Levy argue that institutions help in appropriation of agenda through the "convergence of political and technical consensus about the nature of environmental threats."[27] Institutions mediate in the intergovernmental bargaining and thereby contribute in formulating a comprehensive and specific international policy. Moreover, their contribution is significant in national policy making that are instrumental in checking environmental degradation.[28]

Given this analysis, one may assume that SAARC can suitably play a very effective role in the climate change negotiations. Moreover, the endorsement of observer status of SAARC in the sixteenth meetings of COP under UNFCCC solidifies the same belief. In the climate change discourse the neoliberal institutionalists generally cited the example of European Union to substantiate their claim that regional organisations are effective in climate change negotiations. The members of European Union meet in private to agree on common negotiating positions on climate change. As a regional economic integration organisation, the European Community itself can be, and is, a Party to the Convention. However, it does not have a separate vote from its members.

On deeper analysis, we may however, find some incongruities between EU and SAARC. European Union is a well-organised and cohesive supranational organisation with roughly equal capabilities of all its members. The term capabilities here define the relative capacity and ability of its member states to act as an independent actor in the international deliberation with roughly equal bargaining leverage. On the other hand, SAARC is a supranational organisation of such states whose capabilities are highly uneven.

The convergence of interests on climate change has not taken place among the member states of SAARC because of variation in threat perception arising out of the adverse effects of climate change. Some states of South Asia are more vulnerable to climate change than other. Moreover there is a stark variation in the capability level of SAARC member states. The contribution to the current level of GHG emission also varies highly among the members states of SAARC. The largest contributor to current level of GHG in the South Asian region is India whereas Bangladesh is the most vulnerable state to climate change with negligible contribution to GHG emissions.

SAARC has so far moved as weak party to the climate change negotiations. There are three reasons that explain the relative weakness of SAARC vis-à-vis EU. First, South Asian region is relatively more prone to the catastrophic impacts of climate change than the other developed regions of world. The non-seriousness of US in the climate change negotiations perhaps reveals it. The US was more serious and quick in response to the issue of ozone depletion since ozone depletion was perceived by the US as an immediate environmental threat. This seriousness ultimately paved the way for the adoption of Montreal Protocol on substances that deplete ozone layer after taking into consideration all the issues of developing countries. However, in the case of climate change such an immediate threat is not perceived by the US nor for that matter by other developed states for they are capable to develop new technologies to adapt to the changes caused by climate change. The developing countries on the other hand cannot develop technologies to adapt to climate change on its own as it would require investment of huge resources and thus cannot enjoy bargaining leverage with the developed countries in the climate change negotiations. Moreover, the developed states are in a position to take the *delayed advantage* of the negotiation process of climate change. Second, the internal cleavages among the member states of SAARC due to conflicting political and territorial national interests is another reason that make the SAARC a weak party to the climate change negotiations. Third, SAARC has failed to evolve a collective strategy in the climate change negotiations to persuade the developed states to get their demands accepted. Although, the track record of SAARC is good in terms of issuing Declarations on climate change and signing Conventions on environment but it lack commitment on the part of member states to develop specific common strategy for climate change negotiations under UNFCCC. This is primarily because of the perusal of different relative interests by the member states of SAARC and their different understanding and conception of vital interests involved in the international climate change discourse. For example, the interests of growing energy users, small Island states and small mountainous states often poorer as well as especially vulnerable to climate changes have been at odds in the climate change negotiations. Therefore, the SAARC member states lack shared perception of environmental vulnerability and thus is not able to gain modest bargaining advantage in the climate change negotiations.

Conclusion

The environmental issues are projected by the neoliberal institutionalism as an area where nation states are concerned only with their absolute national interests and not relative national interests. They argue that each state is concerned to protect her absolute interests and do not care about the interests of others. Thus, in case of environmental protection and sustainable development, when each state concentrates on her absolute interests, it leads to the protection of interests of other states. This gives rise to a kind of win-win situation.

This logic, however, is not applicable in case of climate change negotiations. There is a high possibility of relativity at all level of negotiation process. For the developing countries, climate change negotiations beside other must involve agenda to "modify global economic relations in such a way that the South obtains the required resources, technology, and access to markets which would enable [them]...to pursue a development process that is both environmentally sound and rapid enough to meet [their] needs and aspirations."[29] This relativity of interests among the developed and developing states has led to the division of global climate change discourse into north-south discourse on climate change. At the regional level, the relativity of national interests among the member states of SAARC still prevails high. This relativity emanate from the varying degree of impact of climate change on respective nation-states of SAARC causing them to follow their own line of policy on climate change instead of adopting common strategy in the negotiation. Therefore, it would not be naïve to assume that despite its great potential SAARC as a negotiating agent would have little role to play in the future international climate change negotiations.

References

1. The IPCC provides scientific, technical and socio-economic advice to the world community, and in particular to the Parties to the UNFCCC through its periodic assessment reports and special reports. See for details www,ipcc.ch/
2. See for details, http://unfccc.int/essential_background/convention/items/2627.php
3. See for details, http://unfccc.int/kyoto_protocol/items/2830.php

4. I have used the concept of paradigm from the Kuhn's notion of 'Growth of Science and Knowledge', for detailed discussion on paradigm see, Thomas Kuhn, *The Structure of Scientific Revolution* (Chicago: Chicago University Press, 1962); Imre Lakatos and Allan Musgrave, Criticism and Growth of Knowledge: Proceeding of the International Colloquium in the Philosophy of Science, London, 1965, London: CUP, 1970.
5. Garett Porter and J.W. Brown, *Global Environmental Politics* (Boulder, Col.: West view Press, 1991), p. 1.
6. Marc Williams, "International Political Economy and Global Environmental Change", in John Vogler and Mark F. Imber, eds., *The Environment and International Relations* (London: Routledge, 1996), p. 62.
7. Andrew Hurell and B. Kingsburg, "The International Politics of the Environment: A Introduction", in Andrew Hurell and B. Kingsburg, *The International Politics of the Environment* (Oxford: Clarendon, 1992), p. 1.
8. Steven l. Lamy, Contemporary mainstream approaches: neo-realism and neo-liberalism", in John Baylis and Steven Smith, eds., *The Globalisation of World Politics: An Introduction to International Relations*, 3rd ed. (New Delhi: Oxford University Press, 2005), pp. 213-214.
9. Matthew Paterson, "IR theory: neorealism, neoinstitutionalism and the Climate Change Convention" in John Vogler and Mark F. Imber, eds., *The Environment and International Relations* London: Routledge, 1996, p. 63.
10. Weiss, Anita M. and Mughal, Muhammad Aurang Zeb, "Pakistan", in Kotzé, Louis and Morse, Stephen (eds), *Berkshire Encyclopaedia of Sustainability*, Vol. 9. (Great Barrington, Mass.: Berkshire, 2012), pp. 236-240.
11. ul Haq, Mahbub, *Human development in South Asia, 1997* (Karachi: Oxford University Press and the Human Development Center, 1997).
12. For details see http://www.saarc-sec.org/SAARC-Charter/5/
13. See for details, http://www.ipcc.ch/pdf/assessment-report/ar4/syr/ar4_syr.pdf
14. moef.nic.in/downloads/public-information/fin-rpt-incca.pdf
15. Adil Najam, "The View from the South: Developing Countries in Global Environmental Politics." In The Global Environment: Institutions, Law and Policy edited by Regina Axelrod, David Downie and Norman J. Vig, (Washington, DC: Congressional Quarterly Press, 204), pp. 224-243; Adil Najam. 2004. "Sustainable Development and Human Security: Lessons from South Asia." In Broadening Asia's Security Discourse and Agenda: Political, Social and Environmental Perspectives edited by Ramesh Thakur and Edward Newman, (Tokyo: United Nations University Press, 2004); Adil Najam, "The Future of Global Climate Change Policy." In Climate Change: Perspectives Five Years After Kyoto edited by Velma Grover.

Enfield, (NH: Science Publishers, 2004); Adil Najam, Saleemul Huq, Youba Sokona. 2003. "Moving Beyond Kyoto: Developing Countries, Climate Change and Sustainable Development." In Survival for a Small Planet: Issues Addressed at the World Summit on Sustainable Development edited by Tom Bigg, (London: Earthscan, 2003), pp. 46-58; Youba Sokona, Adil Najam and Saleemul Huq, "Climate Change and Sustainable Development: Views for the South". IIED Opinion Series for World Summit on Sustainable Development (London: International institute for Environment and Development, 2002). Adil Najam, Saleemul Huq and Youba Sokona, "Climate Change Beyond Kyoto: Developing Countries Concerns and Interests", *Climate Policy* 3(2003) pp. 221-231.

16. Declaration of Tenth SAARC Summit, Colombo, July 1998, available on www.saarc-sec.org.
17. See for details, www.saarc-sdmc.nic.in/pdf/summit10.pdf
18. Summit Declaration, Fourteenth Summit, New Delhi, 2007, available on www.saarc-sec.org
19. Declaration of Fifteenth Summit, Dhaka 2008 and "SAARC Climate Change Action Plan" available on www.saarc-sec.org
20. SAARC Workshop on Climate Change and Disaster: Emerging Trends and Future Strategies, Dhaka, July 3, 2008.
21. "SAARC Climate Change Action Plan" available on www.saarc-sec.org
22. Declaration of fifteenth SAARC Summit, www.saarc-sec.org
23. Statement by Mr Pema L. Dorji, Director, SAARC Secretariat, on behalf of H.E. Uz. Fathimath Dhiyana Saeed, Secretary General of SAARC, Colombo, 29-30 June 2011 available on www.saarc-sec.org
24. SAARC Statement for COP-15 available on http://www.saarcsec. org/uploads/document/COP%2015%20SAARC%20Statement_20110123094208.PDF
25. *Ibid.*
26. Common SAARC Position for COP-16 available on http://www.saarcsec. org/uploads/document/Common%20SAARC%20position%20for%20COP16_20110123094124.pdf
27. Keohane, Robert O., Peter M. Hass and Marc A. Levy, "The Effectiveness of International Environmental Institutions" in *Institutions for the Earth: Sources of Effective International Environmental Protection*, edited by Peter M. Hass, Robert O. Keohane and Marc A. Levy (Cambridge, Mass: MIT, 1993), p.8.
28. *Ibid.*
29. Adil Najam, "View from the South: Developing Countries in Global Environmental Politics" available on http://people.reed.edu/~ahm/Courses/Reed-POL-372-2011-S3_IEP/Syllabus/EReadings/06.2/06.2.zFurther_AxelrodVanDeveer2010The-Global239-258.pdf

Trends of Regional Integration and SAARC

— *Hari K. Sharma**

Abstract

Contrary to its time and trend the South Asian Association for Regional Cooperation (SAARC)[1] *has been moving in exactly the opposite direction of the current phase of interdependence and functional cooperation. Globalisation, which has emerged as an irresistible force, is fostering economic cooperation and guiding the foreign policy of nations across the globe. Political and territorial disputes are losing their lustre due to the tantalising economic gains, lies in economic cooperation. Although, it doesn't mean that now states have no conflicts; but definitely they didn't dominate all their actions. The winds of cooperation especially in the last two decades of twentieth century were so strong that it has forced the 'Savage Continent' Europe to integrate itself and collaborate on almost all fronts. Putting political rivalry on the backburner, economic factors grabs the driving wheels of states. Numerous examples of rising economic trade and collaboration among bitter political rivals even puts a question mark on the relevance of realpolitik hard power approach.*

But, South Asia presents a unique example of political immaturity, colonial territorial hangover and lack of vision. It defies the global trend of more and more economic integration, initially at the local/regional level and later at the global level.

* Assistant Professor of Political Science, NCWEB, Hansraj College, University of Delhi.

Establishment of SAARC has given the region a new hope of economic cooperation that will have a subsequent spill over effect in other areas which leads to betterment of relations all over. But ever since its inception in 1985, the regional grouping has failed to achieve any breakthrough both in terms of improving trade or reducing political tensions. The region has witnessed political instability, military takeovers, ethnic clashes, arms race, nuclear weapons, terrorism, conflict on borders and even possibility of wars; rather than economic integration. It is not that South Asian economies didn't achieve progress but SAARC has played a very limited role in that. In comparison to other regional groupings SAARC has failed both at the operational and deliverance level.

Emergence of SAARC

Different regions have different reasons for the creation of regional organisations which includes- a strong desire for reconciliation, rebuilding and restructuring after the disastrous Second World War, eagerness of states to manage intra-regional and bilateral conflicts in a different way and also following the global trend of having a regional entity to foster regional cooperation. Although, for some regions, it seems quite difficult but definitely it was not infeasible. What European states have demonstrated after the World War II and what the non-communist, newly independent nation states did in Southeast Asia during 1960s was quite remarkable in the sense that at one point it seems unimaginable. The South Asian experiment of regionalism falls in the third category as it started the process of regional integration fairly late, during 1980s. Although regional organisation have different success ratios and didn't have uniform results across the regions, they have been fairly popular as forums of regional engagements. It is even suggested that regionalism has become the central concept of organising world politics[2].

SAARC was first proposed by Bangladesh and SAARC's founding document, like that of ASEAN Declaration, emphasised on the strict adherence to the principles of the United Nations Charter and pledge... to respect for the principles of sovereign equality, territorial integrity, political independence, non-interference in the internal affairs of other States, and advocated economic, social and technical cooperation, while eschewing formal mechanisms for conflict management. It was never mooted as a formal means of managing inter-state conflicts and disputes in the region rather it was largely conceived as a vehicle to foster socio-cultural and economic cooperation in South Asia, and it was agreed that all decisions were to be made on the basis of unanimity and that all, contentious bilateral issues were to be kept out of the SAARC forum. Many scholars have blamed this particular arrangement as one of the biggest stumbling block in the path of multilateral cooperation as the states still thinks in terms of their bilateral disputes and wary of giving any undue advantage to their opponent. Further they believe that any cooperation in another area might dilute the significance and their grave concerns of their bilateral disputes.

Although member SAARC countries count had initially agreed to work together in the social, economic and technical fields, mutual suspicions—especially Pakistan's fear of Indian hegemony—led to economic cooperation being dropped from the organisation's purview[3]. It was only during the 1990s that SAARC moved into the area of trade, albeit with caution.

New Regionalism and SAARC

Regionalism is a dynamic phenomenon and the theory and practice of regionalism is intrinsically linked with the transforming nature of world politics. With the transition of world politics from cold war to post cold war phase the static and mainly Euro-centric regionalism was replaced with a multi-dimensional, more complicated and global in nature regionalism, where states adopted diverse routes to regional integration. Regionalism has been defined as the body of ideas promoting an identified geographical or social space as the regional project or it is the presence or the conscious construction of an identity that represents one specific region. It is usually associated with a policy program (goals to be achieved) and strategy (means and mechanisms by which goals should be reached), and it normally leads to institution building[4].

After the two disastrous World Wars the resurgence of regionalism in the twentieth century can be understood in terms of three historic waves. Mario Telo identifies the first main wave of regionalism in the form of the revival of the protectionist and neo-mercantilist trend of the 1930s in the aftermath the Great Depression and marked the end of Britishcentered hegemonic stability. The second wave of regionalism was associated with the process of European 'economic integration' that occurred during the 1950s and 1960s. This post-Second World War period of regionalism was influenced by American-centered hegemonic stability. And finally, the third wave of post-hegemonic regionalism emerges as a constituent of a heterogeneous world system marked by the current globalisation process. The wide varieties of regional organisations formed from the mid-1980s onward belong to what has been termed the 'new regionalism'[5].

SAARC was a part of this third post-hegemonic regionalism and acts as a component in a new turbulent and heterogeneous world system. Although SAARC was a constituent of this wave of new regionalism and follows the worldwide trend; it failed to imbibe its underlying thirst. Most regional organisations were the culmination point of their constituents common will to bury their political disputes or at least have a broader understanding of how to go about them and move in the economic direction. They didn't ignore or side-lined their disputes rather they have a common consensus of finding peaceful solutions through bargain or compromise on all existing issues. On the contrary, SAARC countries were not mature enough to march together carrying a legacy of disputes.

SAARC- A New-functionalist Analyses

The theory of neo-functionalism was built on Ernest B. Haas and Jean Monnet's 'community method'[6]. It argues that states should begin integration modestly in areas of low politics, and a high authority should be set up as a promoter of further integration; the first steps will create functional pressures for integration of related sectors and the momentum would gradually entangle national economies and social interests; deepening economic integration will create the need for further institutionalisation, making political integration and a long-term system of peace inevitable[7]. The central dynamic to this process of Neofunctionalism is 'spill-over', which referred that the creation and deepening of integration in one economic sector would create pressures for further economic integration within and beyond that sectorviii. Initial cooperation/integration in economic sector would further foster cooperation in socio-political and cultural sectors. Thus, overall it will become an allencompassing phenomenon.

In the context of European integration, regionalism was closely associated with the theory of neo-functionalism but SAARC was altogether a different case and disowned the very basis of new functionalist analyses. Although, initially its creation evoke much enthusiasm; but disputed boundaries, divisive politics and deep seeded suspicions regarding each other capabilities, motives and initiatives backfired and shattered all hopes of its grand success. Contrary to the stipulations of the neo-functionalists scholars like Stanley Hoffman asserted that regional integration could not spread from 'low politics' (economics) to the sphere of 'high politics' (security)[9]. The incremental approach of regional integration failed to deliver in South Asia and it was argued that rather than having a spill over, it has witnessed a spill back or spill around effect. The political strategy of South Asian leadership has so far failed in translating the economic benefits into political gains. On the contrary, the deep rooted political differences have blocked the prospects for economic growth.

The Philosophical Orientation of South Asian regionalism

Unlike the European Union which was guided by regional integration and mutual economic gains, the foundational philosophy of SAARC was love and truth as underlined by Gandhiji during his valedictory speech at Asian Relations conference "'If you want to give a message again to the West, it must be a message of Love; it must be a message of Truth". Rather than focusing on the economic aspect of cooperation the Indian leaders thought that they can build the future of Asia on love and truth alone, but this philosophical position failed to integrate the region neither in economic nor in political terms.

There were as such no concrete bases for the creation of a regional grouping like SAARC. It was mainly a quest of going with the wind and follows the regional integration modal of both EU and ASEAN. The foundation of that very organisation was weak and fractured enough to predict its failure. Political Conflicts and border dispute is just one part of it. Unlike EU and ASEAN they lack a common enemy against whom they want to unite and protect their common interests. They also lack the political will, effective leadership and strong institutional mechanism to accelerate the pace of economic growth. Upto a large extent India was also failed to act responsibly and play the role of a benign regional ally, knowing the reservations of its weaker partners.

Conclusion

Economic cooperation between countries can occur on three levels i.e. coordination, harmonisation and integration. Coordination is the lowest level of economic cooperation that usually involves the voluntary alignment of national policies and investments in certain sectors of the economy. Harmonisation is a comparatively higher level of cooperation, and it usually involves harmonisation of national legislation or the adoption of common legislation. At this level, all legislation, policies and instruments are nationally controlled and implemented; although they might be regionally agreed. Integration is the highest level of economic cooperation which involves delegation of some of the traditional decision-making powers of nation states to be handed over to the regional level and with high probability of decisions might supersede national legislation. At the integration level at least some economic policies are formulated on the regional level which refers both to the process as a whole, but also to a certain advanced level of cooperation. SAARC still seems struggling at the very coordination level.

Ever since its foundation in 1985, SAARC has not been able to come out of its territorial colonial hangover, mutual suspicions and other disputes. The region constitutes about 23 per cent of the world's population and has 15 per cent of the world's arable land[10] but despite having such demographic factors in its favour; it won't be able to transform them to their economic benefit. The dominant Indian position in the region and lack of a common threat perception, ultimately lead to a fear of dominance from within and the smaller constituents, (especially Pakistan) were particularly wary of India's intensions and possible gains through regional integration. Keeping bilateral issues out of SAARC's forum of discussion without having an effective conflict resolution mechanism to tackle bilateral issues prove counterproductive as the states still thinks in terms of their disputes; rather than exploring the opportunities of economic gains.

The huge size of Indian economy promotes protectionism and lack of unilateral incentives discourages bold steps towards regional integration and opening up of economies. Indian leadership- its postures and policies towards its smaller neighbours- further escalate their fears rather than infusing enthusiasm, and India itself failed to play a pivotal role which was much expected from it, keeping in view of its overriding position. A regional organisation can only function successfully if they were able to utilise the advantages of geographic proximity: limited transfer costs, common policies, and common social and environmental standards that ultimately gives comparative advantage to regions within world competition.

Some scholars have even argued instead of experiencing the spill-over the South Asian region has actually experienced the spill back effect as political conflicts are blocking the way of economic integration. Mario Telo has even argued that religion also have a role to play in its performance and SAARC fail precisely because of political tensions provoked by the instrumentalisation of religious differences[11].

On the economic front, although the region performed fairly well as the gross capital formation of South Asian economies almost doubled from 15.1 per cent during the 1960s to 29.1 per cent during 2008 as against a decline from 23.1 per cent to 21.5 per cent during the same period at the world level[12]. Similarly, the GDP growth in South Asia had been sustained at an average of 5.4 per cent during 1980-1999 followed by higher average growth of 6.8 per cent during 2000-08. But here, the notable thing is that the credit for this impressive economic performance goes to the global trend; rather than their regional membership. It highlights South Asian economies growth potential; but also simultaneously lament on their will to cooperate at the regional level and may be because of this particular reason that despite a number of substantial reforms undertaken in recent period, the region remained one of the poorest in terms of per capita income. Furthermore, the region has significantly lagged behind in the field of infrastructure, social provisions and working of the institutional set-up.

Intra-regional trade in South Asia is another area of grave concern. It is relatively low in comparison with other regions, such as ASEAN in Asia. The South Asian countries have their largest trading partners outside the region. SAARC had a slow start, but gained momentum with the launch of South Asian Preferential Trading Agreement (SAPTA) in the mid-1990s and since the implementation of South Asian Free Trade Area (SAFTA) at the beginning of the new millennium, the intra- regional trade in SAARC

Table 1 : Trend in Intra - Regional Group Trade

(Per cent)

Regional Group	1950	1960	1970	1980	1990	1995	2000	2008
1	2	3	4	5	6	7	8	9
MERCOSUR	6.1	7.6	9.4	9.7	11.0	19.2	19.9	15.5
NAFTA	35.5	30.4	36.0	33.2	37.2	42.0	46.8	40.0
ASEAN	2.8	12.7	22.4	15.9	17.0	21.0	22.7	25.8
ASEAN +3	16.1	21.9	25.8	29.0	26.8	34.9	33.7	34.0#
GCC	...	...	4.6	3.9	8.1	7.5	6.2	5.5
SAARC	11.6	5.0	3.2	3.5	2.7	4.3	4.5	4.8
EU 25	47.9	51.8	61.0	61.8	67.4	66.4	67.2	66.7#
Euro Zone	36.1	41.2	53.7	48.1	54.5	53.2	50.3	49.3
APEC	44.2	47.0	57.9	57.5	67.7	71.7	72.5	65.5
CIS	...	...	...	...	...	33.4	28.4	22.7

 # For 2006: Not available.

Source: **UNCTAD.**

has begun to perform robustly. Despite an overall growth in trade with SAARC region, the intra-SAARC trade continues to remain lowest among all the major regional groups formed so far. In 2008, intra-SAARC trade was merely 4.8 per cent while APEC countries had 65.5 per cent and ASEAN had 25.8 per cent of their total trade within the region. (See Table 1) Despite the formation of regional grouping, trade flows within the SAARC region are not much significant[13].

India's most obstinate disputes with the second largest state in the region, Pakistan over Kashmir, the Siachen glacier, water sharing and on the question of cross-border terrorism has led it to seek external security guarantors against the perceived Indian threat. Pakistan has always tried to balance Indian position in South Asia by inviting China and India further endorse American and Japanese presence to counterbalance the nexus between Pakistan and China. This environment of mutual suspicion and competition has not just destabilised the region but also spoils the prospects of regional integration. SAARC can only emerge as a successful regional block if it side-lined its conflicts, shun all its suspicions, gets ready to shed some of its sovereignty and collaborate- rather than compete- with each other, both in terms of economic and military dominance.

References

1. SAARC includes Afghanistan, Bangladesh, Bhutan, India, Maldives, Nepal, Pakistan and Sri Lanka. The South Asian region (as defined by SAARC) constitutes about 23 per cent of the world's population and has 15 per cent of the world's arable land, but only 6.0 per cent of Purchasing Power Parity (PPP) based global gross domestic product (GDP) and account for around 2.0 per cent of world goods trade, and around 3.0 per cent of world foreign direct investment. It is extraordinarily diverse in terms of country size, economic and social development, geography, political systems, languages, and cultures.
2. Peter Katzenstein, "Regional States: Japan and Asia, Germany and Europe", in Kozo Yamamura and Wolfgang Streeck (eds), The End of Diversity? Prospects for German and Japanese Capitalism. Ithaca: Cornell University Press, 2003, p. 89.
3. Alyson J.K. Bailes (et.al), "Regionalism in South Asian Diplomacy", SIPRI Policy Paper No. 15, 2007, available at http://www.jnu.ac.in/faculty/ssingh/Regionalism_in_ South Asian_ Diplomacy.pdf
4. Helge Hveem, "Explaining the Regional Phenomenon in an Era of Globalisation", in Richard Stubbs and Geoffrey R.D. Underhill (eds)

Political Economy and the Changing Global Order, Oxford: Oxford University Press, 2000, p. 72.

5. Richard Stubbs, "Introduction: Regionalisation and Globalisation", in Stubbs, Richard and Geoffrey R.D. Underhill (eds) Political Economy and the Changing Global Order. Oxford: Oxford University Press, 2000, p. 232.
6. The 'community method' adopted by neo-functionalism blended well with the notion of 'security community' developed by Karl Deutsch in 1957.
7. Ben Rosamond, "Theories of European Integration", New York: St. Martin's Press, 2000, P. 52.
8. Ben Rosamond, *Ibid*, p.60.
9. Stanley Hoffman, "Obstinate or Obsolete?: The Fate of the Nation-State and the Case of Western Europe", Daedalus, Vol. 95, No. 3, Tradition and Change (Summer, 1966), pp. 862-915.
10. Rajeev Jain and J. B. Singh, "Trade Pattern in SAARC Countries: Emerging Trends and Issues", Reserve Bank of India Occasional Papers, Vol. 30, No.3, Winter 2009, p. 74.
11. Mario Telò, "European Union and New Regionalism", Ashgate: September 2007, P. 15.
12. Rajeev Jain and J. B. Singh, *Ibid*, p.75.
13. Rajeev Jain and J. B. Singh, *Ibid*, p. 82.

Mapping SAARC's Role in the Changing Geopolitical and Geostrategic Landscape

— *Bawa Singh**

Abstract

After the end of the Cold War, the globalised world has been undergoing many geopolitical and geostrategic changes and also South Asia has not been left untouched. With the introduction of LPG, regional cooperation has become one of the important dynamics of the international relations. Many regional organisations such as EU and ASEAN proved very successful. SAARC was established in 1985 in order to achieve regional cooperation. Since then 17 Summits have been conducted and many declarations and agreements have been signed to promote regional cooperation. But the geopolitics of the region has always been remained one of the major challenges in terms of implementing its programme and policies. Being strategically located, many external powers are also making strategic foray for their vested interests in South Asia by which geopolitics of the region is becoming more critical. Geostrategic challenges are posing serious security concerns for SAARC. Many serious charges have already been leveled against SAARC not being fully realised its regional cooperation potential as well as not been able to check the strategic challenges. The main focus of this paper is to analyse how emerging geopolitics

* Bawa Singh is teaching in the Centre for South and Central Asian Studies, School of Global relation, Central University of Punjab, Bathinda.

and geostrategic challenges are making it ineffective in realising its regional cooperation as well as has been failed to achieve its set goals and objectives.

Keywords: *SAARC, Geopolitics, Geostrategic Challenges, Regional Cooperation, liberalisation, Privatisation and Globalisation (LPG)*

The South Asia region, by virtue of its geo-strategic location and mineral sources, has been remained a central area of the Great Power struggle for influence since the end of the colonisation. During the Cold War competition among external powers percolated down to South Asia. In order to counter India, Pakistan willingly/unwillingly accommodated the American interests. It has not only brought the external power into the sub-continent but also strengthened its confrontationist anti-India stance. In reciprocation, India had also sought aid from the former Soviet Union. This is how, both the protagonists of the Cold War came into the region. Despite their historical and civilisational bounds, India and China are also not sharing good terms. China wanted to contain the Indian influence in the South Asian region by making Pakistan strong enough in order to check the latter's regional leadership aspirations. After the three decades of SAARC establishment, presently it has also not been remained untouched from geopolitical and geostrategic intervention of the major powers as some of these powers are becoming observers and even pushing for full membership of this institution. The geopolitical expansion and geostrategic intervention of some of the powers such as China and USA and other contiguous neighbours will create serious ramifications for the SAARC.

The South Asian Association for Regional Cooperation (SAARC) was established in 1985, is an economic and geopolitical cooperation among the originally seven member countries primarily located in South Asia continent. Afghanistan is the last one to join SAARC, becoming the eighth member in November 2005. The objectives of SAARC as stated in its Charter are: to promote the welfare of the people of South Asia and to improve their quality of life; to accelerate economic growth, social progress and cultural development in the region and to provide all individuals the opportunity to live in dignity and to realise their full potential; to promote and strengthen collective self-reliance among the countries of South Asia; to contribute to mutual trust, understanding and appreciation of one another's problems; to promote active collaboration and mutual assistance in the economy.[1]

In order to run the functioning of the SAARC, the SAARC Secretariat was established in Kathmandu on 16 January 1987, which is being headed by the Secretary General appointed by the Council of Ministers from member countries in an alphabetical order for a three-year term. He is assisted by the professionals and the general service staff, and also an appropriate number of functional units called divisions assigned to directors on deputation from member states.[2] In order to achieve its objectives, SAARC countries have devised a four tier system. First is at the summit level which is comprised of head of states and governments. Till date 17 Summit have taken place and 18th is going to take place in November 2014 in Nepal. At the second level, comes Charter committee which includes Council of Ministers (CoM) comprising of the Foreign Ministers of the Member States to formulate the policies of the Association and review progress of cooperation under SAARC. The Standing Committee, consisting of the Foreign Secretaries of the member countries has been created to take measures/decisions relating to overall monitoring and coordination of programme under different areas; approve projects and programmes, including modalities of their financing; determine inter-sectoral priorities; mobilise regional and external resources; and identify new areas of cooperation. Standing committee is followed by the Technical Committees to implement, coordinate and monitor the programmes in respective areas of cooperation which covered many areas such as Agriculture and Rural Development, Technical Committee on Health and Population Activities, Technical Committee on Women, Youth and Children, Technical Committee on Science and Technology, Technical Committee on Transport, and Technical Committee on Environment etc. In order to facilitate the Standing Committee, Programming Committees were also setup in December 1985 to select regional projects, including their location, cost-sharing modalities among the Member States and mobilisation of external resources etc.[3]

Since the end of colonisation, this region has always been remained the centre of interest for the major world powers. The US and Russia had developed global rivalry and competition among the two blocs and system. In order to achieve geopolitical and geostrategic interests, the US supported Pakistan both economically and militarily. In reciprocation, Pakistan joined hands not only with the USA but its sponsored defence treaties and pacts such as SEATO, CENTO and NATO etc, whereas on the other hand India was supported by Russia. Since the end of Cold War, bipolarity has come to an end and the world is passing through the phase of transition with the start of New World Order. From the geopolitical and geostrategic perspective, the South Asia has become more significant after India and Pakistan declared their nuclear status in the late 1990s. Nuclear weapon in South Asia is also alarming for the rest of world. In such scenario, most of the major powers as well as regional powers are becoming more interested in engaging themselves with the SAARC. Now the question come geopolitical expansion of SAARC with different ideology and interests would be benefitted for SAARC or it would be other way round?

The social, political and economic development of the region has always been seriously hindered by internal or intra-state conflicts. Being the most ethnically, culturally and linguistically diverse, its challenges have been increased manifolds. It is also host to deeply entrenched ethnic hostility, communal violence and numerous wars, both inter and intra-state and some of these conflicts, such as those in Kashmir and Sri Lanka. The Kashmir issue is not only affecting the bilateral relations rather it has become one the most important factors affecting the geopolitics of the region. Three wars over Kashmir between India and Pakistan took place but it seems that its solution has become the distant dream for South Asia. This dispute has been standing in the way of the lasting peace and prosperity of the Indian subcontinent.[4] The Norwegian Nobel Committee, While awarding the European Union with the 2012 Nobel Peace Prize, stated that,"...Today war between Germany and France is unthinkable. This shows how, through well-aimed efforts and by building up mutual confidence, historical enemies can become close partners."[5] In this context, we can hope that South Asia can become unified just as Europe has become unified under the European Union.

Political dialogue is often conducted on the margins of SAARC meetings which have refrained from interfering in the internal matters of its member states. Exploiting this situation, external powers started making their strategic foray in South Asia which is proving detrimental to the functioning of the SAARC.

Changing Geopolitics of SAARC

SAARC was created in 1985 in order to accelerate the economic cooperation. With the introduction of Liberalisation, Privatisation and Globalisation (LPG), the South Asian region has provided as an opportunity as a big market for the non-member countries. Moreover, the region is strategically located and thus most of the major powers have strategic interests in the region. In order to achieve their vested geopolitical and geostrategic interests in the region, these countries have shown their interests to associate with the SAARC.

The entry of major powers in SAARC would have serious implications for the regional cooperation on account of their own bilateral conflicts as well as external powers involvement in the region. Since the end of the colonisation of this region, the previous masters have been remained involved in this region geopolitically and geo-strategically. Their involvement and intervention heightened the geopolitical and geostrategic challenges of the region. The local bilateral conflicts have become more complicated. The region is well known for its intense poverty and underdevelopment. It is also becoming a theatre of a fresh wave of militarisation.

During the last decade, geopolitics has been changed of the region. Some of the neighbouring countries such as Afghanistan, Iran and Myanmar wanted to be the part of the SAARC. Though Afghanistan is closer - geographically, historically and culturally to the Indian sub-continent and trying to become member of SAARC but it could not become member on account of its civil war, instability, chaos, and brutal regimes. Entry of Afghanistan would have long term implications for the SAARC; however, being a member, Afghanistan can benefit from the various SAARC development programmes, as well as from any collective anti-terrorism measures and consequently promote its own security. It is an indication that SAARC members are concerned about Afghanistan's development and integration with its South Asian neighbours', without that regional peace and stability cannot be enhanced. Abdullah al Ramani, an expert of the Asian Affairs was of the opinion that Pakistan's support for entry of Afghanistan in SAARC was aimed at making Kabul's trade policy more Pakistan-centric and enhancing its influence in Afghanistan, whereas on the other hand India's support for Afghanistan entry stemmed from its policy of supporting the post-Taliban government in Kabul and probably from its view of Afghanistan as a key link to energy rich Central Asia.

SAARC in the Great Game of China

There will be no exaggeration in saying that China is the geo-strategically and geopolitically directly and indirectly affecting the South Asian region. Most of the countries of the South Asia are of the opinion that from geo-political and geostrategic point of view, India is dominant. Recognising this reality, most of the SAARC countries are interested to bring China in the organisation in order to restrain the hegemonistic India. There are some moves have already been floated to include China as a member of the SAARC instead of observer status. Most of the SAARC countries are positive of China's entry into the SAARC. Pakistan became the first country to endorse China's association with SAARC.

The candidature of China received strong support from Pakistan, Bangladesh and Nepal. In the beginning of this, India was not ready to accept China as becoming a member of SAARC on account of the latter's strategic foray in the region. However, during the 13th Summit (Dhaka), it was agreed to accept and grant an observer status to China along with Japan. Rashid Ahmed Khan argued in one of his papers that Indian stand is considered as paradoxical.[6] On the one hand, Sino-Indian bilateral trade has been showing phenomenal growth on the bilateral level whereas on the other hand India had reservations regarding the China's entry in the SAARC. India has apprehension on account of strategic and political reasons as particularly Pakistan, Bangladesh and Nepal have enjoyed close relations with China. Despite India's opposition to China's entry in SAARC, almost all other countries except India are supported China's entry. Only Bhutan sided with India in opposing China's entry into SAARC.[7] China is making strong strategic foray in Nepal and there is a sea change in the bilateral relations of both the countries since the end of monarchy in Nepal. In this changing scenario, Nepal is strongly stood for China in SAARC and threatened to veto Afghanistan's membership in SAARC, which India sponsored, if India did not drop its opposition to China.[8] Bangladesh, Pakistan and Sri Lanka also lined up behind Nepal, leading India to drop its opposition. The whole episode led K Subrahmanyam, a prominent Indian expert in strategic affairs, suggested that "the present impasse in SAARC provides Delhi an opportunity to review its South Asian strategy and progressively shift it away from SAARC."[9] Pakistan viewed China's entry into the SAARC an opportunity to, "counterbalance Indian designs to act as a regional power and dominate SAARC."[10] As a permanent member of the UN Security Council, China continues to play a decisive role in international affairs including the maintenance of peace and security in the world. Geopolitical expansion of SAARC has further weakened and alienated India from its neighbours.

Historically, South Asia and Iran had been sharing many commonalities. Iran has been sharing common borders with two of the eight members of the regional grouping. In such scenario, it has also made strong case for SAARC membership and finally entered as an observer in SAARC. Iran's controversial nuclear programme and its pariah status for the comity of the nations will have serious implications for SAARC but at the same time it would provides ample opportunities for the SAARC region as a whole. Satyajit Mohanty analysed the dynamics how its entry would have ramifications for Iran itself as well as India and SAARC as a whole.[11]

Myanmar joined as an observer in SAARC during the 16th SAARC Summit. Geographically, it is sharing long land and maritime borders with India and Bangladesh and being part of extended sub-continent connects South Asia to Southeast and East Asia. Being part of many regional and sub-regional groupings such Association of Southeast Asian Nations (ASEAN), Bay of Bengal Initiative for Multi-Sectoral Technical and Economic Cooperation (BIMSTEC), Forum for Regional Economic Cooperation among Bangladesh, China, India and Myanmar (BCIM). Some SAARC countries and Myanmar are members of the Ganga-Mekong Cooperation and all these groupings have provided platforms for member countries to interact with each other. After the end of the Cold War and the rise of China-Myanmar's relations have changed geopolitical environment in Asia and consequently have increased Myanmar's geo-strategic importance. Geo-economic factors have also changed the attitude of South Asian a country related to Myanmar and was considered as a "bridge" between South and Southeast Asia. The bilateral relations between India and Myanmar have been rapidly growing which will provide potential opportunities to strengthen the SAARC and ASEAN cooperation. However, other South Asian countries, except India have minimal relations with Myanmar owing to geographical reasons and also because of the low level of development in these countries.

Emerging Geostrategic Scenario in South Asia

The South Asia region is the most volatile region of the world. Many strategic challenges are affecting the common people throughout the region. Trans-boundary terrorism is the common problems which is playing havoc with man and material. Minorities in the SAARC countries are not safe. These minorities are facing human right violations. Drug trafficking, small arms proliferations, maritime terrorism and other security threats are posing serious security concerns for the SAARC countries. Afghanistan post- 2014 will affect the security scenario of the region. China's String of Pearls Theory, India and Pakistan's fight over Afghanistan, USA's Asia Pivot policy, geopolitical expansion of SAARC (China, Japan, Iran, Turkey, USA, and Russia's entry in SAARC) will have geostrategic challenges for the SAARC.

Post 2014 Afghanistan- Strategic Challenge

Afghanistan has become the 8th member of the SAARC. This country is holding a lot of strategic importance for South Asia. It is a bridge link between South Asia and energy rich Central Asia. Much talked about Turkmenistan-Afghanistan-Pakistan-India (TAPI) gas Pipeline, if materialise, would bring not only Turkmen, but also Uzbek and Kazakh gas to South Asia. Kyrgyzstan and Tajikistan have immense hydroelectricity generation potential and can export electricity to Afghanistan and across Afghanistan to Pakistan and to northern regions of India. But at the same it is posing many geostrategic challenges for SAARC. Post 2014, Afghanistan will not be in strong position to control and contain the re-emergence of Taliban which would pose very serious challenges for the regional security. Since the last three decades, Afghanistan has been reeling under the political instability, warlordism and terrorism resulting in havoc with innocent human beings.[12] The economic situation is dismal and current development initiatives may not solve the economic woes of the country. Late 2014, NATO forces going to be withdraw from SAARC. Afghan National Army is plagued by many problems such as shortage of experienced officers, lack of training, arms and ammunitions etc. In such scenario, it will have serious implications for regional security.

Maritime Challenges

Indian Ocean has been remained life line of South Asian's people's life throughout the recorded history. Its role in the expansion of socio-cultural ethos cannot be under estimated. Economically, South Asia has been emerging with the introduction of LPG and consequently Indian Ocean has also become the life lines of South Asian economies. But in the recent year sea piracy, maritime terrorism, drug and gun trafficking via sea have been emerging threats in the Indian Ocean, which is the locus of important international sea trade. Many strategic scholars are of the opinion that the Indian Ocean has many critical choke points such as the Bab el Mandeb, the Straits of Hormuz, the Straits of Malacca, the Sunda, and Lombok-Straits. The disruption of the Sea Lines of

Communication (SLOCs) will have serious strategic challenges for SAARC countries as most of the trade is seaborne and their energy requirement of SAARC countries passes through the Indian Ocean. Approximately, 40 per cent of the global trade also passes through this ocean. It is providing a major bridge between the Atlantic Ocean with the Pacific Ocean. Till date, there is no maritime policy designed by SAARC to check these problems.[13]

India Hegemonistic? Neighbourly Perception- A Major Challenge

India is holding strategic location in South Asia. Its size, economy, military modernisation and advancement, population and political power are being perceived by neighbours as dangerous for the regional stability. In order to check India, its neighbours sought support from external powers. In such scenario, China was ready to extend their hands firmly towards South Asian Countries for building friendly, long-term, stable and futureoriented relations. China strategic foray in South Asia will pose geostrategic as well as geopolitical challenge not for India but for the SAARC as well in the coming years.

Human Rights Violations

The South Asian region is the most volatile region and because of this, many people are facing human rights violation in the SAARC countries. This one-fifth of the world's population is also suffering from formidable challenges resulting from poverty, underdevelopment, and conflict within and among themselves.[14] Though historical, cultural, physical and linguistic terms, South Asia is an integrated region, but since the end of colonisation, no commonalties across SAARC countries have been witnessed on account of deep-rooted divisions and animosities across the whole region. Violations of human rights throughout the breadth and length of the SAARC countries is the order of the day. Internal conflicts, civil strife, poverty and so-called state anti-terror legislation and measures have been resulted in violations of the civil liberties of the people.[15]

Democracy did not take deep root in Nepal and Bhutan and due of this, most of the people deprived of many basic necessities. The people of Pakistan are facing many socioeconomic problems because of its political instability or its pseudo democracy. Since the end of monarchy in Nepal it has been reeling under a serious political crisis from more than a decade.

Consequently, there is no proper government, no constitution, a dead civil society and a partial and state controlled media. Since its independence, India has been enjoying democracy, despite its successful democratic set up, it has been failed to provide the basic amenities to its people. Corruption is rampant. Most of the states are highly infested by the terrorism that is playing with people's life. Minorities, women and children are the most sufferers in the region. The poor are becoming poorer and the rich richer. The dynastic political elites and the corporate families are enjoying the states' welfare facilities and opportunities. In spite of such scenario, SAARC has not even given thought to adopt a specific, detailed and uniform human rights convention or charter despite the existence of these in all other major regions of the world.

Despite many declarations have been made to protect human rights, SAARC has been failed to protect the same. Conventions on narcotics, trafficking of women and children for prostitution, promotion of child welfare have been put in place. Several agreements on food security and various social issues have been signed but their implementation did not show concrete results. There has been no regional agreement that specifically focuses on human rights and fundamental freedoms. A regional instrument would be regarded as an appropriate complement to the universal human rights instruments of the United Nations. Such regional human rights mechanisms are already established in the Americas, Europe, Africa and most recently the Arab States: the last major geographic area, therefore, without its own mechanism is the SAARC region. Most SAARC countries have common problems concerning torture, trafficking, internal displacement due to conflict, refugees, and rights over resources, urban shelter and demolition, domestic violation against women, the practice of the death penalty, and extra-judicial detention and forced disappearances.[16]

Dominent Energy Threats

South Asia is a major region that is housing about 1.5 billion population. On account of this, this region is facing many problems. Shortage of energy is the most critical problem in the South Asia region. India's annual energy demand is growing at a rate of nearly 4 per cent. The gap between demand and supply in India is widening. Pakistan and Nepal are also sailing in the same boat. Pakistan's demand is projected to reach 50,000 megawatts (MW) by 2030 that is three times more than the supply currently available and Nepal is facing more crunch having

20 hours of power cuts per day during the dry season. About 50 per cent of the Bangladesh's total population have no access to electricity. Srinivasan Padmanaban, regional director of the South Asian Regional Initiative for Energy Sarie said, "In many ways, South Asia lags significantly behind most, if not all, the regions in the world in energy trade and regional integration."[17]

Role of SAARC

The role of SAARC is very relevant in the changing geopolitical and geostrategic landscape of the South Asia but since its inception, it has not been able to create this perception yet. In the recent years, other regional organisations such as the European Union and ASEAN have made a niche for themselves in the comity of the nations on account of their contribution to regional peace, stability and economic development. In the changing geopolitical and geostrategic environment, the role of SAARC has become more relevant and significance. The geopolitical expansion of SAARC has provided SAARC with rich opportunities as well as serious challenges as well. In the changing geopolitical and geostrategic landscape of South Asia what role does SAARC have to play in lessening the concerns emerging from such environment? Throughout its inception, SAARC as an intergovernmental body has been remained vulnerable to domestic political issues, intraregional bilateral relations. Exploiting such situations, external powers as well as regional powers such as China have become successful to influence the not only the bilateral relations but at the same time SAARC as well. In such surcharged geopolitical environment it becomes difficult for the organisation to take up contentious issues since they might threaten the survival of the organisation itself.

Without referring to the views of the Michael Haas who has theorised the Asian Way to Peace, the survival and development of Asian regional organisations cannot be understood. He emphasised that peace and cooperation consists of eschewing controversial decision making and minimises unnecessary politicisation and thereby to facilitate collective action where common purposes are discovered. If SAARC is able to overcome the bilateral controversial issues, then the organisation would expand as well as it can face any geopolitical and geostrategic challenges coming from its expansion. It is, therefore, an urgent requirement on the part of SAARC to play a very constructive role in the bilateral issues as well as devise a strong strategy to check the strategic challenges posed by the internal and external environment.

Conclusion

Since the end of the colonisation, the Indian sub-continent has been remained very controversial not only on account of bilateral controversies rather with the intervention of the major powers. Despite rich with mineral sources, Asian countries have not become successful in providing the basic needs of the citizens. In order to sort out these challenges, SAARC was established in 1985 by the South Asian countries. Notwithstanding it's about three decades of existence, SAARC has not become successful. It has been failed to achieve its set targets. With the introduction of LPG, now SAARC is opening to more countries as observers and even some countries are pushing for full membership. Many countries such as USA, Iran, Australia, Myanmar etc. have joined as observers. China is even pushing for its full membership for SAARC. The geopolitical expansion of SAARC will have very serious implications for its own functioning as well as for the member countries. There are many geostrategic challenges are being faced by it but there is no proper strategy has been devised to sort them out. These strategic challenges required urgent attention of the SAARC. In order to sort out bilateral issues and make its functioning more smooth, there is an urgent need for the inclusion of bilateral issues in the SAARC agenda.

References

1. Khan, Saleem M. (1999). Book review essay, South Asian Association for Regional Cooperation. Journal of Asian Economics 10, p. 490.
2. Mohanan B. (1992). The Politics of Regionalism in South Asia. Atlantic Publishers & Distri, New Delhi, p. 46.
3. Khalid, Mohammed. (2013). SAARC: Emerging Security Challenges and need for Strategic Initiatives in the Indian Ocean, in In, Goud Sidda R and Mookherjee, Manisha: India Sri Lanka Relations, Strengthening SAARC, Allied Publishers Pvt. Ltd. New Delhi, p. 49.
4. Jhawar, Shiv R. (2004). Building a Noble World, Brookfield, WI, Noble World Foundation, p. 44.
5. Editorial (2013). Cues from Germany and France, The Japan Times, 11 February.
6. Khan, Rashid Ahmed. (2009). The Role Of Observers In SAARC, IPRI Journal IX (2), pp. 1-16
7. Niazi, Tarique: Asia Between China and India, Japan Focus. Accessed from, http://www.japanfocus.org/-Tarique-Niazi/1756, Accessed on 13 March 2014.

8. Upadhya, Sanjay (2006). "The Unfolding 'Great Game' in South Asia." Scoop, April 12, 2006. Accessed from, http://www.scoop.co.nz/stories/HL0604/S00151.htm, Accessed on 13 April, 2014.
9. Mahmood, Afzaal (2005). "Sino-U.S. Rivalry and South Asia." The Dawn (Karachi-Pakistan), April 16, 2005.
10. Quoted in Siddiqui, Tayyab (2005). "SAARC: New Horizons." The Nation (Lahore-Pakistan), November 10, 2005.
11. Mohanty, Satyajit. (2007). SAARC Observer Status for Iran: Regional Implications, The Institute of Peace and Conflict Studies (IPCS) Article No. 2261, 13 April. http://www.ipcs.org/article/india-theworld/ saarc-observer-status-for-iran-regional-implications-2261.html Accessed on 22 June, 2014.
12. Bakshi, Jyotsna. (2010). Potential Role of Afghanistan in Enhancing South Asian-Central Asian Cooperation, Indian Council of World Affairs, 27 May. http://www.icwa.in/pdfs/VPPotentialMay25,10. pdf Accessed on 22 June, 2014.
13. Khalid, op.cit., pp. 48-59.
14. Mangi, Abdul Qayum. (2005). Prospects of Social Charter among SAARC Countries, *Pakistan Horizon*, 58 (1), pp. 61-76.
15. Basnet, Gyan. (2013). New Identity for SAARC: Establishing a Regional Human Rights Mechanism. http://www.nepalnews.com/archive/2013/others/guestcolumn/may/guest_columns_04.php Accessed on 23 June, 2014.
16. *Ibid.*,
17. Khadka, Navin Singh. (2012). South Asia's Energy Crisis Demands Collective Action, 12 August. http://www.bbc.com/news/business-19107372 Accessed on 23 June, 2014.

Terrorism in South Asia and its impact on Indian Security

— *Madhu Chopra**

Abstract

Terrorism is not a new phenomenon, but it has taken central-if not pre-eminent –role at the global level as one of the main threats to peace and security in the world today. Aside from the dramatic events that were witness to the end of the cold war a little more than a decade ago, no other event has had such a profound impact globally as the terrorist attacks in New York and Washington, D.C. on 11 September 2001. After this attack a new terrorism which is called nuclear terrorism has emerged in world. Nuclear Terrorism involves the actual or potential use of nuclear materials to generate fear to achieve political goals. South Asia emerged as the epic centre of the war against terrorism immediately after words, with the involvement of the American and coalition forces against Al Queda in Afghanistan. The developments brought into focus not only the spectre posed by the threat of global terrorism, but also the dangers which terrorism poses within and among the countries of the region.

South Asia has been the major target areas of terrorism, insurgencies and separatist movements in comparison with other parts of Asia. Afghanistan, Pakistan, India and Bangladesh have been facing serious terrorist activities of the highest form in the world; internecine ethnic, communal and separatist conflicts

* Assistant Professor, Department of Defence and Strategic Studies Kurukshetra University, Kurukshetra

pose a serious threat to stability and inter-state relations in this region. The worst part of this scourge is that the increasing coordination of the terrorists, insurgents and radical groups with their counterparts in neighboring countries has added a critical dimension to the entire management of militancy or terrorism in South Asia.

The three independent countries of South Asia-Pakistan, Bangladesh and Afghanistan have a Muslim majority population following Islam actively while India is a Hindu majority country having the followers of different religions. Within South Asia, Afghanistan and Pakistan along with India have been victims of the decade-long wave of non-state terrorism. For the past over thirty years, Afghanistan has been victim of successive rounds of warfare, with Pakistan bearing the cost of engagement in each such instance. Sri Lanka is suffering the problem of ethnicity and struggling to establish peace and social stability since independence. The communal and ethnic conflicts, the separatist tendencies, inter-state terrorism and the practice of militarisation are the chronic challenges to the nation. Bhutan has faced a threat from the Maoists groups who are active in both India and Nepal.

Almost every country in the India-centric South Asia is faced with the problem of terrorism in one form or the other. But this problem of terrorism puts a serious effect on Indian security which is an emerging power in South Asia. The neighbours of India like Pakistan, Afghanistan and Bangladesh are a great threat to Indian security. The tribal invasion of Kashmir aided and assisted by Pakistan forces, was the first instance of state sponsored terrorism against India to wrest Kashmir. The territories of neighboring countries have been used for launching many of these attacks which put adverse impact on Indian Security.

In this paper an attempt has been made to discuss the meaning and some of the important definitions of terrorism and how this phenomenon has affected the security of India. And some steps are suggested for fighting against the problem of terrorism such as interacting with religious groups, developing institutionalised strategic system, addressing problems of youth, developing Effective Intelligence System.

South Asia has seen inter-state wars and intra-state violent movements during most of its post colonial history, but its experience with terrorism by non-state actors is relatively recent as compared to other regions such as the Middle East. In the last decades or so, South Asia has, indeed, emerged as the centre- stage of international terrorism, with horrendous implications for countries – India, Pakistan, Afghanistan and Sri Lanka. Within South Asia, Afghanistan and Pakistan along with India have been victims of the decade-long wave on non-state terrorism.

The Indian sub-continent or South Asia encompasses today eight very diverse sovereign states of very different sizes: India, Pakistan, Bangladesh, Sri Lanka, Nepal, Bhutan, Maldives and Afghanistan. The term South Asia and India refer, in the first instance, to a vast geographical space stretching from the Himalayan mountain ranges in the north to the Indian Ocean in the south from the valley of the Indus in the west to the plains of the Brahmaputra in the east. The subcontinent carries the weight not only of its people but also of their ancient history, stretching back five millennia, and a modern history encompassing the British colonialism compressed it tumultuous developments within the past couple centuries.[1]

The region South Asia and its peoples present a picture of diversity in Unity, indeed of immense diversity within a very broad contour of unity. Among them there is great diversity in natural attributes-imposing hills and mountains, lush green river plains, arid deserts and brown plateaus. The South Asian societies are marked by their plural character in terms of languages, cultures, regions and religions. The people of South Asia speak at least twenty major languages and if we include the more important dialects, the count rises to over two hundred. The very diverse languages and language families of South Asia have made enormous contributions to world literature from ancient to modern times. In a broad historical and cultural sense all states of the region may be viewed to be belonging to the Indian family of nations.

It is a fact that the major countries of South Asia share a common historical past in the form of the British colonial rule, however in terms of political stability, economic regeneration and socio-cultural change they remained poles apart in post-Independence period with the exception that they cooperated each other both at the bilateral as well as multilateral levels under the umbrella of forums, such as Economic and Social Commission for Asia and Pacific (ESCP), Non-Aligned Movement and Commonwealth.

Likewise the region South Asia share certain things in common and they are the religious-cultural heritage of the ancient and medieval times and the administrative, political, educational, economic institutions.[2] Adherents of major world religions, Hinduism, Islam, and Buddhism are found in the sub-continent. Hinduism with ancient roots, modern transformation and multiple interpretations plays a vital part in the culture and politics of the sub-continent. The greatest cultural and political achievements of Islam have taken place in the subcontinent, where more that 400 million of the world's 1.3 billion Muslims live today. Each of the three most populous countries of South Asia – India, Bangladesh and Pakistan has nearly 140 million Muslims, nest only to Indonesia as the largest Muslim countries in the world.[3] Buddhism, apart from the formal adherents in the land of the birth, continues to flourish in Sri Lanka and the Himalayas as well as in East and South-east Asia. South Asia has also significant number of Jain, Zoroastrian, Christian and Sikh minorities.

The states of South Asia emerged as sovereign entities after their prolonged struggle against colonialism. In the post-colonial era, nation building became an arduous task. It was all the more challenging for multicultural states to blend the diverse religious, linguistic and ethno-cultural groups into a national mould.[4] Majority of these states devised the mechanism of a secular democratic order to achieve his objective. But lack of popular participation or the inadequacy of participation has, rather, contributed to political fragmentation. The absence of a political mechanism to settle who will get what and how has given rise to conflicts among ethnic groups.[5]

The withdrawal of empire leaves a legacy of uncertain frontiers and other disputes among the legatee states. It was complicated further by the lack of self-confidence in the leadership elites of the new nations who frequently direct the fears of their citizens against neighboring nations in a mistaken belief that this will strengthen the spirit of nationalism and inspire internal cohesion.[6] Real problems among neighbours do exist and in the South Asian System we can easily discern two types of dialectical struggles that have influenced the nature of ties in the region. One type of struggle is by India for a regional role of dominance, maturing into either a sphere of influence or a hegemonic order. Another is primarily influenced by India's ambitious role the struggle by Pakistan and others for autonomy security perceptions of the South Asian states remained at the top they, however, have developed stronger economic links with the countries outside the region.

Terrorism has profoundly influenced inter-state relations in South Asia. With the world's fastest growing markets, fastest – rising military expenditures and most serious hot sports coupled with a toxic stew of boiling religious, political, ethnic, strategic and historical animosities, made all the more volatile by endemic poverty, illiteracy and the sheer agony of daily existence, Asia holds the key to the future international security order. Much of Asia's terrorist violence is concentrated in its southern belt, which in the past decade emerged as the international hub of terrorism. This southern part of the Asia, encompassing Afghanistan, Pakistan, Uzbekistan, Tajikistan, Chinese ruled Xinjiang and Tibet, India, Nepal, Sri Lanka, Bangladesh, Myanmar, is wrecked by terrorist, insurgent, and separatist violence in a manner unmatched elsewhere in the world.[7]

After the partition political development secularism emerged as an issue in both India and Pakistan. The Constitution of India has two main objectives to achieve through secularism. First, Secularism is adopted as an ideology, which confers a well defined identity to the nation and second as a state policy for governance.[8] In opposite the government of Pakistan and the terrorists nurtured by the government agencies strongly believe that the Indian secularism is humbug. Baba Saheb Ambedkar, the chairperson of Constitution Assembly of India, declared that the state will not uphold or adopt any religion of its own but protect all religious faiths. Then Qaed-e-Azam Jinnah had a dream of making Pakistan a secular state. But his dream was buried along with him. In his absence political leadership in the country became weak and fragile and the vacuum created by his departure provided fertile ground for religious clergies in Pakistan to intervene in the political affairs. This gave good opportunity to Islamic clergies and institutions to profit from the situation and maneuver towards making Pakistan an Islamic Republic. The clergies belonging to the *Deoband School of Islamic thought* and the *Wahabi Takfir* played their move cautiously but diligently to share political power along the religio-political vision and the successive military regimes had the geo-strategic purpose. The combination of the two set right atmosphere for creating religiously motivated militant outfits to undermine the influence of Indian secularism. The creation of Bangladesh and later invasion of Afghanistan by the erstwhile Soviet Union brought the two schools further closer to each other.

In December 1979's invasion of Soviet Union posed not only threat to Indian security but to the entire South Asian region. This invasion was done during the cold war. The USA took this event very seriously and decided to teach the lesson to the Soviet Union. In the US war against the Soviets, Pakistan became the most important ally and this Jihad was waged with Pakistan's order regions with Afghanistan acting s a launching pad for Afghan and other militants from the Muslim world. The weapons for *Afghan Mujahedeens* were passed on through Pakistan. It also enabled Pakistan to receive substantive military aid as well as quiet acceptance of its indulgence in nuclear technology extended by China. Be it the critical issue of Pakistan's tribal areas acting as safe haven for *Taliban*-led insurgents in the Afghanistan or the worrying affair of the growth of extremism and its terrorist consequences in Pakistan, the root, cause lies in the globally sponsored Afghan Jihad of 1980s.[9] The South Asia, which had experienced very low levels of organised terrorism until the early 1980s, has undergone a dramatic transformation to become the scene of the bloodiest terrorist violence in the world.

Building a strategic relation with Pakistan has been a persisting feature of US policy in South Asia and the new development in Afghanistan had precipitated its urgency. In the context of policy requirements Pakistan was used by the US as a conduit of arms supplies to the Afghan *Mujahideens* who were fighting against the Soviet forces in Afghanistan from their bases in Pakistan. These arms came mainly from America but also from China, European countries and the Muslim world. Besides supplying arms to the *Mujahideen*, Pakistan also provided them with training. Without all this assistance, the US objective of bleeding the Soviets while in Afghanistan could not have been achieved.[10] When in Feburary 1989 the Soviet takeover in Afghanistan ended, the supply of US arms and assistance to Afghan *Mujahideen* also halted simultaneously. The Government of Pakistan very tactfully turned the face of Afghan rebels and others towards Kashmir. The pace of terrorist activities increased suddenly in Jammu and Kashmir and along the line of control.[11]

What is Terrorism

Terrorism as a means of advancing a political agenda has existed for centuries, but technologically advancing have bought the potential damage irregular groups are able to inflict to an unprecedented scale, requiring those concerned with international security to look beyond just state actors, classical deterrence, and other conventional ways of thinking in order to address this very real threat. A concomitant concern is the way in which this threat has been abused by governments to justify political repression and engage in acts of war, most notably the 2003 US invasion of Iraq, which have actually increased the threat from terrorism.

The term "terrorism" comes from French '*terrorisme*', from Latin: terror', "great fear", "dread", related to the Latin verb '*terrere*', "to frighten". The terror cimbrics was a panic and state of emergency in Rome in response to the approach of warriors of the Cimbri tribe in 105 BC. It is originated in reference to state violence, specifically the "terror" practiced by the French government following the revolution in the late 1700s. The French National Convention declared in September, 1793 that "terror is the order of the day". The period 1793-94 is referred to as *La Terreur (Reign of Terror).* Maximilien Robespierre, a leader in the French revolution proclaimed in 1794 that "Terror is nothing other than justice, prompt, severe, inflexible." The Committee of Public Safety agents that enforced the policies of "The Terror" were referred to as "Terrorists". The word "terrorism" was first recorded in English-language dictionaries in 1798 as meaning "systematic use of terror as a policy".

Although the Reign of Terror was imposed by the French government, in modern times "terrorism" usually refers to the killing of innocents by a private group in such a way as to create a media spectacle. This meaning originated with Russian radicals in the 1870s. Sergey Nechayev, who founded People's Retribution in 1869, described himself as a "terrorist". German anarchist writer Johann Most helped popularise the modern sense of the word by dispensing "advice for terrorists" in the 1880s.[12]

Internationally terrorism has been defined as an act that has international consequences and includes incidents in which terrorists go abroad to strike their targets, elect victims very easily with the tacit assistance of a foreign state. As a result, mostly air hijackings, attack on nerve centre of another state fall easy prey to such attacks. The U.S. Army on the other hand, defines terrorism as the calculated use of violence or the threat of violence to attain goals-political, religious or ideological in nature. Insurgency on the other hand is a bigger exercise where organisational structure is far too large amounting to an armed build up in a systematic manner. The two phenomena may be treated as similar insofar as the basic objective is struggle for power.

In India, the Anti-Terrorist Act 1985, defines a terrorist as "a person who indulges in wanton killing of persons or violence or in the disruption of services or in damaging property or disrupting means of communication essential to the community with a view to putting the public or any section of the public in fear, affecting adversely the harmony between religions of different races, coercing or over awing the government established by law or endangering the sovereignty and integrity of India". In brief terrorism can be defined, "it is an unlawful act aimed at injuring the society and disrupting its harmony and peace.

There has been no consensus over the meaning of terrorism throughout the universe. The main objective of such terrorists is just to create terror in the public by unlawful method may be by using weapons both lethal as well as chemicals, hijacking, kidnapping, destruction of property, disruption of services essential to the life of people or any other act not confronting to humanitarian norms. The purpose of such activities is to induce a state of fear in victim. The causes of terrorism may be diverse. The terrorist generally depend on their own myopic perceptions of the social vision. The socio-economic condition of a particular society has its effects on crime situation. With the advancement of science and technology, industrialisation is no longer dependent on all available labour. It needs and relies exclusively on trained and experienced workers. As a result of which the bulk of migratory youth reaching the cities fail to get adequately suitable jobs. This results in unemployment and under – employment creating frustration among the youth and children. No doubt, industrialisation in itself cannot be considered a cause of crime, the interaction of social processes and relations that follow industrialisation serve a strong contributory factor in the creation of crime –prone opportunity structure. Young people who are highly vulnerable to such influences, out of frustration, easily fall prey to delinquent way of life and resort to terrorist activities. On occasions they are more influenced by communal tendencies like religion and casteism or they may be led by lingual and geographic or regional considerations, or the variables like political and economic constraints may be the emotive forces operating behind the acts of terrorism. Terrorism cannot be understood in naked isolation of the conditions around the terrorists. They are always in search of soft targets so as to attract world attention and make their presence felt. Whether the motivation is economic, political or ideological but the rapid spread of violence seems to be eating up the vitals of an organised social order. Has the world ever witnessed such threats or not but the fact remains that terrorism hammers hard at the very essence of human achievements mainly measurable in terms of good social order and protection accorded to a citizen in general and even to the terrorist in particular at municipal and international levels. The main issue at stake is that can a developing democracy like India withstand the pressure which the terrorism is likely to generate.

Terrorism is a war of attrition fought by an invisible- but vocal army. The state has no need to act of attention. It has the tools to exercise its will immediately. While the terrorist plants bombs to sow a mood of insecurity, the states act bluntly to make political opposition very bad for the health of the opponents, and quickly. State terror can often be the breeding group for terrorism or of its military cousin, guerrilla warfare, though they turn are not at all the same thing. Terrorists kill one man to threaten a thousand, or to intimidate an industry, to breed public insecurity; and to blackmail governments into reconsidering the policies which generate these violently consequences in otherwise orderly states.

Terrorism is one of the serious problems being faced by the contemporary world. The terrorists do not only hold the democratic institutions to ransom but dilacerate every bit of human civilisation in particular, explicable in terms of legal abstractism and the principles like rule of law. The terrorists are literally engaged in war against the state and the institutions operating other it so is, the state at war with them. In either case the innocent citizens who may be remotely connected with terrorism or the terrorist cause become may be remotely connected with terrorism or the terrorist cause becomes the major victims of terrorist violence. The increase in terrorist violence and incidence of terrorist activities has usually been a cause of panic giving birth to fear psychosis among the people both at vertical as well as horizontal levels.

Terrorism may also be defined as an act of organised violence to create chaos and disorder for achieving the goals which in normal course cannot be realised within the framework of legal and constitutional institutions. It is an act of intimidation seeking to subjugate the people and the governments into acceptance of their point of view and also the methodology to propagate it. Terrorism may further be elaborated as a deliberate attempt to strike terror among the people by use of abnormal force. It creates a fear-psychosis so that the people do not muster courage to speak against it. Although the administration of terror is ruthless, there is a systematic planning and organised build up of the cadres charged with its execution. It may differ from insurgency to the extent that the latter has a pronounced political back up. These days, however, it is believed, to a large extent, that the two are same.

Terrorism is neither new nor a recent phenomenon in the human society. It has existed in all ages. It has grown in form and size along the evolution of society. There has always been dissent against the established authority irrespective of the fact that the authority is established under a feudal system, a monarchic system or a democratic system. From the rule of the dominant to the rule of law, many a stages have been witnessed in the evolution of human society and at each stage of evolution did terrorism exist in one or the other form. It has been identified with anarchists, with revolutionaries and with fundamentalists at different times of history.

Contemporary terrorism is more complex phenomenon. It is neither the by-product of twentieth century up-surges, nor the by-product of the two-global wars fought during the first half of this century nor even the by-product of the freedoms won by most of the nations of Asia, Africa and Latin America after the Second World War, it may more appropriately be treated as the by-product of the national and international politics after the world took its present shape.

The emergence of the contemporary world community with sharp historical, ideological and political conflicts provided scope for sustenance and growth of terrorism is one or the other form. "Contemporary terrorism has more to do with the alienated educated youth rather than with the working class movement that Marx talked about. It is a movement of small groups who may have a strategic logic of their own, who may make their own rational choice and who are definitely not psycho-pathological cases."

Forms of Terrorism

The terrorism is known as different forms like:

- Religious Terrorism
- Political Terrorism
- Ideological Terrorism
- Regional Terrorism
- International Terrorism
- Urban Terrorism
- Nuclear Terrorism
- State Terrorism

Except these forms another form of terrorism has recently developed which is essentially criminal in character and resorted to for different considerations than are associated with the known forms of terrorism such as an illegal trade in narcotics or smuggling of precious metals etc.

Effects of Terrorism

Terrorism produces harmful effects in several ways. The normal life is disrupted and the smoke of devastation hovers all around. Terrorism puts effects on every sphere of life. Broadly the adverse effects of terrorism may be classified as:-

- Economic Effects
- Socio-Cultural Effects
- Political Effects

Terrorism in South Asia

Today terrorism has become a method. As a method, it gets manifested in almost every conflict, be it an insurgency, an ethnic conflict, state-led law and order or security operations, or even an interstate proxy war. Both state and non-state actors are prone to employing extreme intensity of violence, often bordering on terror or actually being terror, either as a means of conveying political messages, or as an instrument in securing tactical or even strategic military and political advantages.

No doubt, every corner of the world has been affected by terrorism. South Asia has been the major target areas of terrorism, insurgencies and separatist movements in comparison with other parts of Asia. It is in South Asia is as old as history. In the Ramayana epic, which is read and revered all over South and South-East-Asia, perhaps the abduction of Sita by the Lankan King Ravana by luring her to the glitter of a golden deer was an act of terrorism. And so also was the burning of Ravana's "Golden Lanka" by the monkey god, Hanuman, as an act of retaliation. The political consequences of Ravana's first act of terrorism led to a war between his sate Lanka and the refugee king of Ayodhya, Lord Rama, resulting in the elimination of Ravana and destruction of his Lanka.

Today, South Asia generally evokes the image of a region that is plagued by violent religious extremism where groups like the Taliban, Al-Qaeda and Laskar-e-Tayyba (LeT) are active. This is also known to be a region where Maoists groups are running riot in large parts of its territory. Presently, Afghanistan, Pakistan, India and Bangladesh are facing serious threat. In South Asia, the number of fatal casualities in terrorist attacks is the highest in the world; internecine ethnic, communal and separatist conflicts pose a serious threat to stability and inter-state relations in this region. This part of the globe, in particular, is witnessing multiple conflicts in which ideological, ethnic, communal and political issues are intertwined.

Terrorism operates in this region under the façade of different terminologists and varies in its nature. It ranges from the practice of internal colonialism as manifested by contrast regional disparity as in Baluchistan, Pakistan, to demand for political independence by the Sri Lankan Tamils in the north-east of Sri-Lanka; and brutal and massive human rights violations ranging from social discrimination and disenfranchisement as in southern Bhutan to economic alienation manifested in naxalite movements in Andhara Pradesh, Chhattisgarh, Orissa, Bihar etc. The poor side of the river is that these South Asian countries have also been clearly involved in encouraging, hosting and aiding terrorists from neighboring countries. The ULFA's presence in Bhutan, insurgents in Bangladesh and the well known support extended by Pakistan to terrorist activities in Jammu Kashmir are blatant manifestation of cross-border abetment of terrorism. The worst part is that the increasing coordination of the terrorists, insurgents and radical groups with their counterparts in neighboring countries has added a critical dimension to the entire management of militancy of terrorism in South Asia.

Five countries of South Asia-India, Pakistan, Afghanistan, Bangladesh and Sri Lanka have tradition of political violence the problem of terrorism erupted in last four decades. It is a region of *Jihadi*-dominated terrorism which is nowhere near containment and it propagates the pernicious ideology of hate, revenge, and violence. It treats all conflicts with non-Muslims worthy of *Jihadi* and even considers liberal Islamic regimes, organisations and individuals as non-Islamic.

Effects on Indian Security

Almost every country in the India-centric South Asia is faced with the problem of terrorism in one form or the other. It is known by all that India is an emerging power in South Asia. Yet it is bearing the burnt of the terrorist violence in South Asia which has risen sharply in recent years. It is multifarious challenges in the management of its internal security. There is an upsurge of terrorist activities and insurgent groups in different parts of the country. The neighbours of India like Pakistan, Afghanistan and Bangladesh are a great threat to Indian security. The tribal invasion of Kashmir aided and assisted by Pakistan forces, was the first instance of state sponsored terrorism against India to wrest Kashmir. The territories of neighboring countries have been used for launching many of these attacks which put adverse impact on Indian Security.

Tensions have also been generated between India and other neighbours, like Bangladesh, Nepal and Bhutan on account of the latter's connivance or cavalier attitude towards the threat of terrorism posed to the former. In the case of Bangladesh, India's complains of continuing ISI activities and shelter and support provided to the North-East insurgent constitute an area of tension, because some of the North-East insurgent leaders' move freely, have bank accounts, and run profitable businesses in Bangladesh, possibly with the connivance of the government and the security agencies. In the case of Nepal, the hijacking of IC-814 brought the relations between the two neighbours to their lowest ebb in the past few decades. Except it, Nepal's territory has been used by ISI activities against India. These activities put a serious effect on Indian security. In recent years the problem of Naxalism is posing a serious threat to the security of India. It is said that near about 230 districts in the country are in the grip of Maoists, Naxalites etc. Definitely these Maoists have been helped by Nepal's Maoists.

The reasons of terrorism in India may vary vastly from religious to geographical to caste to history. Islamic terrorism in India is essentially of an imported variety. The manpower weapons. Finances, ideological motivation and plans that go in terrorist actions largely has its origin in its neighbourhood. The terror has affected not only Kashmir, Punjab, Mumbai, Delhi, but other regions of the country and the North-East for more than 50 years; where the draconian Armed Forces Special Power Act has been in force for the last 50 years. Ethnic unrest and rebel violence have been major Indian security concerns since the Chineseaided Naga and Mizo separatist insurgencies flared in the 1960s. Terrorism covered a large number of Andhara Pradesh, Orissa, MP, Chhattisgarh and Jharkhand right up to the Nepal border. We had insurgency and terrorism in Tamil Nadu. We lost of two our former prime ministers to this kind of terrorism.

Effective strategies to combat terrorism in South Asia

Evolving effective strategies to combat terrorism in South Asia is important as this region accounts for the highest terrorism-related deaths. Here are some strategies:-

(a) By Good Governance

(b) Role of civil society

(c) By early warning and response mechanisms and regional cooperation

(d) By restriction on State sponsored terrorism

(e) By weakening of theories like clash of civilisations

(f) By curbing on individual liberty- which strengthen terrorism

(g) By regional cooperation

(h) By interacting with religious groups

(i) By developing institutionalised strategic system

(j) By addressing problems of youth

(k) By developing Effective Intelligence System.

It is extremely important to deal with various security issues, including terrorism, in the changed global security and economic environment. For this purpose, the creation of a Security Organisation for South Asia (SOSA) is necessary. So it can be truly said that a great determine must be done to know the main root cause of terrorism. Only then terrorism can be ended. The government's theory that terrorism is caused by people in other cultures that want to hurt the people. Their recommended remedy is to kill everyone who would be bold enough to cause us fear, and scare the rest of the world into submission, through threats, innuendos or outright violence. But it has not been seen that their remedy is working. It seems that more people get mad to kill the terrorists who threaten them. But this does not look like the end to terrorism. It looks more like growing vicious cycle of terrorism.

Lastly, it can be said that "in view of the inherent human instinct terrorism cannot be altogether eliminated but, by changing the psychology and behaviour of terrorists, terrorism can be minimised to the level of humanisation".[13] This is the bottom line for terrorism. They must be realised that the value of life is more than death.

References

1. Sugata Bose, Ayesha Jalal, *Modern South Asia –History, culture, Political Economy*, (New Delhi: Oxford University Press, 2004), pp. 3-4.

2. D. N. Malik, *Post-war International Politics-A Quadripartite Survey*, (Muzaffarpur: Veena Mandir Publishers, 1973), pp. 594-95.

3. Sugata Bose, Ayesha Jalal, *Modern South Asia- History, Culture, Political Economy,* op.cit., p. 4.

4. *The Hindustan Times*, 4 August, 1988.

5. Tahir Amin, *Ethno-National Movements of Pakistan: Domestic and International Factors,* (Islamabad: Institute of Policy Studies, 1988).
6. Eric Gonsalves and Nancy Jelty(eds.), *The Dynamics of South Asia Regional Cooperation and SAARC,* (New Delhi: Sage Publications 1999), p.11.
7. Rashed Uz Zaman, WMD *Terrorism in South Asia: Trends and Implications,* (Dhaka:University of Bangladesh), p. 5.
8. D.D. Basu, *Constitution of India,* (Delhi: Printice- Hall India, 1976), p. 264.
9. Ishtiaq Ahmad, *Terrorism in South Asia: Retrospect and Prospect, 15 July 2011.*
10. S.D. Muni, "The United States and South Asia: The Strategic Dimension', in Shelton U. Kodikara (ed.), *External Compulsions of South Asian Politics* (New Delhi: Sage Publications,1993). pp. 68-69.
11. Manvendra Singh, "Threshold of Patience', *The Hindustan Times,* 15 January 2002.
12. Niranjan Das, "*Terrorism-Understanding the New Security Challenges*" (New Delhi M. D. Publications Pvt. Ltd.), pp-3.
13. Madhu Chopra, "Terrorism- An Anatomical and Chronological Analysis" in Rajindra Prasad, *et.el.*, (Eds.) , *Terrorism in South Asia-Issues and Challenges*, (New Delhi, Radha Publications), p. 454.

Mapping SAARC: Towards a Cooperative Security Framework in South Asia

— ***Sujit Lahiry****

Abstract

Regionalisation is neither a new, nor a unilinear phenomenon, but a phenomenon in which countries of a particular region voluntarily cooperate on all issues to resolve bilateral and multilateral problems existing between them. One of the most apt examples of a successful regional organisation can be reflected in the regional security structure of the European Union. However, the phenomenon of regionalism received a major boost in the post-Cold War scenario in a globalised world. And, regionalism is regarded as one of the most effective ways to counter neo-liberal economic globalisation. The disintegration of USSR, expansion of European Union, the changed US strategy, as well as shifting perspectives on foreign investment and regional trade in the developing world – all these factors have reinforced the need for regionalisation. Regionalism is viewed as a form of cooperation in which states cooperate to achieve political stability, economic modernisation and development and to boost regional trade.

Most of the regional organisations, like SAARC (South Asian Association for Regional Cooperation) have been guided by the basic

* Assistant Professor of Political Science, Panjab University Regional Centre, Sri Muktsar Sahib, Punjab.

assumptions of the functionalist theory. The functionalist theory states that cooperation in 'low politics' areas (technical, economic and social) will lead to cooperation in 'high politics' areas (i.e., political cooperation, Security). But, the bitter relations which exist between two of the most powerful countries in South Asia – i.e., India and Pakistan, rules out any fruitful cooperation. It can be firmly affirmed that SAARC's record is dismal in terms of institutional development and programme implementation.

The core and central argument of this paper is that the domestic politics of these seven South Asian states, i.e., India, Pakistan, Bangladesh, Sri Lanka, Nepal, Bhutan and Maldives had led to the formation of SAARC. Accordingly, SAARC was institutionalised on 8 December 1985, with the signing of the Dhaka Declaration and adoption of the SAARC Charter. Afghanistan was included as the eighth member of SAARC on 13 November 2005.

This paper will also discuss the emerging frontiers of SAARC, like, SAPTA and SAFTA. This paper concludes by arguing that there is an urgent need to move towards a cooperative security framework in South Asia, which will concomitantly lead to the creation of a South Asian identity as well as, a strengthened SAARC.

Regionalisation is neither a new, nor a unilinear phenomenon, but a phenomenon in which countries of a particular region voluntarily cooperate on all issues to resolve bilateral and multilateral problems existing between them. One of the most apt examples of a successful regional organisation can be reflected in the regional security structure of the European Union. The genesis of European Union can be traced back to the formation of European Community in 1951.

However, the phenomenon of regionalism received a major boost in the post-Cold War scenario in a globalised world. And, regionalism is regarded as one of the most effective ways to counter neo-liberal economic globalisation. The disintegration of USSR, expansion of European Union, the changed US strategy, as well as shifting perspectives on foreign investment and regional trade in the developing world – all these factors have reinforced the need for regionalisation. Regionalism is viewed as a form of cooperation in which states cooperate to achieve political stability, economic modernisation and development to boost regional trade.

Most of the regional organisations, like SAARC, have been guided by the basic assumptions of the functionalist theory. The functionalist theory states that cooperation in 'low politics' areas (technical, economic and social) will lead to cooperation in 'high politics' areas (i.e., political cooperation, Security). But, the bitter relations which exist between two of the most powerful countries in South Asia – i.e., India and Pakistan, rules out any fruitful cooperation. It can be firmly affirmed that SAARC's record is dismal in terms of institutional development and programme implementation.

The core and central argument of this paper is that SAARC's functioning is always influenced by the domestic politics of these South Asian states. Further, there is a constant fear-psychosis between India and the other smaller states in South Asia. Most of the states in South Asia consider India as a regional hegemon. However, India needs to adopt the stance of a big brother and not a regional hegemon in South Asia. There is a need to move towards a cooperative security framework in South Asia, which will help us in rejuvenating SAARC. This paper has been divided into three sections. The first section traces the genesis and origin of SAARC, and the compulsions of the South Asian countries to form a regional grouping called SAARC. The second section eulogises the emerging frontiers of SAARC, as reflected in SAPTA, SAFTA and other conventions of SAARC. The third and last section elucidates the evolution of a South Asian Identity. It can be concluded that a cooperative security framework in South Asia will make SAARC one of the most successful regional organisations in the twenty first Century.

I

The idea of South Asian regional organisation was primarily mooted by late Zia-ur Rahman, former President of Bangladesh. As has been argued earlier, this idea of South Asian regionalism was the outcome of a series of developments in domestic politics of the South Asian states as well as external factors. Rahman overthrew the India-supported popular civilian regime of Sheikh Mujibur Rahman and assumed power through a military coup in 1975. To begin with, President Zia-ur Rahman first discussed the issue of regionalism with Prime Minister Morarji Desai of India in December 1977. It was followed by Nepal's King Birendra's call for regionalism in South Asia, primarily in sharing river waters. Further, as Kishore C. Dash has argued, "President Zia-ur Rahman had also informally discussed the idea of regional cooperation with the leaders of South Asian countries during the Commonwealth Summit in Lusaka (1979) and the Non-Aligned Summit in Havana (1979). Finally, the Bangladesh President seemed to have given a concrete shape to the proposal after his visit to Sri Lanka and discussion with the Sri Lankan President J.R. Jayawardene in November 1979" (Dash 2008: 82). It was followed by two substantive meetings – one in Colombo (1981) and the other in Islamabad (1983).

Most of the states in South Asia decided to form SAARC in order to bring about economic development within their national economies and counter India's hegemonic aspirations, as well as to have a say in South Asian regional affairs. Bangladesh, the key architect behind SAARC, believed that SAARC would help her in having a say in South Asian affairs and also provide her with the much needed security to counter India's expansionist policy. Pakistan joined SAARC primarily to counter Indian influence and its growing clout not only in South Asian affairs, but also in the international arena. Sri Lanka's ethnic crisis compelled her to join SAARC (Lahiry 2007: 25-26). The political considerations played heavily before Nepal joined SAARC. These were "attainment of individual and collective regional security necessary for economic development, preventing India from supporting anti-monarchy political groups, securing support for Nepal's zone of peace proposal and raising the political profile of Nepal in the region. Harnessing Nepal's river water was one of the key considerations. Nepal wanted to diversify technical cooperation on hydroelectricity with other countries, as it sought to avoid dependence on India in harnessing the potential of Nepal's rivers, and key initiatives, such as the Karnali multipurpose project" (Pattanaik 2006: 142). Thus, almost all the states in South Asia decided to join SAARC to achieve greater economic power and leverage vis-à-vis India.

The early 1980s witnessed turbulent changes in the domestic politics of the South Asian states. The Congress party under Mrs Indira Gandhi came back to power. The two reluctant partners in South Asian regional cooperation were India and Pakistan. The bilateral relations between India and Pakistan deteriorated following US military aid to Pakistan. Indo-Sri Lankan relations suffered a severe setback following the beginning of a violent separatist movement in Sri Lanka under the leadership of the Tamil Tigers. Zia-ur Rahman, Bangladesh President was assassinated in May 1981, and Vice-President Abdus Sattar became the President following elections held in 1981. At the international level, the economy of the South Asian countries received a major setback following the oil crisis of 1973 (Dash 2008: 86).

On 8 December, 1985, SAARC was institutionalised with the signing of the Dhaka Declaration and adoption of the SAARC Charter. SAARC

Charter includes a long Preamble and ten articles. The very raison d'etre of establishing SAARC was to forge cooperation among all the seven member states of South Asia. The assumption was that a common culture, civilisation and heritage among all the seven post-colonial states of South Asia would bring about unity and cooperation among them, gradually bring about social and economic development in the region, and possibly create an integrated market that could remove poverty, illiteracy and unemployment, which are some of the common problems and unifying objectives of the seven South Asian states. It was believed that regional cooperation would bring about economic cooperation, despite the political differences existing among them. But, in reality, suspicion, mistrust, geographical disparities, domestic political considerations, inter and intra-state disputes, and divergent security objectives and goals have hampered the prospects of regional cooperation in South Asia.

Sovereign equality, territorial integrity, political independence and non-interference in internal affairs are some of the major principles behind the establishment of SAARC, which was clearly defined in its Charter. The SAARC Charter kept bilateral issues out of the purview of SAARC and emphasised on multilateral cooperation. The member-states of SAARC were free to forge any other bilateral and multilateral cooperation, as they would deem fit. But, in reality, bilateral disputes have always stymied the prospects of multilateral cooperation through SAARC. Most of the South Asian states look to itself as the 'self', and the other member-states as the 'other'; and, this construct between the 'self' and the 'other' leads to mistrust, suspicion, hostility and conflicts. Consequently, regional cooperation continues to remain an utopian dream.

SAARC initially consisted of seven South Asian countries – India, Pakistan, Bangladesh, Sri Lanka, Nepal, Bhutan and Maldives. In the SAARC Summit held at Dhaka on 13, November 2005, Afghanistan was included as the eighth member. By including Afghanistan, SAARC countries now have links with Central Asia, Myanmar (part of ASEAN) as well as West Asia. SAARC has also granted Observer Status to European Union, People's Republic of China, Japan, US and South Korea. The increased membership of SAARC has given a boost to regional cooperation in South Asia. At the 14th SAARC Summit held at New Delhi on 3-4, April 2007, the Indian Prime Minister, Dr Manmohan Singh, argued that "connectivity – physical, economic and of the mind, enabling us to fully use our geographical and resource endowments, has historically been the key to our region's peace and prosperity. South Asia has flourished most when connected to itself and the rest of the world" (Singh 2007). In other words, the theme of connectivity is of paramount importance, if SAARC has to remain relevant.

II

All the major South Asian states are producers and exporters of raw materials and importers of finished products from the economically developed countries. This has adversely affected their intra-regional as well as inter-regional trade and industrial development. Intraregional trade as a share of total exports of South Asia is a mere five per cent. As one study points out,

> The US, countries of the European Union and Japan together are the largest trading partners of the SAARC countries accounting for more than 50 per cent of total trade. Furthermore, a substantial proportion, i.e., 40 per cent of the trade of SAARC countries is with the APEC region, including China. In contrast, the South Asian countries formally do not trade with each other (Bank 1998).

To facilitate free trade among the South Asian states, the member-states of SAARC signed the SAARC Preferential Trading Arrangement (SAPTA), which was operationalised in 1995. SAPTA gave tariff concessions on more than 4000 items of trade. It also encouraged trade with less or no duties. Till the twefth SAARC Summit in Islamabad in 2004, SAPTA remained operational. In 2004, SAPTA was converted into South Asian Free Trade Area (SAFTA). SAFTA, which envisages free trade among the South Asian countries, was ratified and came into force on January 1, 2006. The SAFTA Agreement, argues Mahwish Hafeez, 'aimed to eliminate all sorts of barriers in trade and facilitation of free and fair movement of products, promoting fair competition and free trade environment in respect of the existing economic conditions that ensures maximum benefits and establish an institutional frame to promote and expand regional cooperation' (Hafeez 2013: 75).

SAFTA ensures phased tariff liberalisation programme (TLP). While, LDCs (Least Developed Countries) will bring down tariffs to 30 per cent, non-LDCs were supposed to bring down tariffs to 20 per cent. It was further agreed that LDCs will reduce tariffs in eight years, tariffs in non-LDCs will be reduced from 20 per cent to 0-5 per cent in five years (and Sri Lanka in 6 years). In order to promote greater economic integration,

SAFTA 'involves integration of capital and financial markets, liberalisation of cross-border investment and the creation of regional supply chain networks facilitated by multi-national investment' (Baru 2014: 283). This can be expanded to create a South Asian Economic Union (SAEU). This would entail, argues Sanjay Baru, 'to adopt policies that facilitate the establishment of such regional supply chain networks, involving both regional and global corporations. Improved physical connectivity, supportive financial systems that facilitate cross-border business connectivity and regional integration of markets would facilitate this process' (Baru 2014: 283-284). In other words, SAEU will facilitate the integration of markets, remove the bottlenecks regarding trade and travel, and facilitate increased economic integration between the countries of South Asia.

Table 1: Bilateral/Regional Trade Initiatives Involving India and Other SAARC Partners

Country With India	Bilateral Initiatives PTAs	Other Exports Subject to India's	Value of Indian Exports SAFTA Sensitive List (%)	Value of Subject to SAFTA Sensitive List (%)
Afganistan PTA (2003)			n.an.a	
Bangladesh	Trade Agreement (2006)	APTA, BIMSTEC	11.2	66.0
Bhutan	FTA(1995)	BIMSTEC	36.8	n.a
Maldives	Trade Agreement (1991)	3.6	65.2	
Nepal	FTA (1991)	BIMSTEC	46.2	64.2
Pakistan			16.4	14.5
Sri Lanka	FTA(1998)	APTA, BIMSTEC	41.5	53.5

Notes: n.a. = Not Available; PTA=Preferential Trade Agreement; APTA= Asia Pacific Trade Agreement, in which Bangladesh, India and Sri Lanka are signatories; BIMSTEC= Bay of Bengal Initiative for Multi-Sectoral Technical and Economic Cooperation, in which Bangladesh, Bhutan, Nepal, India and Sri Lanka are signatories.

Source: Weerakoon, Dushni, "Towards a Cooperative Framework for South Asia: Economic Development and Regional Integration", in

Nihar Nayak, ed., *Cooperative Security Framework for South Asia*, New Delhi, IDSA and Pentagon Press, 2013, p.134. For details, see Weerakoon, Dushni, "The Political Economy of Trade Integration in South Asia: The Role of India", *The World Economy*, Vol. 33, No. 7, 2010, pp. 851-957.

Table 1 shows that almost all the countries of South Asia have Preferential Trade Agreement, trade agreement and Free Trade Area/ Agreement vis-à-vis India. Apart from SAPTA, Asia-Pacific Trade Agreement (APTA) and the Bay of Bengal Initiative for Multi-Sectoral Technical and Economic Cooperation (BIMSTEC) stand out as leading PTAs vis-àvis India and other SAARC member-states. One just hope that increased volume of trade between India and other member-states of SAARC would help all the SAARC countries equally.

SAARC Cooperation on Environmental Issues

In order to tackle the problem of climate change, a SAARC Convention on Cooperation on Environment was signed by the leaders of the SAARC countries, held during the sixteenth SAARC summit at Bhutan on 28-29 April, 2010. Over the next five years, it was decided to plant 10 million trees. To tackle the capacity building needs posed by climate change, India declared *India Endowment for Climate Change* in South Asia. To develop sustainable energy technologies, India proposed to set up climate innovation centres in South Asia. 'Towards a Green and Happy South Asia' was the central theme of the sixteenth SAARC Summit.

SAARC Cooperation on Terrorism

On 4th November, 1987 the 'SAARC Regional Convention on Suppression of Terrorism' was adopted by the SAARC countries, which, however, came into force on August 22. During the twelfth SAARC summit in January 2004, the member-countries of SAARC signed an Additional Protocol to the SAARC Regional Convention on Suppression of Terrorism. It entered into force on January 12, 2006. Both these acts were essentially meant to contain the phenomenon of global terrorism.

Similarly, there is a SAARC Disaster Management Centre (set up in October 2006); SAARC Energy Centre in Islamabad (set up on March 1, 2006); and SAARC Development Fund meant to provide financial assistance for social, economic and infrastructure development of member countries of SAARC. All these measures were primarily emphasised to ensure comprehensive and cooperative security in South Asia. At a bilateral level, India signed the *Ganga* Water Treaty with Bangladesh in 1996, and also signed the *Mahakali* Accord with Nepal in 1996. Added to it, India signed a Free Trade Agreement with Sri Lanka in 1998.

In SAARC, we have two levels of interaction and integration – one official, and the other non-official. While, the integration between the governments of the eight South Asian statesis what I refer to as Formal/Official/Governmental/Public Diplomacy. The other type of integration is what I refer to as Informal/Unofficial/Non-Governmental Integration based primarily on civil society interaction and people-to-people contact. Let us now evaluate both these types of integration within SAARC.

The government-to-government interface is reflected in the meetings of SAARC summits, where the heads of the government of the eight South Asian states takes up burning issues confronting the South Asian sub-continent. Even the meetings of the Foreign Ministers and Foreign Secretaries are being characterised as the official and government-to-government level interaction and integration. The establishment of South Asian University at New Delhi is one of the most landmark projects and a pioneering achievement of the member-states of SAARC. It is definitely going to herald the boom of connectivity of the mind. Teachers, researchers and students will henceforth be able to move across the border and be able to take the University to new and greater heights.

The non-governmental/un-official/informal interaction will involve people from all walks of life, be they be academicians, researchers, business leaders, social activists, etc. They can collectively put pressure on the political elite of the eight member-states of SAARC and thereby enhance greater civil society interaction between them. The Neemrana talks between India and Pakistan is one of the apt examples of this type of integration. It will greatly facilitate social, economic and cultural integration within SAARC. The recent meeting between the business leaders of SAARC at New Delhi on 16-17, January 2014 will give boost the business-to-business interaction within SAARC. All these measures will give fillip to more and more people-to people contact within the SAARC region.

Perhaps, then, one can argue that the basic assumption of the functionalist theory will come into fruition. Trade, commerce and economic integration within SAARC will pave the way for political cooperation. The settlement of political, territorial and ethnic disputes between India on the one hand; and Pakistan, Bangladesh, Sri Lanka and Nepal will be much easier. Moreover, one of the ways to counter hegemonic globalisation is to promote regionalisation. Regionalism within South Asia will give boost to making these eight South Asian states more economically independent and autonomous, but also promote greater industrialisation within these member-states of SAARC. Further, it will promote more effective regional cooperation in South Asia and work as a potent weapon to counter hegemonic globalisation. This will also give a fillip to the fledgling South-South cooperation, to contain the imperialist Western Europe and especially, the United States.

III

The countries of South Asia will need to think of their identity as a South Asian Identity and as an integrated community, instead of their narrow and parochialnational identity. As Sanjay Baru argues:

> Regional associations have two characterestics – first is geographical proximity, if not necessarily contiguity, and the second is shared economic, cultural and other characterestics of a community. Thus, 'neighbourhood' and 'community' are two dimensions of a regional association.....The SAARC has both characterestics. It is a geographically well-defined 'neighbourhood' and a 'community' with several shared characterestics. Hence, it is only natural that SAARC has been able to emerge as an active association of nations, despite its slow start and persistent bilateral problems between some members.

In other words, South Asia is a geographically wide region with several shared characterestics and commonalities existing between them. Most of them are post-colonial states with similar society, economy, culture and civilisational characterestics. Most of them do not adhere to democratic systems barring India. For example, in Pakistan, civil-military relations is at most times in a flux, and oscillates between each other. Civilian governments have often been uprooted by military dictatorships. In others, like Nepal, Bhutan and Maldives, democracy is still at a very nascent stage. In India, the upsurge of Hindu Right, or more appropriately, the communal Sangh Parivar pose a great threat to the security and integrity of the Indian state.

Moreover, most of these states in the South Asian sub-continent face similar daunting challenges of nation-building, and are still confronted by endemic socio-economic problems, like, dowry, poverty, unemployment, malnutrition, corruption, female foeticide, rising inflation, etc. Added to all these, the forces of liberalisation and globalisation have pushed these South Asian states to peripheries in the contemporary world. The bilateral problems between India and most of these states in South Asia have acted as stumbling block before SAARC. What ails SAARC is that lack of political will among the leaders of SAARC countries impede the regional integration process. Further, bilateral disputes, divisive politics and mutual distrust between member-states of South Asia stand as stumbling block before SAARC.

The South Asian states have to realise that they can curtail the offensives of the hegemonic West only through collective action. In this regard, SAARC can learn some lessons from European Union and ASEAN. While, in EU, pooling and sharing sovereignties is regarded as a standard practice. In ASEAN, Arvind Gupta argues that "the ASEAN Regional Forum (ARF) has provided a useful platform to discuss political and security issues, devise Confidence Building Measures (CBMs), and move on to economic cooperation which is what matters" (Gupta 2009: 135).

Moreover, there is a need for the South Asian states to move towards a cooperative security framework in SAARC. In cooperative security, the paradigm of relations will move from conflictual relations to cooperative relations. It is assumed that regional states will gradually develop Confidence and Security Building Measures through discussion, negotiation, cooperation and compromise (Snyder 1999: 115). As Craig Snyder aptly observes :

Cooperative Security is primarily focused on preventing interstate conflict and as such tends to work to preserve the *status-quo* between and within states. Cooperative Security can, however, also be used to maintain the security of individuals or groups within states. Not only can non-governmental organisations be involved in the management of international crises, but nonstate actors gain a voice on security issues, be they internal or external in many international fora. This is not to suggest that cooperative security is designed to allow external interference in the domestic affairs of states, or even to assist on democratic forms of governance, but merely that non-state voices should be heard (Snyder 1999: 115).

Thus, cooperative security not only gives the non-state actors to play a vital role in the international arena, but it is also the most effective regional security structure, as it allows the establishment of multinational institutions and provides the mechanism by which the substate groups can peacefully gain independence.The South Asian states need to realise that they can carve a niche for themselves in the contemporary world only through a strengthened SAARC. They need to comprehend that a strengthened SAARC will act as a counterhegemonic project against the policies of the imperialist West and restructure the dependency relationship between the North and the South.

References

- Baru, Sanjay, "India's Role in the Economic Re-integration of the Indian Subcontinent", in Sumita Kumar, ed., *Stability and Growth in South Asia*, New Delhi, IDSA and Pentagon Press, 2014, pp. 275-299.
- Dash, Kishore C., *Regionalism in South Asia: Negotiating Cooperation, Institutional Structures*, New Delhi, Routledge, 2008.
- Gupta, Arvind, "Prospects for Stability and Growth in South Asia", in Sumita Kumar, ed., *Stability and Growth in South Asia*, New Delhi, IDSA and Pentagon Press, 2014, pp. 311-313.
- *Towards Greater Connectivity*, Review of Book by Dipankar Bannerjee and N. Manoharan, eds., *SAARC:* New Delhi, Kondrad Adenauer Stiftung, 2008, in Strategic Analysis, Vol. 33, Issue 1, January 2009, pp. 133-135.
- Harshe, Rajen, "South Asian Regional Cooperation: Problems and Prospects", *Economic and Political Weekly*, Vol. 34, No. 19, May 8, 1999.
- Lahiry, Sujit, "India's Relationship With Its South Asian Neighbours: Contemporary Trends", *World Affairs*, Winter (October-December) 2013, pp. 70-79.
- ___________, "India's Foreign Policy in South Asia: Retrospect and Prospect", in EmanualNahar, *The Foreign Policy of India in the twenty first Century: Challenges and Prospects*, New Delhi, Pearson Education, 2011, pp. 193-198.
- ___________, "SAARC: Old Dilemmas and Emerging Prospects", *Journal of Peace Studies*, Vol. 14, No. 2, April-June 2007, pp. 17-37.
- Lahiry, Sujit, "Concept of Security: A Theoretical Analysis", *Journal of Peace Studies*, Vol. 11, Issue 4, October-December 2004, pp. 57-77.
- Nayak, Nihar, ed., *Cooperative Security Framework for South Asia*, New Delhi, IDSA and Pentagon Press, 2013.
- Snyder, Craig A., "Regional Security Structures", in Craig A. Snyder, ed., *Contemporary Security and Strategy*, Great Britain, Macmillan Press, 1999.

- Weerakoon, Dushni, "Towards a Cooperative Security Framework for South Asia: Economic Development and Regional Integration", in Nihar Nayak, ed., *Cooperative 12 Security Framework for South Asia*, New Delhi, IDSA and Pentagon Press, 2013, pp. 127-139.
- ________________, "The Political Economy of Trade Integration in South Asia: The Role of India", *The World Economy*, Vol. 33, No. 7, 2010, pp. 851-957.

Indo-Pak Disputes: Impact on Regional Cooperation in South Asia

— **Harinderjit Kaur**

Abstract

The formation of SAARC is a landmark step taken by the leaders of the member nations. The main rationale behind its establishment is to develop a congenial environment through summit diplomacy where all nations may interact peacefully with each other, cultivate sustainable peace and promote mutual economic well being, by harnessing available resources in the region through the peaceful process of economic integration. Nevertheless, after 28 years of establishment, neither South Asian nations have been able to push the process of integration into full swing nor the organisation itself has become viable enough to promote peace, harmony and economic integration or prevent conflicts in the region. Indo-Pak bilateral disputes and conflicts accompained by suspicion and mistrust have severely hampered the process of much needed regional cooperation in the South Asia. Pakistan's approach towards SAARC from the very beginning has been political and its expectations from SAARC has been limited. Paskitan seems to be least interested in regional economic interactions especially with India. In order to achieve the objectives of the SAARC, it would have to evolve into a full-fledged regional entity that can cultivate peace in the region. The realisation of durable peace and the future of economic integration through SAARC depend upon the ability and interest of India and Pakistan to resolve domestic as well as long-standing differences through peaceful deliberations.

Introduction

In International Politics Regionalism is assuming greater significance. It is a multi-dimensional phenomenon. In the most objective and realistic sense, it is a common meeting ground between national intrests and global forces. Regionalism is an effective instrument that emerged as an important part of the western strategy, wherein economic as well as military arrangements were worked out to fulfill the objectives of the concerned areas. Regionalism encompases efforts by a group of nations to enhance their economic, political, social or cultural ineractions. (Goldstein and Pevehouse, 2009, p.352)

In contrast to other areas of developing world, where such organisations like the Association of South East Asian Nations (ASEAN) in South East Asia or Organisation of African Unity (OAU) in Africa gradually took shape, the level of organisational or institutional set-up in the South Asian region has been minimal. Countries in this region, which has one fifth of the world's population and fourth of the people of all developing countries have no common political institutions, defence plans, growth strategies or foreign policy perspectives. Although those nations have been getting together bilaterally as well regionally at such world forums such as Non- Aligned Summits, United Nations and Commonwealth, these interactions have not led to the creation of viable political or institutional framework for better exploitation of the vast natural and human potential or cooperation for their mutual benefit, either in the bilateral sense or in terms of collective regional cooperation.

There are various schools of thought regarding the preffered methods and approaches to International Integration.

The Federal School of thought conceives of integration in legal and institutional terms and it stands for bringing together previously separate, autonomous or territorial units to constitute a new form of Union. For Federalism the aim of the Union is to integrate different entities but not to assimilate them. It is about finding the balance between self rule and shared rule, about being a unified entity and maintaining diversity and difference. This is one of the greatest appeals of Federalism; it formally acknowledges these differences which are so vital to a pluralism political system and society. Within the Union, although bodies are working in partnership, difference and diversity is acknowledged. Previously discrete, distinct, or independent entities come together to form a new whole a union- in which they merge part of their autonomous selves while retaining certain strategic and important powers, functions and competences which are fundamental to the preservation and promotion of their particular cultures, interests and identities. Federalism in the context of the EU is the application of federal principles to the process of European integration where the term integration refers to the sense of a coming together of previously separate or independent parts to form a new whole. (Weiner and Diez 2004, p. 31).

Functional School of Thought proposed to build a structure based on funtions and common interest and needs shared by states which linked authority with increasing weight of scientific knowledge, aided by technology and expertise. The benefits rendered by regional functional organisations would attract the loyalty of population, stimulate their participation and expand the area of integration. According to functionalists regional integration is material interdependence between various nation-states which further leads to Collective Governance . This theory argues that technological and economic development leads to more and more regional structures as states seek practical means to fulfill necessary strategic and economic functions. According to David Mitrany, the creator of functionalism in International Relations, functional approach provides the states the opportunity to successfully cooperate in non-political context, Such a developmental cooperation would lead to process called autonomous development towards multiplication, expansion and deepening of functional international organisations. Functionalism proposed to build a form of authority based in functions and needs, which linked authority with needs, scientific knowledge, expertise and technology, i.e, it provided a supraterritorial concept of authority. Neofunctionalism is a theory of **regional integration,** building on the work of **Ernst B. Haas,** and also **Leon Lindberg,** both American political scientists. Neofunctionalists focused their attention in the process of integration among states, i.e. regional integration. Initially, states integrate in limited functional or economic areas. Thereafter, partially integrated states experience increasing momentum for further rounds of integration in related areas. According to this school of thought, economic integration (functionalism) generates a political dynamic that leads to further integration. Closer economic ties will further strengthen political cordination in order to work effectively and eventually lead to political integration as well – a process called 'spillover'. (Goldstein and Pevehouse, 2009, p. 353). According to neofunctionalists, there are two kinds of spillover: functional and political. **Functional spillover** is the interconnection of various *economic* sectors or strategic areas, and the integration in one policy-area spilling over into others. Political spillover is the creation of supranational governance models as the **European Union.** (Joseph S Nye Jr, 1968, p. 157).

All the above mentioned schools of thought are based on European experience, and have made notable contributions in the process of Regional Integration of European Nation-States, for enhancing their development in various aspects. However, the social, Political, cultural and economic conditions of developing states are significantly different from that of developed states. Therefore it is neccessary to look into historical background of conflicts and issues prevailing in developing socities, for understanding the origin and expansion of regional organisations operating there.

The modern age is an age of International co-operation and inter-dependence of the states. No state, however, powerful, can afford to live or act in isolation. Relations of the peolple and the governments all over the world are greatly affected even by the actions of the weakest and smallest of the states. To avoid anarchostic situations and develop international cooperation in varoius fields, regional organisations came into being. Regional organistaions emerged because of the urge to solve regional problems in a cooperative and common framework. The Modern regional organisations which came into existence after World War-II can be divided into three parts: (i) Regional Defence organisations such as NATO, CENTO and WARSAW pact; (ii) Hybrid Organisations such as OAS, OAU and the Arab League etc.

But this study is not concerned with these two type of organisations, infact the the primary concern of this study is the third type of organisations, i.e. (iii) The Functional Organisations.

Functional Regional Organisations are in a sense, **International Organisations** as they incorporate international membership and encompass **geopolitical** entities. However, their membership is characterised by boundaries and demarcations characteristic to a defined and unique geography, such as continents, or geopolitics, such as **Economic Blocks.** They have been established to foster cooperation and political and economic integration or dialogue amongst states within a restrictive geographical or geopolitical boundary. Regional integration agreements have led to major developments in international relations between and among many countries, specifically increases in international trade and investment and in the formation of regional trading blocs. As fundamental to the multi-faceted process of globalisation, emergence of regional economic organisations has been a major development in the International Relations of recent years. As such, Regional Integration Agreements has gained high importance. Almost all the industrial nations part of such agreements, number of developing nations too are a part of at least one, and in cases, more than one such agreement. Regional integration arrangements are a part and parcel of the present global economic order and this trend is now an acknowledged future of the international scene. It has achieved a new meaning and new significance. Regional integration arrangements are mainly the outcome of necessity felt by nation-states to integrate their economies in order to achieve rapid economic development, decrease conflict, and build mutual trusts between the integrated units. This study is based on such a regional arrangement : The South Asian Association for Regional Cooperation (SAARC).

About South Asian Region

Geographically, South Asia consists of Bangladesh, Bhutan, Nepal, Maldives, Pakistan and Srilanka. All of them constitute inseparable natural region, they have tropical monsoon type climate, common history and share similar religious traditions and cultural values. Religions like Hinduism, Islam ,Christianity and Buddhism cost significant influence in determining the social organisation of South Asia. As the entire region was under the British Colonialism, this factor led to the development of common political institutions and legal administrative structures. The historical commonality of all the nations of South Asia, inspite of the subsequent political turmoils, has imparted a sense of solidarity to the countries of this region. The problems that South-Asian nations are facing are similar in nature like poverty, population explosion, unemployment, inequality of income, excessive dependency on agriculture, lack of industrial development, corruption, terrorism etc. Common factors like geographical features, historical roots, religion, and similar set of problems provide some kind of unity among the people of South Asia. Economic. Social and political compulsions of South Asian Nations makes it essential for them to work together in various fields. Due to the to presence of similar kind of problems, pressures within these countries are forcing them to look in and outward and seek larger regional co-operation.

SAARC is an organisation of **South Asian** Nations comprising the Governments of Bangladesh, India, Pakistan, Sri Lanka, Bhutan, Nepal and Maldives. They formally adopted its charter providing for the promotion of economic and social progress, cultural development within the South Asia region and also for friendship and cooperation with other developing countries. It is dedicated to economic, technological, social, and cultural development emphasising collective self-reliance, and the areas chosen for cooperation are those where political concerns are least involved. The first concrete proposal for establishing a framework for regional cooperation on the basis of functional approach in South Asia was made by the late President of Bangladesh, **Zia-ur-Rahman,** on May 2, 1980. SAARC emphasis on closer integration of neighbouring economies as a first step in creating a larger regional **market** for **trade** and **investment.** This was claimed to spur greater efficiency, **productivity** gain and **competitiveness,** not just by lowering border barriers, but by reducing other costs and risks of trade and investment. Though Economic growth of the South Asian Region was mentioned in its charter as its aim and objective, cooperation in the economic field, in practical terms, was taken up much later by the member States.

Attitude and Perceptions of India and Pakistan During SAARC Summits

From 1985 to 2011, 17 summits have been held. All the members expressed a seriousness over growing linkages between drug trafficking and international arms trade and terrorist activities (Murthy, May 2008). The head of states or governments recalled the adoption of the 1996 Undeclaration on measure to eliminate international terrorism (Chakraborti, March 2012) SAARC has undertaken several initiative to tackle this crisis, like the terrorism convention of 1987, the Additional Protocol of 2006, the joint declaration against terrorism at the colombo summit in August 2008, the proposal by the Bangladeshi Prime Minister, Sheikh Hasina on 28 January 2009 for establishing a joint South Asian Antiterrorism task force.

The Kathmandu Summit (2002) declaration unanimously accepted that terrorism in all its forms as a challenge to all nations. But there were differences of opinion between the countries during this summit especially between India and Pakistan that make it difficult to arrive at a consensus. Terrorism is a major issue which could not strengthen the SAARC. It has been seen in the past, terrorist have threatened to derail peace process between India and Pakistan as happened in the case of Parliament attack in December 2001 and later the Mumbai blasts (Gopal 2009 : 119). India strongly held that Pakistan based *Kashmiri* militant, groups *Jaish-e-Mohammad* and *Lashkar-e-Taiyeba* are responsible for these attacks and put pressure on Pakistan to ban these groups and take appropriate action, including extradition to India. Problems faced on account of lack of effective implementation of these conventions, which appears toothless in the absence of concerted and firm political will and mutual trust among the countries in the region.

There are so many problems which create obstacles in the way of working of SAARC and hamper the process of regional Co-operation within its arrangement and purview.

Bilateral issues are a setback to the SAARC Process when the SAARC summits were put off due to Political Reasons, SAARC summits have played an important role in developing contacts among the leaders of the SAARC States. It also provide opportunities to the leaders for informal bilateral contacts and consultations on the sidelines of the summits. (Bahadur, July 2001) The summits have been postponed without really considering. It created adverse impact on the institution of SAARC. For example SAARC Summit of 1989 was postponed because of the presence of Indian peacekeeping forces in Sri Lanka (Lama, July 2001). The Sri Lankan Prime Minister Rana Singhe Premadasa said that he would not attend the SAARC meeting unless Indian forces were withdrawn from his country. After colombo Summit 1998 which was to be held in November 1999 it was postponed because of the clashes between India and Pakistan, on grounds of a military coup in Pakistan. In 1992, the Dhaka Summit was cancelled in the affermath of the Babri Masjid demolition due to threats issued to the then Indian Prime Minister Narsimha Rao by fundamentalist forces, clearly demonstrating that an internal matter of a country has the capacity to derail SAARC (Patnaik, July-Sep 2004).

The thirteenth Summit of SAARC was to be held in January 2005. It was postponed due to the tragedy of Tsunami and then refixed on February 2005. It was again postponed. New Delhi denied to be part of the Summit and blamed security environment in Bangladesh was not suitable for the summit. It is deep-seated distrust between India and Bangladesh on Political dispute that has created barriers before a fruitful dialogue.

Ironically, though Article and (General provisions) mentions that 'bilateral and contentious issues shall be excluded from the deliberations'. It has been the political issues which have never allowed SAARC to take off. (SAARC Secretariat, 1985) it has been primarily India-Pakistan bilateral issues which have always taken the driving seat pushing the remaining five member states to the backstage.

Economic co-operation with in the SAARC started in 1993, when the first regional agreement on economic cooperation formed, Called the South Asian Preferential Trade Agreement (SAPTA) was signed at the seventh summit in Dhaka which came into force on 7th December 1995. The SAARC preferential tariff concessions aimed to achieve a Free Trade Agreement (FTA) decided to liberalise their economies in Trade. It proof to be unsuccessful and did not do much to integrate the region economically. In 2004 the preferential Trade Agreement was replaced by South-Asian Free Trade Agreement (SAFTA) that finally came into effect in 2006 (Mehta, March 2012).

According to this Agreement, SAARC states are to reduce or eliminate tariffs, Pakistan India and Sri Lanka will cut tariffs up to 5 per cent within 7 years of the start of agreement. The SAARC countries will also maximise their lists of items that are give preference for intra SAARC trade. All countries can however, "Maintain a list of sensitive products" which they will not have to reduce tariffs (Kumar, March 2012). The share of intra SAARC trade in global trade of SAARC countries is today at 5.5 per cent in 2008, which is far below compared with 58 per cent in NAFTA, 54 per cent in European Union, 25 per cent in ASEAN (Mehta, March 2012). During the course of the 13th SAARC summit at Dhaka, Dr Manmohan Singh correctly stated that; Regional economic co-operation in South Asia has fallen for short of our expectation and the dreams of our founding father. It remains for behind the more successful examples in both Asia and other regions of the world (Maini, 2007 : 34).

Though the SAARC countries have agreed upon free trade areas, tariff concessions need to be structured in such a way that it facilitates the flow of products. However, in the past tariff concessions which have been given by various countries of South Asia are on those products which are not tradable items between the countries or are on the negative list. Also Pakistan has been reluctant to restore normal trading relations, With India until the Kashmir issue was not settled. Gen. Zia had reportedly said: 'I do not want to see the emergence of Indian lobby in Pakistan.

SAARC is still a long way from fulfilling its potential of being a powerful regional bloc. A clear distinctions needs to be made between bilateral and multilateral relations on the issue of free trade, This is one of the reasons why products are largely smuggled and rerouted through third countries. Both the countries have similar socio-econornic needs which can be fulfilled through mutual cooperation. Bilateral investment is the most effective trial to create mutual stake of India and Pak which would help in defusing tension and subsequently resolving all such issues, which create obstacle in the way of economic growth of the entire region. Strong economic relations will serve as a catalyst role towards the peace-building process.

The problems in the working of SAARC arise due to differences in perception of member-nations regarding the nature, role and structure of this organisation. Such differences are the result of different vintage points determined by respective national interests of the member-nations. Pakistan's approcah towards SAARC has been mainly political and it has shown least interest in regional economic interactions. Nepal's major demand from SAARC is to develop South Asia as a Zone of Peace. Sri Lanka wants to tackle its domestic problems through cooperation of this South–Asian Organisation, whereas Bangladesh's primary concern is the management of river–waters. SAARC summits have been reflection of such differences. It was, in-fact, Kathmandu Summit, where the things began to change in the right direction, a step towards regional cooperation. However still prevailing diffrences in perception of member-nations especially regarding institutional framework of SAARC, different economic structures of member-nations, vast disparities in the working of respective Political Systems and the resultant diffrences in attitude and interests, does not provide favourable ground for regional cooperation.

SAARC is failure to take up bilateral issues and have been attributed as one of the major cause for the failure of regional Co-operation in South Asia. The heads of SAARC nations have stressed that important political issue affecting bilateral ties need to be taken up for SAARC to be successful, However, the inclusion of bilateral issues has many advantages and sometimes leads to mistrust and suspicion among the nations. Resolving bilateral issues can be achieved through bilateral negotiations rather than diluting the SAARC platform to find solution to such disputes. The SAARC charter prohibits the discussion of bilateral issues. Some Pakistan analysts have accused India of being the main culprit and feel that hampered SAARC. However, India's point of view most of the problems, it has with its neighbour are bilateral in nature and do not concern with other member states (Patnaik 2004).

Indo-Pak Conflicts in the Way of Regional Cooperation

Bilateral disputes and conflits between India and Pakistan create major hindrances in the succesful working of SAARC.

Indo-Pak relations has been mainly a story of conflicts and discord, mutual distrust and suspicion. Even though the two **South Asian** nations share historic, cultural, geographic, and economic links, their relationship has been plagued by hostility and suspicion, and strained by a number of historical and political issues. Legacy being a major determining factor of the both countries and conditioned their bilateral relations. The other major determining factors are: (a) Environmental Factors: exogenous and indigenous.The problems emerging from the partition are Border disputes, Kashmir problem and utilisation of the river waters. The first important problem that emerged after the partition was that of minorities. Millions of Muslims living in India Hindus and **Sikhs** living in Pakistan emigrated in one of the most gigantic transfers of population in the modern era. Both countries accused each other of not providing adequate security to the minorities emigrating through their territory. This served to increase tensions between the newly-born countries. Differences between them resulted in communal riots on various occasions which created a tense and hostile environment between both countries.

Ideology also played an important role in Indo-Pak relations.The Muslim League was a Muslim Organisation and fought for Pakistan to provide a Homeland for Muslims. On the other, Indian National Congress was a multi-religious organisation, committed to secularism and cotinued to reject the Two-Nation Theory ofThe Muslim League. The Two different ideologies perpetuated their dispute over Kashmir, Pakistan claims Kashmir for the fulfillment of the Two-Nation Theory, while the Government of India continues to hold that Jammu and Kashmir is an integral part of India on the basis of its secular character and image.

Issue of Kashmir:- Kashmir issue is the root cause of all tension between India and Pakistan, The question arises that how will India take the Kashmir question? India says that Kashmir is not the "Core Issue" and the issue is more about the problem in Kashmir rather than the problem of Kashmir, It does not recognise Kashmir as a dispute, therefore discussing the loyalty of its accession to the Indian Union does not arise at all Whereas for Pakistan, the disputed territory of Kashmir is the core issue, two definition of the problem, which implies that parties are infect, looking at two different aspects (Narang 2006 : 108).

Pakistan has been consistently harping on its stand that no worth while progress could be expected unless India resolved the problem of Kashmir to her satisfaction. India's strongly opposed these attempts. It is no doubt that Kashmir has been the focal point of discord between India and Pak Since the partition of the country. Three wars 1965, 71 and Kargil War between them could not solve this problem.

Jammu and Kashmir and Kashmir region has resulted in frequent fighting along the line of control (LOC) which both countries accepted in 1972 Simla Agreement. Both nations have maintained troops along the line. But the occupation of the Siachen area by Indian and Pakistan troops in April 1984 this portion was termed as the Actual Ground position line (AGPL). The eastern boundary of Pakistan is thus a line composed of the international boundary, the LOC and the AGPL, Despite the various rounds of bilateral negotiations no solution has been found (Pillai 2003, 255).

The 60-Kilometre long Sir Creek lies on the boundary between Pakistan and India in the marshes of Rann of Kutch and flows into the Arabian Sea. It was not included in the 1968 Tribunal Award on the Indo-Pakistan Western boundary because both sides had agreed to exclude the area from the deliberation of the tribunal. The Sir Creek area is rich in fish, is a breeding ground for prawns. Any change in the land boundary will greatly affect the External Economic Zone (EEZ). The dispute is over the interpretation of the boundary line dividing the Creek. India's position on Sir Creek is that it wants boundaries to be demarcated from the centre of the creek while Pakistan wants the bank of the Creek is international boundary. Another problems about Siachen Glacier, highest battle field of the world, situated in the north reaches of Kashmir.

Kashmir is important for Pakistan because all of its rivers from Kashmir and water is vital for Pakistani side as the latter is facing a major water shortage. In 1960, India and Pakistan signed the Indus Water treaty which divided the use of rivers and canals between the two countries. Pakistan obtained exclusive rights for the three western rivers, Indus, Jhelum and Chenab. India retained rights to the three eastern rivers Ravi, Beas and Sutluj. Baglihar Dam is a dam project in the Chenab River in the Doda district of Jammu and Kashmir. Pakistan feels that India is violating the Indus treaty by constructing this dam on the river Chenab and also feels that the construction of spiliway-gated structure will deprive it of up to 7000 cusecs of water daily and will have an adverse impact on its irrigation system. India has clearly stated that the construction of Baglihar project is not the violation of Indus water treaty. The Indian side has said, that all water which has been with held will be released after being used for power generation (Maini 2007 : 49).The Wular Barrage is a project started by India in 1984 at the Wular Lake downstream from the Shelum river. It consists of a darn with a navigating lock of permit navigation during the lean winter, months. In 1987 work was stopped following a protest by Pakistan that this was a violation of the Indus Water Treaty of 1960 in that it was meant for water storage. Indus stand is that it is meant to enhance navigation, which is permissible under the treaty. Various rounds of talks have been held so far but an agreement has remained elusive (Piilai 2003 : 256).

The two largest state of the region India and Pakistan were born as twins, but rival twins, through a baptism of blood and fire. Tensions between India and Pakistan, in particular, become high pitched from time to time (Aditya 2006 : 33). The fight over Kashmir in 1948 added fuel to fire and till now Kashmir the major bone of contention, The two countries again engaged in war in 1965 and 1971. As a result of 1971 war the east wing of Pakistan became an independent country and to be known as Bangladesh. Pakistan firmly believes that 'Mukti Bahini' which eventually led to the creation of Bangladesh, was created by India." There have been occasional happenings of cross-border firing by both the countries since then. The alleged Cross- border terrorism in Jammu and Kashmir became another serious problem between India and Pakistan. At his press conference in July 2001, President of Pakistan, General Musharraf justified the Kargil aggression and asserted that Pakistan's support to 'Jehadis' in Kashmir was like India's arming the 'Mukti Bahini' (Ghuman 2006 : 295).

India-Pakistan fought three wars (1965, 71, 99) and now both are nuclear power countries. A major source of tension in the region was the nuclear tests carried out by India and Pakistan in May 1998. Their congenital hostility is symbolised in their missile nomenclature: India's 'Prithvi' and Pakistan's 'Ghauri'. The 1999 battle over Kargil remains history's first direct combat between nuclear powers. In this time when defense spending is generally declining, military budget is being hiked up in India and Pakistan (Gopal 2009: 119).

The issue of terrorism has been on the agenda of SAARC since the first summit held in 1985. With the passage of time, the issue of terrorism have taken a more complex character and there is clear realisation among the member countries of SAARC that there is no other alternative to have coordinated strategies to respond effectively to curb terrorism. From the very beginning, SAARC took terrorism issue approved that the standing committee should set up a study group to examine the problem of terrorism. During the summits all the members agreed to fight against terrorism and also recognised to importance of the principle laid down in UN Resolution 1373. Even the heads of state expressed happiness at the signing of SAARC Regional convention on suppression of terrorism and considered it a historic step towards the prevention of terrorism from the region.

Conclusion

Most of the SAARC members have suspicion and mistrust towards India which has weakened India's position in South Asia and left the space for China. India needs to give a re-look in its policies with SAARC countries. An Analysis of socio-economic agenda within the purview of SAARC reveals that the organisation has achieved limited success. Actually, political conflicts have become obstacle in the way of SAARC. The history of Indo-Pak relations suggest that inspite of three wars and Kargil setback to the Lahore process, India and Pakistan can achieve peace and concilliation. Such things do happen in the real world among bitter rivals, once they begin addressing the root causes of tension nad insecurity and realise the merits of cooperation. If the leadership of the major countries in the region can set aside their history of conflict and animosity, then SAARC could well reinvest itself as the South-Asian equivalent of the European Union. This requires both India and Pakistan to make unilateral concessions for each other as well as for the smaller countries in the region to address economic insecurity among them. India, in particular is placed geographically in an unenviable position that also gives it a bad image. This calls for extra efforts by New Delhi to correct any misperception (Narang, 2006:111). To develop SAARC into a successful-working regional model, emphasis should be laid on removing fear, suspicion, distrust and feelings of jealousy among the member-nations. Such negative attitude waver the attitude of members and severly hamper the process of steady and continous cooperation. Study of the speeches of member-nations at various SAARC Summits clearly reflect that they are alive to the needs and advantages of regional cooperation, and willing to acccept the new international economic realities. SAARC can prove to be a highly beneficial organisation for South Asian Nations, if all the members work together on one platform. Considering the vast natural and human potential of South Asian Nations, economic coopereation among them could develop South Asian region as competitive International market. For This, it is essential that they understand present geopolitical realities and do not allow their political conflicts come in the way of regional economic cooperation. It will further depend upon the prudence and wisdom of the member nations in taking advantage of cooperative environment. For resolving their bilateral disputes to create a climate of regional peace and stability. (VP Dutt, 2005, pp. 193-197).

Regionalism in the Age of Globalisation: Reinventing the SAARC through New Regional Approach

— ***Rajiv Kumar****

Abstract

The globalisation process marked the rapid and far reaching changes in the world economy and politics. Many traditional structures of international politics and economy were rendered obsolete by these changes. Many others were forced into redefining and reinventing themselves. Old regionalism becomes inadequate to face the challenge of globalisation, because it was state centric in nature. Where the nation state is itself on the decline, how the old regionalism will remain adequate to the challenges of globalisation? As an institution, SAARC is still working in old regionalism framework which is very state-centric in nature. The association has allowed the political logic to dominate over economics and therefore lags far behind several other regional and multilateral initiatives. Thus it has failed to provide adequate responses to globalisation. It has remained an intergovernmental mechanism which had little relevance for people of South Asia. So, there is a need for SAARC to redefine and reorient itself from old regionalism to new regionalism where it becomes more people-centric.

* Assistant Professor, Department of Political Science Panjab University Constituent College Nihal Singh Wala, Moga, Punjab.

Introduction

Regional approach to development and cooperation was the major development in the post-world war II international politics. In the process of regional cooperation varied and creative attempts has been made by groups of nation for sharing geographical, historical and political benefits in an increasing interdependent world. During the first twenty years of the post-war period, alliance-politics remained a key, almost a deterministic part of international relations. Later on, their role, particularly of the military or security alliances appears to have declined; nevertheless, these continue to be regarded as important instrument of international intercourse. Non-security functional-regional alliances have gained a good and healthy ground in contemporary times. European Union (EU) and Association of South East Asian Nation (ASEAN) are example of this. Regionalism in international politics meant a collective action at regional level to achieve national objectives. This process involves the idea that of promoting cooperation and collaboration among a group of states which consider themselves bound by geographic, cultural and political interests. But it has various dimensions. The term regionalisation is often used to refer to the growth of societal integration within a region and… the often undirected process of social and economic interaction *(Hurrell: 1995: 39)*. This process produces interdependence and also constitutes deepening perceptions of common interests and identity, including self-awareness as a region. A regional arrangement include military or economic or political or a limited purpose or a multipurpose organisation and there are different forms of interaction between 'regionalisation' and the range of ways in which states may promote regional cohesion. In some cases, state-led actions have been responsible for an increase in 'real' interaction. In other words, the development of ties has been more one of 'marked-led integration'.

This paper is an attempt to understand the process of regional cooperation in South Asia, in the form of South Asian Association for Regional Cooperation (SAARC). It explore the changing phase of regionalism in the globalisation context where the forces of globalisation transnational flows of capital, people, goods and information-are progressively undermined the authority, legitimacy and effectiveness of the nation state. In this context paper seeks how 'new' regionalism emerges a failed nation state response to globalisation? Why SAARC still not become a vibrant regional grouping for regional cooperation in South Asia?

Globalisation and Regionalism

Regionalism in terms of international politics is closely associated with functionalism. The functionalist theory laid main emphasis on reducing or sidetracking political aspects by initiating regional action on non-political, non-controversial issues at lower or any other appropriate and possible level of decision making authority *(Gopal, 1996:12)*. One of the most important assumptions of the functionalist school is based on the concept called "spillover" effect. The underlying belief of the "spillover" concept is that cooperation in one area would open new avenues for similar cooperation in other areas. For example, successful forging of cooperation in the area of coal and steel production would spillover functional areas like transport, pollution control etc. According to the functionalists such a process of cooperation, would eventually lead to political unification of a given region. Cooperation and integration both the approaches followed within a regional system but distinction is often made between the two.

Cooperation, particularly, economic cooperation refers to an agreement which foresee some degree of commercial preferentialism but with no harmonisation of domestic rules, nor any obligation for common action in international affairs. Politically, it entails mutual support and commitment regarding the implementation of certain values and practices within the countries. On the other hand, regional integration refers to the process by which states go beyond the removal of obstacles to interact between their countries and create a regional space subject to some distinct common rules *(Best and Thomas, 2008: 436)*. Regional economic integration involves various steps. The first step is a free trade area in which tariffs are eliminated among the member states. The second step is a customs union which establishes a common policy of protection for the members with other countries. The custom union which is also a free trade area is difficult to form because each nation has its own industries that face international competition. A further step in regional integration is a common market which is a custom union without any kind of restriction in the movement of labour and capital across member states. A final stage of regional economic integration will be an economic union, with member states sharing a common currency. Cooperation and integration are not commonly exclusive general approaches for regional governance so much as options which may be pursued for different sectors and dimensions of regional relations. All regional systems, including the EU today, contain a mixture of both.

Globalisation is generally defined as the growing interconnectedness and interrelatedness of all aspects of society' *(Jones: 2006:2)*. It becomes the central driving force behind the rapid social, political and economic changes that are reshaping modern societies and the world order. Most significant impact of this process is on the very nature of the state because forces of globalisation have challenged the very authority, legitimacy and effectiveness of the nation state. The rapidity with which capital, technology and idea can transfer between states has transformed international economic relationship. 'Economic globalisation is bringing about a denationalisation of economies through the establishment of transnational networks of production trade and finance *(Held, et. al: 1999: 4)*. Marked by new forms of information and communication technologies and mirrored by global financial integration, the global productive economy has moved beyond the scale of nation states.

New technology has also brought about the time-space compression of the globe. Its implication for the national sovereignty is that no government can effectively control the international flow of information. Even the emergence of the institutions of global governance like Human Right Commission, Amnesty International etc, states has become the subject of external security. In addition no single state is able to respond to globalisation similar to terrorism, climate change, energy security on its own.

So the globalisation forces have undermined the very sovereignty of the nation state. In this process 'new regionalism' which is multidimensional and consistent with the modern interconnected world can be seen as a failed nation state response to globalisation. 'New regionalism being the political corrective to globalise market driven disorder and turbulence, not only on the level of the world but also at local system'. *(Hettne, et al: 1999: XXXI)*. It foster a trend where countries whether big and small try to seek cooperation and act together to seize the opportunities but also jointly face the challenge and down sides of globalisation. Present wave of regionalism is known as 'new regionalism' which is very different as compared to the debates on regional integration some thirty years ago.

Difference between Old and New Regionalism

The recent wave of regionalisation throughout the world warranted a new type of analysis which went beyond the classical integration theory.

Where the old regionalism was created from above (by the superpowers), the new is more spontaneous process from within the region and also from 'below' in the sense that the actor behind regionalist projects are no longer state only, but a large number of different types of institutions, organisations, non state actors etc. Old regionalism was specific with regard to objective, some organisations being security oriented and other being economically oriented; the new has a more comprehensive, multidimensional process. It includes not only trade and economic integration but also environment, social policy, political, security; democracy includes the issue of accountability and legitimacy. Unlike the old regionalism, new regionalism becomes 'open' regionalism. Regional grouping are extending their orbit beyond the doctrinal limit and become much more inclusive that can pave the way for more collaborative and viable performance.

In fact, new regionalism has become much more comprehensive, open, multidimensional and consistent with the modern interconnected and interdependence world. It not only includes economic affair but also takes into account the socio-political and environmental security and thereby pushing the countries towards the platform of cooperation and establishing regional coherence and identity. European Union (EU) and Association of South East Asian Nation (ASEAN) are example of successful new regional groupings. They reinvented and reorient themself form old regionalism to new regionalism.

Against this background, the following part of the paper, explore the regional cooperation in South Asia in the form of South Asian Association for Regional Cooperation (SAARC). It looked into the questions of how SAARC has responded to this global transformation. Why it has been failed to become a vibrant regional grouping? What should be the way to make SAARC a vibrant regional grouping? These are some of the key questions that the paper tried to be answered?

SAARC in the Globalise world

The geographical contiguity and socio-economic similarities among the South Asian countries found expression in the form of SAARC in 1985 for launching the process of regional cooperation and development in South Asia. The seven countries of South Asia-India, Nepal, Bangladesh, Bhutan, Sri Lanka, Maldives and Pakistan are the founder members of this organisation (Afghanistan was admitted the 8th member of SAARC during 14th SAARC Summit, held in India).

As a form of regional organisation SAARC was a product typical of the 1980's. Domestically this was the period in which two dominant features of post colonial economic nationalism- the goals of self-reliance and self-sufficiency, had not yet lost their appeal but severe limitation on their pursuit had been revealed in practice. Internationally, this was period when the north-south dialogue had reached a dead end. Countries of the south began to see south–south cooperation as the only viable route to their development. The SAARC was the product too sought, too promote and strengthen such collective self–reliance. At the same time, however another legacy of the post colonial territorial nationalism continues to have strong hold over south Asian countries. So the SAARC was the product of typical circumstances of that period.

Particularly after 1990's, the process of economic cooperation in South Asia has accelerated on the agenda of SAARC. Virtually all South Asian states have responded to globalisation by liberalising their economies, opening up their market. Number of declarations has also been made in SAARC summits to make SAARC as trade grouping. On December, 1995 SAARC Preferential Trading Agreement (SAPTA) was operationalised to promote and sustain mutual trade and economic cooperation within SAARC region through the exchange of trade concession. This was the effort to establish itself as a budding trading block in the changing global order. Infact, SAPTA was a prelude and a tool of realising the final goal of South Asia Free Trade Area (SAFTA). 'Notwithstanding some achievements that have taken place with reference to SAPTA, it has failed to prove itself as a strong, unified economic block. Due to the lack of restraint of the member countries from bringing in their mutual political conflicts on the promenade of SAARC deliberations' (*Chakraborti: 2008: 201),* SAARC countries moved further towards South Asia Free trade Area (SAFTA). In the 12th SAARC summit of 2004 held at Islamabad, SAARC countries implement SAFTA in order to make South Asia as a free trade region. After the signing of an agreement on SAFTA, the earlier agreement of SAPTA has been replaced by this new agreement. Under SAFTA, the member countries will reduce their custom duties to 0-5 per cent by the year 2016. However, in case of Sri Lanka, India and Pakistan this time limit is the year of 2012. Beyond these time limits, the region will go for zero custom duty. Under this agreement, each member country is permitted to declare a list of sensitive goods in which no duty concession shall be made.

Despite all the efforts, regional cooperation in South Asia has remained non-starter even after 26 years of SAARC existence. The notion of South Asian solidarity or South Asian identity is yet to take shape. Infact, the leaders of the SAARC have always raised their voice on the burning issues of the region but it has hardly done anything to solve the core problems of the region like poverty, food security, preventing terrorism or drug smuggling etc. South Asia accounts for nearly 23 per cent of the total world population. However its share in the global GDP is less than 3 per cent of global trade. The region is home to the world's 400 million, which means nearly 30 per cent of region's population lives below poverty line *(Chakraborti: 2010: 510)*. South Asian countries account only 0.25 per cent of the world's GNP. In fact with income levels lingering below US $ 400 in term of per capita GNP, they rank among the world's poorest countries *(Singh: 2010: 46)*. Even the World Bank repot shows that 2/3 people of South Asia live on less than two dollars per day. The Human Development Report 2010 unveiled by United Nation Development Programme (UNDP) shows that South Asia is the home of half of the world multidimensionally poor population or 844 million people.

For the first time, member countries expressed their frustration with its sluggish progress in the 16th Summit held in *Thimphu* (Bhutan) which is also the silver jubilee year of formation of SAARC. The Prime Minister of India, Dr Manmohan Singh expressed his disappointment by saying that "*the glass of regional cooperation, regional development and regional integration is half empty.*" This apprehension was expressed by the member countries both large and small. The major reason for the failure of SAARC is that it continues to operate in old regionalism framework, which has very state centric in nature. Where the globalisation process denationalises economy through the transnational production system, the SAARC nations still work in territorial nationalism framework. It is substantially government centric, government driven and government controlled with a top down approach, its programs have generally left no mark on the common man who has remained largely marginalised' *(Nath Ram: 2008: 2-3)*. In this framework bilateral tensions among the member's countries have hampered the successful working of SAARC. In every SAARC Summit, declaration and issues like-combating terrorism, infrastructure connectivity, poverty alleviation, people-to-people contact, gender development, energy security, economic integration etc. are on the agenda of SAARC but they are not yet implemented due to bilateral conflict between the countries. SAARC never allows multiple voices from non state actor, in its ambit. 'It is increasingly realised that the South Asian civil society has never found SAARC to be the people's institution. It has rather remained far alienated from the South Asian masses, their aspirations and development. They have always found it much more convenient and effective to work outside the official SAARC framework' *(Lama: 2001:*83). South Asian academia and professionals are meanwhile meeting quite regularly. Even after the 26/11, where both Indian and Pakistani government became suspicious of each other and create hysteria of war. On the other hand, South Asian civil society group like media, social activates, academicians are on the forefront to normalise the situation. That is why there are question asked on SAARC credibility, relevance and sustainability.

The SAARC charter prohibits the raising of bilateral problems in the meeting of SAARC. The bilateral issues of the member countries unfortunately have always thwarted the attempt to give SAARC its role as regional forum. The bilateral problems between the member states like India-Pakistan tensions, India has differences with Nepal and Bangladesh etc, on certain issues which negatively affect the growth of closer regional cooperation. The Afghanistan-Pakistan relations are constrained by allegations of support for the Taliban from sources in Pakistan. Similarly securing the immigration and security issues in the India-Bangladesh border areas is another source of concern. During SAARC summits, bilateral issues overshadow the official agenda of meeting. For example, during the 16th summit in *Thimphu* (Bhutan) and the 17th summit in *Addu Island* (Maldives) held in April 2010 and November 2011, respectively, the meeting between the Indian and Pakistani Prime Minister assumed greater significance. India –Pakistan talks on the sidelines of SAARC have also always diverted the focus of the media. Media always made these talks on sidelines of SAARC a big ticket event. Instead of highlighting the SAARC issues, media devoted its entire energy to the India-Pakistan engagement on the sidelines of the SAARC. Consequently, the regional organisation has not got the media attention that is necessary to popularise the concept of SAARC in a region that is divided by history and where the scars of partition have provided fertile ground for mistrust and suspicion to grow. That is why South Asia, despite 'share a civilisation, architecture, art, literature and language', physical and institutional infrastructure, has failed to make much the headway and emerge as a strong regional grouping, thanks to the India-Pakistan rivalry.

The much hyped SAFTA success has another inside story to this bilateral conflict. It is revealing to note that the total intra-South Asian trade was $ 11 billion in 2009 out of which the intra-regional trade through SAARC mechanism was merely 5.29 billion dollars. Even the combined trade of all these countries accounts for less than 2 per cent of global trade. The region account only 1.7 per cent of world exports and 3 per cent of global Foreign Direct Investment (FDI) inflow *(Chakraborti: 2010: 510)*. 'In sharp contrast to the success of ASEAN and EU in boosting interregional trade, the proportion of inter SAARC trade remains modest in both world and interregional trade.' Their share of inter-regional trade was 3.2 per cent in 1991, increased to mere 4.9 per cent in 2008 *(The Asian Age:2008)*. After the implementation of SAFTA the increase in intra-SAARC trade is due to merely increase in Indo-Bangladesh trade through the mechanism of SAFTA. Although there is good sign for regional trade that Pakistan government has announced its willingness to implement SAFTA with India or to grant status of Most Favoured Nation (MFN) to it under W.T.O. rules. Since its recent announcement, Pakistan has waffled over the actual status. For long, the hostility between India and Pakistan had derailed progress on the trade front and had rendered ineffective the efforts to establish a SAFTA that could transform the region's economic growth. A Free Trade Area (FTA) in South Asia has very little meaning and significance if it does not cover potentially the largest segment of trade in the region i.e. that between India and Pakistan. Another countries of the region also believe that the organisation can truly make a mark only if India and Pakistan, resolves their bilateral differences and become engines of regional economic growth. Most countries preferred bilateral free trade agreement than trade through SAFTA e.g. India-Sri Lanka, India-Bangladesh free trade agreement.

India, overwhelmingly dominate in the region over other members in terms of size, population and economy, created its big brother image among the member countries. India is really the *Big Daddy* in the region, the one with an Everest of an economy compared to its South Asian counterparts. It accounts for 74 per cent of the region's population, 75 per cent of its GDP, 79 per cent of its trade and 81 per cent of region's FDI inflow. *(Chakraborti: 2010: 511)*. India has trade surplus with all other South Asian countries except Bhutan. In addition, India is the largest military power in the region and together with Pakistan, a nuclear state. Other members, due to various reasons are apprehensive of India's domination in the region. This factor hampers the closer regional cooperation among the member states of the region. Whereas economic globalisation provides the opportunity for growth and development through integration of economic entities, South Asia misses this opportunity, due to their political tension and still run in poverty trap. That is the reason why India which is emerging as the fast growing economy of the world is not able to find any hope for growth within the gamut of South Asia are forcing India to engage more with the other equitable partner i.e. China, Central Asia, ASEAN etc. India also signed FTA with the ASEAN in 2009 which operationalised with the countries like Malaysia, Singapore, Thailand, Myanmar and Vietnam. India participates in the international affairs not as a member of SAARC but in her individual capacity. Indian participation in other regional or international groupings like G-20, IBSA and BRICS is more pronounced and broad based rather than her participation in SAARC process.

New Regionalism a way out

It is time to search for an alternate and workable model of regional cooperation which goes beyond the SAARC. It does not mean to jettison SAARC. There is a need to rediscover, redefine and reinvent SAARC according to the changing realties of South Asia. It will become a vibrant regional grouping only when its benefit will reaches to the people of South Asia. There is a need for closing the huge gap that remains between the promises of SAARC and reality of South Asia. If it wants to justify its location as the only viable grouping of the region it should reorient itself from state centric to people centric SAARC or SAARC from below. Civil society, business groups should be allowed more space in the ambit of SAARC. 'it should adopt a four pillar approach based on knowledge, technology, commerce and culture and a host of multiple partnerships could be created at the lever of civil society, business, scientific community and culture groups which would be a manifestation of 'People SAARC' or a 'SAARC from Below' (*Tripathi: 2008:41).* The official SAARC should play more role of facilitator rather than initiator of these exchanges. It should be multilateral in nature and global in vision.

Even the presence of a dominant member country is not necessarily threat to cooperation and shared gains. It is found that regional integration particular among developing countries, can succeed only if the economically stronger members' states adopt measures for enabling the weaker member's states to derive equitable benefits from the integration process. Others members' countries should consider India's rising economy as opportunity not as a threat. Because of its formidable position in the South, India bears a major responsibility to act as a leader of this region by playing a positive proactive role which makes SAARC a vibrant regional grouping. To do this, India should follow the "*Gujral Doctrine*" to provide the unilateral concessions to its neighbouring countries without demanding the reciprocity. It gives the other partners greater visibility in regional affairs and makes them an equal partner in the region which is Indo-Centric in Nature.

Conclusion

As an institution, SAARC has remained an intergovernmental mechanism which had little relevance for people of south Asia. The association has allowed the political logic to dominance over economic and therefore lags far behind several other regional and multilateral initiatives. So there is a need that SAARC will redefine and reorient itself from old regionalism to new regionalism where it becomes more people centric.

The truth is that SAARC has so far been moderate in its accomplishment. But there are potential benefits of economic cooperation in the region. According to Human Development in South Asia 1998 report, greater South Asian Cooperation could also lead to a revolution in the communication and energy sectors. It has been estimated that the cost of non-cooperation in the area of transport and communication would lead to a loss of intraregional trade, amounting to $ 1.8 billion annually by 2015. From 2007 summit onwards, SAARC has focused on the development of institutional framework for strengthening regional cooperation. The leaders of SAARC members highlighted the need for more efficient, focused, time bound and people centric activities and incorporating the same in the national programmes of the member states. The "Partnership for Growth for Our people" and "Towards a Green and Happy South Asia" and "Building Bridges" was the themes of the 15th, 16th and 17th SAARC summit respectively. These summit adopted people-centric model which is a good sign for south Asia. Or to put it even more dramatically SAARC is an idea whose time has finally arrived. That is also indicated by the fact that there are now nine countries that have been given 'Observer' status at the Maldives Summit outnumbering the number of member countries. These are the US, Australia, China, EU, Iran, Japan, South Korea, Mauritius and Myanmar. That is a good sign as many of these countries had written off SAARC regarding it as a lost course.

In the fourth meeting of SAARC interior ministers held in *Thimpu* on 23 July, 2011, leaders have agreed on the need for greater regional connectivity, better transport infrastructure, enhanced flow of material and goods and taking further steps to facilitate integration. Towards the achievement of the objective, the challenge before SAARC is to translate institutions into activities, conventions into programmes, official statements into popular sentiments. Declarations at summits and official level meetings do not amount to regional cooperation or integration. Regional cooperation should enable free movement of people, of goods, of services and of ideas. It should help us re-discover our shared heritage and build our common future.

References

Best, Edward and Thomas Christiansen (2008), 'Regionalism in International Affairs', in John Baylis, Steve Smith and Patricia Owens (eds), *The Globalisation of World Politics: An Introduction to International Relations (4th ed),* Oxford University Press, New York. Chakraborti, Tridib, (2008), 'SAARC Expands its Wings: Insinuations in the New Global Order', *World Focus*, Vol. 26, No. 5, May, pp. 201-208.

______(2010), 'India's Relations with South Asia in 2010: A Journey of Crests and Troughs', *World Focus*, Vol. XXXI, No. 11-12, Nov-Dec, pp. 510-519.

Gopal, Krishan (1996), *Geopolitical Relations and Regional Cooperation: A Study of South Asia,* Trans Asia Publications, New Delhi.

Held, David , Anthony McGrew, David Goldblatt and Jonathan Perraton, (eds) (1999), *'Global Transformation: Politics, Economics And Cultural,* Cambridge.

Hettne, Bjorn, Andras Inotai and Sunke Osvaldo (eds) (1999), *Globalism and New Regionalism,* Macmillan Press, London.

Hurrel, A. (1995), 'Regionalism in Theoretical Perspective', in L. Fawcett and A. Hurrell (eds), *Regionalism in World Politics: Regional Organisation and International Order,* Oxford University Press.

Jones, Andrew (2006), *'Dictionary of Globliasation'*, Polity Press, Cambridge.

Lama, Mahendra P. (2001), 'The Future Ahead', *World Focus,* Vol . 22, No.7, May, pp. 82-86.

Ram, Amar Nath (2008), 'South Asian Regional Cooperation,' *Man and Development*, Vol. 31, No. 1, March, pp.1-12.

Singh, Vivek Kumar (2010), *India's International Relations*, Unique Publishers, New Delhi. The Asian Age (New Delhi), *'India must Breathe Life into SAFTA'*, 5 August, 2008, p.10. Tripathi, Rahul (2006), 'The Regional Discourse on South Asia: Vision for a People SAARC', *South Asian Survey,* Vol. 13, No. 2, July-Dec, pp.13-19.

______(2008), 'Bringing SAARC closer to South Asia', *World Focus,* Vol. 26, No. 5, May, pp-39-43.

The authors are Junior Research Fellows (JRF) in Department of Political Science, Panjab University, Chandigarh.

China's Attitude and Perceptions towards SAARC: An Overview

— **Shayama Bangar and **Priyanaka*

Abstract

South Asian Association for Regional Cooperation (SAARC) was established in 1985 to enhance cooperation among the countries of South Asia in a political and areas of mutual interest. SAARC is only an organisation where are an observer country is much more than member countries. Though the Chinese involvement in South Asian Association for Regional Cooperation (SAARC) is a statement of China's adherence to the theory of multilateral practices; it is Beijing's orderly contact with the SAARC members and systematic 'good-neighborhood' policy that have fetched adequate space to China in South Asian politics today. China's involvement in Asian regionalisation is a main axis of its foreign policy and a part of China's multilateral strategy which aims at increasing its regional role in Asia and multilateralism in global arena. The engagement with the regional institutions such as SAARC, on the one hand facilitate China's role as an effective player in the peripheral politics and on the other hand, maximizes PRC's strategic interest for further regional integration. The article seeks to analyze the China's role in SAARC and why China wants to be a part of the SAARC (full member). This article also highlights the positive effect of China and SAARC cooperation.

Introduction

The emergence of SAARC however is a historic and positive event as it is for the first time that the South Asian countries have come together

* Research Scholar, Department of Political Science, Panjab university, Chandigarh.

** Assistant Professor, Rayat and Bahra college, Roper.

on common forum to solve common problems. Like many regional organisations, South Asian Association for Regional Cooperation (SAARC) was formed to provide a forum to the people of South Asia where they could work collectively for peace, development and economic cooperation in their region.

However, despite having close geographical, cultural and historical affinity, the Organisation has failed to achieve the desired results for certain reasons.[1] It remained confined to holding summits from time to time and to pledges made by the leaders of South Asian countries to develop the region into a potential economic market. The SAARC has a vision quite unlike that of other groupings like the NATO, SEATO, CENTO and the Warsaw Pact which were more pronouncedly military blocs. The foremost objective and their principal activities were not fostering economic cooperation or communal collaboration. Economic considerations, on the other hand, provided the impetus to the formation of the SAARC and forging of regional arrangements to enhance trade and commerce between them and among countries in South Asia.[2] During its twenty-five year journey, SAARC as an institution has made little progress in forging regional cooperation in South Asia. Other regional blocs in different parts of the world came into existence more or less with SAARC, have moved forward at a much faster pace in enhancing economic cooperation within their respective regions. Political and security issues, lack of trust, particularly amongst relatively smaller member states vis-a-vis the larger ones, the member states interest in looking extra regionally for enhancing trade and investment relations, and persistence of trade restrictive non-tariff barriers in the region are some of the factors responsible for the lackluster performance of the SAARC.[3] A regional bloc of 1.5 billion people, SAARC has thus far away to gain respect and command the attention of the world community. States except India within the Asian region are smaller and weaker. They felt a threat to independent and sovereign existence from a big and strong neighbour like India. Nepal perceived a fear of Indian supervision over their matters and continues to nurse a threat of Indian interference. But Bhutan and the Maldives, however, have not exhibited any overt signs of being under siege or anxiety from Indian dominance. On the other hand, independent Bangladesh does nurse a fear of India and has been most anxious about the designs or intentions of her powerful neighbour. The SAARC is increasingly becoming dysfunctional, due to most of the countries being poor as well as India-Pakistan rivalry hampering progress.

But still China joined SAARC as an observer member and wants full membership in this regional organisation.[4]

Why does China want SAARC?

Most of the member countries of South Asian Association for Regional Cooperation (SAARC) and the People's Republic of China are close neighbours linked together by common rivers and mountains. There is a great possibility of inter-regional cooperation as a model of South-South Cooperation. China and South Asia are positive forces for peace and development. The cooperation and closeness between China and South Asia will contribute to the strengthening of Pan- Asian unity. The twenty first century can be changed into an era of modernisation of Asia through the joint efforts of China and South Asia. China is the development partner of almost all states in the SAARC.[5] It has been involved in several construction and infrastructure projects in these countries. It has a special relationship with Pakistan, which it cultivates, in a bid to keep India on its toes. Along with China also wants stability in this region. It can be stable and prosperous only when the neighbourhood is stable and prosperous. Where there is a fire in the neighbourhood, it is likely to catch your own house. Throughout history, negative developments in the region have tended to impart instability to the states present in those regions. Take the Arab Spring, or West Asian turmoil. Even closer to home, India's Kashmir is unstable because of Pakistan's attempts to create a warlike environment. Therefore China has a vested interest in keeping this environment stable. Also, being a member of the largest growing demographic would have significant advantages when it comes to exports. China could use its clout to increase the exports to the member nations of SAARC.[6]

The 18th summit of the South Asian Association for Regional Cooperation (SAARC) is underway in Kathmandu, Nepal. SAARC consists of Afghanistan, Bangladesh, Bhutan, India, Maldives, Nepal, Pakistan and Sri Lanka. The prime ministers and presidents of each of those countries gathered in Nepal for the summit, along with diplomatic representatives from SAARC observers – including China. In addition, the rise of China offers greater scope for both South Asia as a region and SAARC as an institution to expand and grow. Given the complexities that rising powers pose in global politics, it goes without mentioning that China in its affiliation to SAARC would aspire for a greater purpose in South Asia and that could shape the regional power politics in coming future.[7] China has been an observer at SAARC since 2006, but is interested in pursuing full membership. China's "all weather friend" Pakistan helped push for China's full inclusion during the SAARC summit but, as has happened in the past, reluctance from India kept the proposal from moving forward. China's delegation to the SAARC summit was headed up by Vice Foreign Minister Liu Zhenmin. While in Nepal, Liu pledged that China will seek deeper ties with South Asia, especially on the economic front. "China has put forward a series of initiatives, (including) increasing trade between South Asia and China to 150 billion US dollars and investment to 30 billion US dollars in the next five years. The US $30 billion will go to road construction, Liu said.

China's offer of increased trade and infrastructure development is an off-shoot of the Silk Road Economic Belt, China's plan for an integrated trading network that will stretch from western China to Central Asia, South Asia, the Middle East, and Europe. Many of the SAARC members (including Afghanistan, Pakistan, the Maldives, Sri Lanka) have already expressed interest in joining either the Silk Road Economic Belt or its oceanic equivalent, the Maritime Silk Road. In addition, Bangladesh, India, Nepal, Pakistan, and Sri Lanka joined China's Asian Investment Infrastructure Bank, which is expected to act as a major source of funding for Silk Road infrastructure projects. India is especially wary of increased Chinese influence over its near neighbours.[8] In part as a response to increased Chinese attention to the region, Indian Prime Minister Narendra Modi has made a special point of reaching out to the South Asian nations. This regional outreach includes a new vision for SAARC a point Modi made clear from the very beginning of his term by inviting all the SAARC leaders to his swearing-in ceremony in May. Given this, India will look askance at China's own goals for SAARC, which tie so neatly into China's larger foreign policy vision for the entire Eurasian continent – a vision that puts China back at the center of the world. On their face, China and India share common goals for SAARC: increasing regional integration, through infrastructure connections and increased economic ties. The issue, of course, is that both India and China ultimately want to be at the center of this regional integration process.[9]

China's Role into SAARC

SAARC as a regional forum has been able to attract the attention of big powers that are more competitive than cooperative. Ever since 2006, SAARC has been undergoing some outstanding transformations. After more than two decades stagnation, political uncertainty and various kind of violence in most member countries. SAARC has completed the first ever expression with granting observer states to many other outsider countries. After the inclusion of observer SAARC has gone regional to global level. The extra regional power as observer SAARC might make some waves. Some observers appear to be optimistic that association the leading world power would nudge and support regional economic integration. The emerging economic strength of some of the SAARC members in global order has opened the eyes of many external associates to be its partners. SAARC is one of the few (if only) regional organisations in the world that has more observers than its actual member states. Among those observers are Australia, China, the European Union, and the United States. China's role is perhaps the most discussed – not least because Beijing seeks to expand its role, potentially through full membership.[10]

13 November 2005, SAARC Summit in Dhaka is significant for sever important policy initiatives. But one of most important outcome is the decision to grants to state to China which has significant foreign policy implications for India. The moves for inclusion of China in SAARC as on observer came as rude shock to India. China entry into SAARC demonstrates China's rising diplomatic and economic clout in the region. India was the only SAARC member state that strongly opposed Chinese bid to join the regional alliance. India believes that China's entry into SAARC would eclipse India's importance and standing as a major regional power in the grouping. [11] China also faces challenges from the South Asian region, including concerns about instability in Pakistan and extremism. But South Asia also provides economic opportunity and strategic benefits, especially as China seeks a greater role in the Indian Ocean. Thus, China has been developing economic and political links with SAARC member states. A number of SAARC countries have reportedly supported full membership for China, including ally Pakistan, as well as Nepal and Sri Lanka. For the smaller SAARC states, China is a growing economic player in their countries; moreover, having another large Asian state in SAARC presents the possibility of limiting India's influence or playing one off against the other to elicit maximum benefits. India has not been a supporter of full membership for China in SAARC. It has traditionally frowned upon too much external influence in South Asia (though it has worked with other third parties in the region to curb Chinese influence). Those in India who support Chinese membership assert that, through geography and its links with SAARC members, China

is a "South Asian" country.[12] They admit that the region and the Sino-Indian relationship could benefit from Chinese membership. Some analysts state that SAARC is not that relevant any way and thus there would be little harm in including China. Yet others admit that China is already engaging with South Asian countries bilaterally in a way that excludes India; this way India could be part of that engagement.

Those who oppose Chinese membership, including within the Indian government, question the inclusion of a non-South Asian country. Their concerns include China potentially dominating the organisation and working against India interests within it; Sino-Indian political difficulties limiting SAARC's effectiveness and activities, as India-Pakistan ones have done; and Sino-Indian interactions within SAARC exacerbating China-India mistrust. Any assessment of China's role needs to factor in India's perception, as well as the current and future direction of the relationship. It also requires analyses of China's relations with individual SAARC members and its approach to the region. Policymakers and analysts have to assess what China will bring to the table as a full member and whether its inclusion will advance or impede SAARC's mission. [13] The implications of full membership are crucial, given that it comes with a veto. After all, in other fore like the Asian Development Bank, Beijing has vetoed some Indian projects for political reasons. Moreover, if there is a membership expansion, why only China? Why not others, such as Myanmar and Iran from the broader region, and Japan and the U.S. from beyond it?

Beyond China's role in SAARC, Indian policymakers are faced with the reality of Chinese influence in the neighbourhood that will only likely increase in the future. The implications are not all negative – India and its companies, after all, can potentially benefit from Chinese investment in South Asia, especially if it improves connectivity, livelihoods and, ideally, stability. However, expanded Chinese activity has caused apprehension. There is still — and perhaps growing — concern and uncertainty about Chinese behavior and its leadership's intentions. There are also questions about whether China's leaders will use economic influence as a tool of political pressure. On the flip side, it hasn't been clear that China is willing to use political leverage to enhance regional stability (as opposed to its own security), for example, with Pakistan. Moreover, hopes of economic interdependence enhancing strategic cooperation between countries have delivered mixed results. It is also natural that the smaller SAARC states have been increasing their links with China. They see economic benefits from engaging with this rising Asian giant – as do many Indians – and also a way to garner Indian interest and some competitive courting. Indian policymakers and analysts objecting loudly to these links is futile and, arguably, counterproductive.

An effective Indian approach requires presenting a viable alternative. It means convincing SAARC countries that it wants to take them along on the path to economic prosperity. This wouldn't be doing these countries a favor – rather, it is in India's economic and security interests. This does not mean backing down when India has security concerns (e.g. counter-terrorism). It does mean showing favor at times (for example, giving up on certain demands for larger gains over all).

Positive effect of China and SAARC cooperation

China and South Asian countries are linked together by mountains and waters. Even the towering Himalayas cannot block the mutual economic attraction between China and SAARC. China has a large consumption market and the fastest growing economy in the world, while South Asian countries are rich in both natural and human resources. Combined, the economic integration of China and SAARC will create a huge market with 2.8 billion people, which will bring new force for economic development to China, South Asia and the whole world.

The economic integration of China and SAARC will enhance the economic development of South Asian countries and China in at least three ways. First, most SAARC countries remain at the lower end of industrialisation, and unemployment problems are pressing for South Asian governments. China is now at the medium level of industrialisation, and Chinese capital is increasingly "going global." With the restructuring of the Chinese economy, a lot of labour-intensive industries will move abroad. Although some Chinese economists assume that Africa is the best choice for these industries. It could be beneficial for South Asian countries – especially those with large populations – enjoy better geographic advantages and conditions. It is of vital importance that South Asian countries resolve their employment problems, increase the proportion of manufacturing in their economies and improve economic growth. At the same time, continued Reform and Opening in China will forge a huge market for these countries.

Second, China has been playing an active role in power projects, transportation, and other infrastructure construction overseas, particularly in developing countries. In doing so, it is taking advantage of state financing as well as experience and technology acquired during its three decades of economic growth. Most SAARC countries are behind in terms of their infrastructure. If South Asian countries absorb China's infrastructure financing and experience, this will change their national infrastructures, promote social and economic development and create better conditions for absorbing even more FDI. Prime Minister Modi's economic priorities are infrastructure construction and labour-intensive manufacturing sectors, both of which will provide great space for China-India economic cooperation.

Third, over the past three decades of economic Reform and Opening, China has acquired considerable experience that is applicable beyond just economic development and infrastructure construction. In an era of globalisation, countries must first have social stability and a peaceful periphery if they want to experience economic development. Political leaders and society should have an open mind towards the outside world, especially toward foreign investment. Political leaders must be willing to reform unsuitable rules, regulations and laws. China is very cautious when communicating with other developing countries about its experiences, so as to avoid Western countries condemning the so-called "China model." But these experiences can be helpful to South Asian countries, along with China's economic and technological aid and people-to-people communication. Such communication will improve South Asian countries' social and economic development, strengthen the integration of SAARC, and create better conditions to resolve regional conflicts. Moreover, China-SAARC cooperation on international financial issues will enhance South Asia's capability to respond to international financial crises, while benefitting the reform of the international financial system.[14]

References

1. Mahmood, Tehmina (2000), "SAARC and Regional Politics", *Pakistan Horizon*, Vol. 53, No.4, pp.7-21. See also in Muhammad Jamshed Iqbal (2006), "SAARC: Origin, Growth, Potential and Achievements", *Pakistan Journal of History & Culture,* Vol. XXVI I/4 (2006) p. 32.
2. Chabbra, Alka (2011), SAARC: SAPTA to SAFTA (eds) in The foreign Policy of India in the twenty first Century Challenges and Prospects by Emanual Nahar, Pearson, New Delhi pp. 313 -324.
3. Khan, H. Ashfaque (2011), China and SAARC, www. Nust.edu.pk/s3h/china and SAARC.pdf

4. Shinde, Rohit (2008), What are pros and cons of China joining SAARC www.quora.com/foreign policy/what-are-pros and cons-of-china-joining-saarc.
5. Lal, Hiranya (2003), SAARC, China and Pan-Asian Unity in (eds) South Asia and China towards inter-regional cooperation by Upendra Gautam, China study Centre-Published Kathmandu, pp. 55-56.
6. The diplomat.com/2014/11/china –makes- inroads –into- India-backyard.
7. Panda, P. Jagannath (2010), China in SAARC, China Report 46:3 293-310. Chr.sagepub.com/content/46/3/299.abstract.
8. Sroosh, Nabi and Yosuf Sabir (2009), Towards an Asian Century: Future of economic cooperation in SAARC countries, Hanns Seidel Foundation, pp.119-126.
9. The diplomat.com/2014/11/china –makes- inroads –into- India-backyard.
10. Bhattacharya Abanti (2005). "China's entry into SAARC, *World Focus*, Vol. XXI, No.5 May 2008, pp. 193-196. Also See Bhattacharya, Abanti, (2005), China's 'Observe' Status : Implication for SAARC www.ipcs.org/china-oberver-status-implicatios-for-SAARC-1891.html.
11. Dutta, Sujit (2011), China in SAARC? To what Effect, *Strategic Analysis*, Vol. 35, No. 3, pp. 18-27. Also see in Ghimine, Yubaraj and Shubhajit Roy (2014), Saarc: China pushes its case for seat through Pakistan www.indianexpress.com
12. Abdujjaher, Md. (2005), China as a saarc member: A debate www.academia .edu/china -as-a-saarc-member.
13. Dutta, Sujit (2011), China in SAARC? To what Effect, *Strategic Analysis*, Vol.35, No.3, pp. 18-27.
14. Zongyi, Liu (2014), China's economic relations with SAARC: Prospect and hurdles www.ciis.org.cn/english/2014-12/01/content-7409453.htm

SAARC at Twenty-Eight: Bridging Bridges through Energy

*— Reema Duggal**

Abstract

It is now generally accepted that energy security could be significantly enhanced through sustained cross-border exchanges in many regions. In South Asia, however regional energy security cooperation has seriously remained entangled in geopolitics. The possibility of over-exploitation of natural resources such as coal, natural gas and oil reserves and the low level of political confidence in sharing hydro resources have placed serious obstacles to enhancing the level of energy security in the region. This article looks at the bountiful opportunities that exist for South-Asia to collectively harness diverse energy resources so as to increase the level of energy security in the region and thus sustain higher economic growth.

The **politics of energy security** has emerged as a key concern worldwide and national energy strategies are increasingly treated as part of the traditional security agenda. The global demand for energy is slated to grow dramatically over the next 20 years, with the most rapid incremental consumption becoming evident in Asia, particularly in China and India. All governments will therefore need to develop comprehensive policies to meet the challenges posed by the growing demand for energy globally. Energy security will thus become an increasingly important component of foreign and security policy agendas in the countries world over. As the strategic importance of energy rises, both globally and

* Research Scholar, Department of Political Science, Panjab University, Chandigarh.

nationally, the more it is going to be focus of intense public and political debate. Energy security has been conventionally defined as 'the availability of energy at all times in various forms, in sufficient quantities and at affordable prices'[1]. Whereas in the context of growing focus on environmental sustainability issues and climate change, the International Energy Agency (IEA) would re-define long-term energy security as, mainly linked to timely investments to supply energy in line with economic developments and environmental needs[2]. Securing sustainable energy supplies to meet energy needs at reasonable/affordable prices has become a major policy imperative of countries. For a long time 'energy security' has had a different meaning, depending on the perspectives from the producer, consumer and transit states. Whereas consumer nations are primarily interested in security of supply, producer countries are more focused on security of demand from foreign markets. Transit states are interested in their own national security of supply and security of demand from neighbouring markets in order to benefit from stable and ever-higher transit fees. In addition, the concept of 'national energy security' also depends on the individual country's geographical location, domestic policies and the traditional state, economic and business ties it maintains with its partners. Integrated solutions to the energy-climate nexus are needed to balance energy security priorities with economic and environmental objectives. While there may be agreement that energy security is often defined as a national priority everywhere, there are very different ideas about the best ways of achieving it. Therefore, regionalisation is accepted as one of the most fastest and favourable route for prosperity, for promoting collective interests, ensuring protection against the negative fall-out of globalisation and enhancing security through intraregional interdependent relationships. Over the last several decades, Asia has become increasingly integrated with the rest of the world, its rapid development driven largely by exports to the US and EU. However, the regional global financial crises and economic fallout is quickly changing that dynamic, however Currently, over half of world trade takes place between members of regional trade agreements and Asia is no exception. However, in Asia, as in other parts of the world, regional integration is uneven. While South-east Asia is shooting up its economic integration efforts through ASEAN Economic Community Blueprint for 2015, with plans to continue attracting FDI, capitalise on the growth of its neighbours and accelerate the pace of its trade facilitation measures through a single market strategy. South Asia remains weakly integrated through the South Asian Association for Regional Cooperation

(SAARC) both economically and politically.[3] SAARC is a relatively young economic integration project and appears to be very small compared to other existing regional blocks. Since its foundation in 1985, SAARC is meant to pursue and unite the sub-continent under the noblest aims of social and economic development; mutual understanding and crucially the creation of an order based on mutual respect, equity and shared benefits. Needless to say, there is no mention of South Asia as we know it: a region sadly famous also for being ridden[4]. It is well known that SAARC is unable to fulfil the aspirations of the people of South Asia. Many scholars argue that it is a story of missed opportunities, compounded by absence of political cohesion and a shared vision. Being excessively government driven, it has substantially failed to impact positively on the life of the common man[5].

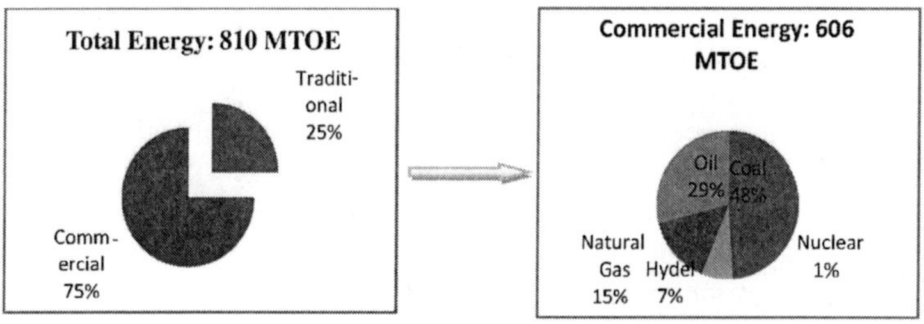

Source: IEA official site[12]

Since twenty eight years, eighteen summits have taken place and meetings have been held, but the result or success achieved is rather modest. Within SAARC there has been little progress even in respect of intra-regional trade, which accounts for 5 per cent as compared to 62 per cent for the EU and 55 per cent for NAFTA. No wonder that as a region we count for so little in the world: less than 1 per cent of the share of global trade, just 1.5 per cent of the World Gross Product, even as we count 450 million among the world's poorest people and 50 per cent of the world's illiterates within our seven nations. Lot many shortcomings can be seen as an obstacle in the uneven progress of this major body: most have to do with intra-regional political tensions, trust deficit and most involve India.

South Asia possesses significant indigenous energy resources, but nature has not distributed these resources evenly throughout the region and they remain underdeveloped. For instance, India with an oil resource potential of 5,576 million tonnes of oil equivalent stands at the top followed by Pakistan 3,600 million tonnes and Bangladesh 0.96 million tonnes. Pakistan, India, Afghanistan and Bangladesh have gas resources ranging from 120 billion cubic meters in Afghanistan to 7,985 bcm in Pakistan. On the coal front, the resource potential for India is 245,690 million tons, Pakistan 185,000 million tons and Bangladesh 2,715 million tons. Hydropower potential represents one of the largest energy resources in the region and India's potential is 301,000 MW, Bhutan 50,000 MW, Nepal 42,915 MW, Pakistan 40,000 MW, Sri lanka 2000 MW and Bangladesh 775 MW, totalling 437,000 MW of which only 9 per cent has been explored[6]. Sustainable energy supplies with economically viable and best energy solution have become imperative to major energy policy and procedures in-order to meet increasing energy demand in SAARC member states. As we have discussed earlier that the region remain energy deficit in aggregate, so energy cooperation is in demand which would mean efficient utilisation of region's resources, increase in reliability of energy supply, economically in operationalisation of initiatives, mutual support in contingencies and confidence building measures for geopolitical solution strategy[7]. So trust and confidence between SAARC member states are of prime importance for the success of SAARC Energy Ring concept and promotion of Energy Trade. What is critically lacking in all scholarly and journalistic studies on SAARC is a reasoned record of this side of SAARC existence. How politics have always been entangled, at different level but often crucially with SAARC activities. So the important question remains-how much more energy will the region need during next 10-30 years and from where will this energy will be supplied?

The Need for Energy Security in South Asia: Demand and Supply Forecast

South Asian countries are highly dependent on imported crude oil and petroleum products. The imports range from 25 per cent of commercial energy consumption in the case of Bhutan to 100 per cent in the case of Maldives.[8] The recent volatility and sharp increase in world oil prices has placed an unexpected and enormous burden on foreign exchange reserves, to the detriment of national economies. While countries like Sri Lanka and Maldives, which lack indigenous fossil fuel sources, are especially hard hit, even countries like India, Pakistan, and Bangladesh now meet less of their demand with indigenous fuel sources and face mounting energy import bills.[9] All countries in South Asia rely heavily on non-commercial energy, primarily biomass. Securing and expanding the use of commercial energy is essential, however, for the future economic growth of the region. Afghanistan and Bhutan currently have no long-term plans. Each country study forecasts energy demand up to 2020, based on an indepth analysis of future energy plans and prospects. The demand for different forms of energy is also discussed in each study. The oil consumption growth rate is expected to be over 6 per cent in all countries. Per capita energy consumption ranges from a low of 16 kilograms of oil equivalent (kgoe) in Afghanistan to a high of 759 kgoe in Maldives. Oil imports meet roughly 25 per cent of the commercial fuel demand in Bhutan, India, and Pakistan and 100 per cent of the commercial fuel demand of Maldives. Much of the imported oil products are used as fuel for the transportation sector as well as to meet some urban cooking needs. At the same time, the demand for electricity is growing at a rate of 7 per cent per year in most countries except Afghanistan, Bhutan, and Maldives, which expect growth rates of over 13 per cent in the first decade to meet rural electrification needs.[10] Within this context, there is sustained shift from traditional and commercial sources of energy to commercial sources. South Asia possesses significant indigenous energy resources, but nature has not distributed these resources evenly throughout the region and they remain underdeveloped. Energy use in South Asia has been increasing at over 5 per cent per annum during recent years. Energy use is likely to double by 2020, resulting in a projected consumption of about 1,200 million tons oil equivalent of energy per year.[11] Below is the diagram showing the Energy use in South Asia in MTOE (million tonnes of oil equivalent).

According to the SARI Regional Energy Report, India with an oil resource potential of 5,576 million tones of oil equivalent (mtoe) stands at the top followed by Pakistan 3,600 mtoe and Bangladesh 0.96 mtoe. Pakistan, Bangladesh, India and Afghanistan have gas resources ranging from 120 billion cubic meters (bcm) in Afghanistan to 7,985 bcm in Pakistan. On the coal front, the resource potential for India is 245,690 million tons, Pakistan 185,000 million tons, and Bangladesh 2,715 million tons (the other countries do not have viable coal resources). Hydropower potential represents one of the largest energy resources in the region, and India‘s potential is 301,000 MW, Bhutan 50,000 MW, Nepal 42,915 MW, Pakistan 40,000 MW, Sri Lanka 2,000 MW, and Bangladesh 775 MW, totalling 437,000MW of which only 9 per cent has been exploited. The countries in the region have developed energy use strategies based on the resources available and the expected demand. While Bangladesh intends to meet most of its commercial energy needs from natural gas in the near term, Bhutan and Nepal intend to develop their hydro-resources to both meet their energy needs and to export electricity to neighbouring countries. Pakistan anticipates that it will have to import gas from 2010 and begin to utilise its lignite/coal resources, while Sri Lanka is planning to develop indigenous hydro and biomass resources and to import coal for power generation. India is focused on optimal utilisation of its coal and hydroelectric sources as well as diversifying its supply mix by introducing more renewable energy and nuclear energy, as well as exploring and sourcing oil and gas resources beyond its boundaries. Therefore, South Asia is thus a huge importer of commercial fuels and depends on imported oil products, which are used as fuel for the transport sector. To exacerbate the problem, the world energy prices have risen sharply over the past two years. Crude oil prices are continuously rising which will have a debilitating impact on the economies of South Asia, which have relatively meagre foreign exchange reserves to meet ballooning fuel import bills.

As we all know that this South Asian region has the capability and the potential to become an economic giant but the endemic problems within South Asian countries are an obstacle in its economic growth rate. The geopolitical situation of South Asia also leads to energy insecurity, therefore South Asia is slowly moving towards greater insecurity as they are largely dependent on energy imports from foreign countries. India's centrality in the region is a function of both its size and a geographical location that enables it to share a common border with almost all its neighbouring countries. So India should utilise its geopolitical location to increase the level of energy security in the region.

India needs to play a major Role in SAARC

India should play her role not as a big brother but as an equal partner for the stability and cooperation in South Asia. SAARC is not an unimportant forum rather its significance has increased in the face of changing global and regional patterns so India should be aware of this scenario. Most of the disputes in South Asia are Indo-centric so India should adopt a low profile to get the confidence of its smaller neighbours. India must play a more trustworthy and accommodating role in taking economic initiatives to build up trust among the smaller neighbours, e.g. road transit between Nepal and Bangladesh should be allowed to flourish.[13] India has been a very active member since the beginning of SAARC but the hurdle that continued in its progress is due to Kashmir disputes with Pakistan. This is a prime cause of ineffectiveness in South Asian integration. The SAARC has failed to improve regional integration amongst South Asian countries which has led to several economic and political problems in this region. In addition to it, India superior power status in South Asia is creating fear of dominance amongst its neighbouring South Asian partners, like fear of Nepal that India will took control of its trade because of its geographical location. Besides, the tension prevailing between India and Sri Lanka over liberation Tigers of Tamil-Eelam are enough to prove that SAARC as failed as an organisation and is merely a *Talking Shop.* On the economic front, India has been selective amongst the countries of the SAARC in signing free trade agreements. Similar free trade agreements with Bangladesh and Pakistan have been stalled due to political and economic concerns on both sides. As a result, the trade amongst member countries is insignificant. Intra-SAARC trade makes up less than 5 per cent of the region's total gross domestic product, and only 3.7 per cent of its global trade. In the areas of exports, for a number of commodities SAARC member countries compete intensely with one another in all international markets. Market share of SAARC countries in the non oil producing countries is only around 4 per cent. SAARC countries have to look no further than its closest regional organisation ASEAN which is vibrant, dynamic and progressive all through. It has now covered a mileage which will soon disappear from the site of SAARC in terms of economic progress. Political differences and deficits of trusts amongst the member countries are the major obstacles to the advancement of this group. The two largest economies of the group, India and Pakistan, should take the credit for its failures. India has accepted SAARC as a voluntary independent organisation of sovereign states for regional cooperation, so it should become an active member in improving its healthy and cordial relations amongst South Asian countries.

Why the potential remain untapped?

Among the pre-requisites for energy trade, are the availability of energy resources potential for their economic exploitation, competitive cost advantages, adequate infrastructure, harmonious and enabling policies, lack of trade barriers, a climate of mutual trust and strong political will to cooperate for gaining mutual benefits. Currently less than 0.5 per cent of the regional trade comes from within the region and the total intra-regional trade in energy is less than 5 per cent of the total trade taking place between SAARC members. Formulating policies that promote and at least that do not impede energy trade is a challenge that is facing the SAARC members. Hydropower is the largest indigenous energy resource of the region and can meet a large part of the energy requirement of the member states. They need to adopt a collaborative approach for the exploration of the resource and possible CDM opportunities from a regional than a national perspective alone. For the SAARC region, it is suggested that the member states may first come together and develop an Inter-Governmental Agreement to promote regional energy trade. This agreement should define the areas where the governments of the member states shall commit to work towards regional energy trade.

Like many regional organisation, SAARC was formed to provide a forum to the people of South-Asia where they could work collectively for peace, development and economic cooperation in their region. However, despite having close geographical, cultural and historical affinity, the organisation has failed to achieve the desired results for certain reasons. It remained confined to holding summits from time to time and to pledges made by the leaders of South Asian countries to develop the region into a potential economic market. Arguably, SAARC so far has not been able to meaningfully respond to the aspirations of the people of South-Asia. Many believe that it is a story of missed opportunities, compounded by absence of political cohesion and a shared vision. Being excessively government driven, it has substantially failed to impact positively on the life of the common man[14].

What is critically lacking in all scholarly and journalistic studies on SAARC is a reasoned record of this side of SAARC's existence. How politics have been always entangled, at different levels but often crucially, with SAARC activities?

Key elements that are absent in current energy policies in the region include:

- **Lack of Regional Energy Grids:** This concept has been under discussion in SAARC since 2004 and the SAARC Working Group on Energy is currently considering this concept. Regional Energy Grids like regional electricity Grid and Regional Natural Gas Grid are pre-requisite in power trading in the region. Though these grids participating countries can import gas from outside the region through pipelines, jointly developed by nations.

- **Energy Sector Master Plan: Promoting Indigenous Resource Development:** The South Asian countries should also emphasise joint development mechanisms aimed at increasing investments in shared energy infrastructure and resource development. For example, South Asia has an economic hydropower potential of over 190,000 MW (Bhutan 23,760 MW, India 84,400 MW, Nepal 43,000 MW, and Pakistan 40,000 MW) which, when developed, would provide an excellent opportunity for energy trade within the region to bridge the demand-supply gap. So, the countries of the region need to develop a regional energy sector master plan that will take a realistic view of energy resources, demand profiles, and growth scenarios.
- **Shared Development of Coal Technologies:** There are tremendous opportunities for sharing technology on low-grade coal/lignite use and coal-based power generation equipment manufacturing. India, Bangladesh and Pakistan are serious about utilising their coal reserves; there is merit in sharing knowledge regionally. Currently, there are no institutional mechanisms for joint development of coal or clean coal technologies.
- **Sustained Cooperation on Regional Energy Issues:** The SAARC Energy Working Group, SAFIR, and SARI Energy have been facilitating discussions on energy security issues. However, the existing arrangements and institutions that have been working toward a regional energy security plan are not adequately equipped with a mandate and adequate resources to secure such plans in the foreseeable future. To supplement these efforts in a sustainable manner, there is need to establish a regional facility to support information sharing on techniques and technologies, training, renewable energy research and development, for promotion of a common strategy to address energy security concerns.[15]

The Road to Energy Security

To meet the growing aspirations of the people and economies of South Asian, each of the country are under immense social and political pressure to secure reliable, sustainable and reasonably priced energy supplies to meet the ever increasing demand for commercial energy.

Energy Security is no longer merely a catchphrase but an indisputable reality for vital economic development throughout South-Asia[16]. Though each of these countries is trying to evolve its own strategy to address the issue, there is growing realisation of the need to address energy security from a regional perspective. A regional approach facilitates a more comprehensive, cost-effective and sustainable set of solutions to the challenges of energy security. Initiatives should be taken to promote integration of Energy systems and enhance cross-border energy trade among the South Asian countries by focussing on the following initiatives for overall socio-economic development of the region.

- **Promoting Regional Energy Trade**

Policy makers in the public sector need to look upon trade as diversifying the forms of energy and their sources of supply, thus enhancing energy security, rather than focussing on the costly and ill-affordable goal of full national energy self-sufficiency. Possible evolution of regional energy trade within the SAARC region and between the SAARC region and its neighbours; towards one of the largest integrated markets in the world. Opportunities should be promoted for and possible evolution of intra and extra regional energy trading for these two clusters. In the Eastern cluster (Bangladesh, Bhutan, India, Nepal and Sri Lanka) opportunities include–

1. Expanding India's bilateral electricity trade beyond Bhutan to electricity imports from Nepal.
2. Possible gas and electricity imports from Bangladesh.

This would create a good basis for integrated electricity trading among the four countries, which could link with Mynamar (especially for gas imports) and Sri Lanka[17]. In the Western cluster (Afghanistan, Pakistan and India) the priority options include expanding electricity imports from Central Asia beyond Afghanistan to Pakistan and subsequently to India. Imports of gas from Central Asia, as well as from Iran, to Pakistan and India are also of significant interest. India would eventually bridge the two clusters into a unified energy market, with integrated electricity and gas networks.

- **Develop a Structure for a Regional Power Exchange:** after reviewing the power system structures in individual countries, along with their operational procedures and regulatory and commercial requirements for cross-border trade[18].

- **Harmonise Policy, Legal and Regulatory Issues:** The key result of this is to create the enabling systematic conditions for a sustainable market for investment and implementation of cross-border Energy Trade[19].

- **Advance Transmission Systems Interconnections:** The key result is to create the enabling, systematic conditions for a sustainable market for investment and implementation of sub-regional bilateral transmission interconnections beginning with the eastern sub-region of South Asia. The Electricity Energy should be traded among the member states by pooling all the resources and controlled through a centralised regulatory mechanism at SAARC level. As its well known that India is rich in coal resources, Bangladesh in gas reserves and Nepal and Bhutan in hydro-resources, so member states should thus provide a promising option for cooperation.

- **South Asian Energy Dialogue:** Training in designing, manufacture, installation and maintenance of energy systems should be contributed by private institutions and industries which can help in energy management. NGO's should come forward for promoting regional confidence and understanding. Within the aegis of regional forum there is a need for discussion on bilateral energy issues amongst members from Pakistan, India, Bangladesh and Nepal. This could take the form of Energy Dialogue comprising experts, academics, environmental bureaucrats and NGO's [20]

- **Energy Cooperation through South Asia Sub-regional Economic Cooperation:** Energy cooperation is the main focus of the SASEC program. The existing intra-regional energy trade is among the SASEC countries is limited to electricity trade between India-Bhutan and India-Nepal in 2011, within the framework of SASEC cooperation, it was around 5600 gigawatt-hour and trade in petroleum products between India and Nepal, Bhutan, Bangladesh and Sri Lanka. The enhanced electricity trade will be based on the expansion of power transfer links between Bhutan and India, and India and Nepal.[21]

The association is no longer in its infancy, therefore, the main challenge before the association is to prove its effectiveness in terms of bridging the gap between the promises made and achievements, contribute to reducing poverty in the member nations and take concrete steps for easy access to the people of one country to the other and easy flow of goods and services within the region so that a win-win situation is created from all member nation.

For promoting regional trade this very important question of 'What should be done?' need to be answered firmly. Policy makers in the public sector need to look upon trade as diversifying the forms of energy and their sources of supply, thus enhancing energy security. So it is viable to develop a better understanding at SAARC level so that regional trade can be evolved at a better pace.[22]

Conclusion

Securing long-term energy supplies to power expanding economies and meet the rising aspirations of a growing population is no longer a concept. Rather, the need for national and regional energy security has become a compelling reality for South Asia, as evidenced by the fact that each country in the region is seriously exploring avenues and options to meet future energy demand. At the same time, South Asia possesses indigenous energy resources and high-quality labour, in addition to a well-established governance system. Leveraging these advantages, a platform for action must be created to move quickly toward developing a regional energy market that can alleviate the risks associated with national energy security goals. Development of regional energy markets will require governments, institutions, academics, and all segments of society to come together to discuss openly and freely the issues involved—including the apportionment of costs and benefits—in a transparent, fair, and equitable manner. Creating a South Asia Regional Energy Foundation would be an important first step in this regard. The planning and progress for the reality of the concept of 'Energy Ring' is not up to mark and special initiatives are required at the level of Pakistan and India for long-term sustainable solutions to the region. The key challenges include transforming bilateral power exchange into multi-lateral, vision beyond 4-nation Power Grid (Bangladesh, Bhutan, India and Nepal), competition and low-carbon development. Private institutions and industries should contribute in energy management by imparting training in designing, manufacture, installation and maintenance of energy systems. This could take the form of a South Asian Energy Dialogue comprising experts, academics, environmentalists, bureaucrats and NGO's [23].

According to the World Bank Report,

'South Asia is one of the least integrated regions in the world. Regional Trade can potentially benefit the lagging regions of South Asia. For the region to be part of the 'Asian Century' the vision of South Asian integration and cooperation needs to be embraced by governments and citizens alike'.

In sum, it is pragmatic and unbiased acknowledgement and commitment to the fact that regional problems need to be tackled regionally, beyond any kind of border and barrier, what will make SAARC an association for cooperation in South Asia and worldwide. To conclude, in the context of SAARC moving at a very slow pace, whether or not it would be able to meet the challenges set for itself and within what time frame, only time will tell. Above all, there has to be a suitable political and economic environment within the region, without which SAARC would not be able to achieve these challenges.

References

1. Umbach, F. (2004) 'The Intersection of Climate Protection Policies and Energy Security', *Journal of Transatlantic Studies,* 10(4), 374.
2. Energy Security, http://www.iea.org/topics/energysecurity/
3. Lozach, S. V. (2013), *The Key to Asia's Future,* The Diplomat, January 18, p.1
4. Obino, F. (2010), *SAARC: The Political Challenge for South Asia and Beyond*, EPW, vol.15, no. 26, p. 44.
5. Nath, A. (2009), *SAARC in a Globalised Era: Imperatives and opportunities,* India Quaterly, 65(4), p. 441.
6. http://www.saarc-sec.org/
7. Sankar, T.L. (2000), *Regional Energy Security for South Asia,* Regional Report, SARI/Energy Program.
8. Iqbal, Kanwar (2012), *Energy Policy in South Asia: the Way Forward to Promote Regional Trade*, SAARC CCI, p. 333
9. Sankar. T.L. (2000), *Regional Energy Security for South Asia*: Regional Report, SARI/Energy Program.
10. *Ibid*
11. Siddiqi, T.A. (2008), *Developing Integrated Energy Policies in South Asia*, Saarc Energy Centre, Report no.1.
12. International Energy Agency, www. IEA.com
13. Shahhen. I. (2013). *South Asian Association for Regional Cooperation (SAARC): Its Role, Hurdles and Prospects,* IOSR Journal Of Humanities And Social Science, Vol. 15, Issue 6.
14. Nath, A. (2009), *SAARC in a Globalised Era: Imperatives and opportunities,* India Quaterly, 65(4), p. 449.
15. Sankar. T.L (2000), *Regional Energy Security for South Asia*: Regional Report, SARI/Energy Program.

16. Kumar, R., (2009), *India's Role in South Asia Trade and Investment Integration*, ADB Report, Regional Economic Integration Working Papers
17. Fowler, P., (2012), *Energy and Security in South Asia: Cooperation and Conflict,* Asian Affairs, 43(2), p. 312.
18. World Energy Council Report (2000), *Renewable Energy in South Asia,* London, p.2.
19. SARI/Energy Program www.sari-energy.org 2000.
20. Report of RIS Policy Brief on *Energy Cooperation in South Asia: Potential and Prospects*, No. 8, Dec 2008.
21. ADB Report, (2013), *An Overview of Energy Cooperation in South Asia,* South Asia Working Papers.
22. Report of RIS Policy Brief on *Energy Cooperation in South Asia: Potential and Prospects*, No. 8, Dec 2008.
23. www.worldbank.org/website/External/Countries/SouthAsia/Ext/

India's Approach Towards SAARC

— *Anjna Malhotra**

Abstract

Regional cooperation means developing friendly relations among nations in solving problems which are economic, social, cultural and humanitarian in character. Regionalist organisations, regionalist systems and regional doctrines are the basic features of regionalism. Regionalism has become the remarkable feature of world politics. In the era of Liberalisation, Privatisation and Globalisation, nations are desperate to seize the opportunity of taking active part in international economic arena and pursuing all round economic and social developments. All countries are now desperate to involve in regional organisations as members, as strategic partners, as observer members etc. Regional cooperation is crucial to achieve desired objectives set by all countries. This is also essential for economic development by facilitating free flow of trade and to coordinate economic policies among countries of same economic region.

After Second World War the concept of regional cooperation came into existence with the advent of European Integration model. This model has proved a test bed for ideas and doctrines to increase regional integration and to solve economic problems. Regionalism is one of the most contested doctrines for the students of political science. It is widely analysed by various political thinkers at international, regional and local level. At each level this doctrine assume specific connotation with serious

* Anjna Malhotra, Assistant Professor in Political Science, SDAM College, Dinanagar, Punjab.

academic and political implications. For some it is a formula to check the hegemony of super power and to safeguard the basic principle of sovereignty, for some is essential for regional growth, for some it is a method of developing friendly ties with many at low cost much benefit theory.[1] Several schemes for regional economic integration were established in Europe in the decades following World War II. In 1952 the ECSC (European Coal and Steel Community) came into existence which eventually developed into the European community in 1957.

Economic regionalism is now-a-days becoming a regular feature. Nations are ready to cooperate with rival countries also. ASEAN is the best example of this. On the lines of ASEAN, SAARC was established by seven sisters of south Asia namely India, Bangladesh, Nepal, Pakistan, Sri Lanka, Maldives, Bhutan in the year 1985. Afghanistan became its eighth member in 2005. Australia, China, the EU, Iran, Japan, Mauritius, Myanmar, South Korea and United States are the observer members of SAARC.

South Asia is one of the most disintegrated regions of the world.The culture, civilisation and human resources of this region are at par with the best in the world. Be it art, philosophy, science, religion, language etc. everything has flourished in this region and has left a deep impact on the rest of the world. But today the scenario is that the south Asia region belongs to the deprived regions of the world.

Now we have entered the twenty first century and 25 years have passed since a step was taken for the common future of South Asia through SAARC. Now its time that we look back and take stock of the situation as regards a bright future for this vision. More than 1.3 billion people are concentrated in this region that form 23 per cent of the worldwide population. At such a juncture it becomes imperative that all the member nations of this region come together and pool their sources for the realisation of the common objectives and aims. Enthusiastic and aggressive steps are the need of the hour if we want to prosper in a substantial way. A good way can be to increase the budget allocation for SAARC by each of the member nations. Side by side empowering of SAARC bodies, SAARC secretariat and SAARC regional centers also needs utmost attention. Up till now, South Asia has not fared well. Keeping in view the rich human resources and other assets, many factors have created hindrance in the realisation of the aims of SAARC.

1. 1st such prominent factor is the prevalence of inter and intra state conflicts in this region.
2. Free interaction between the member countries has not been achieved and different kinds of barriers march the success of this economic region.
3. Various kinds of resources have not been utilised for each other's' benefit; for example water resources have not been explored for the common benefit of all SAARC countries.
4. Official trade in this region is limited and has given birth to illegal forms of trade.

Commercial relations among SAARC member-states

Plentiful natural and human resources are available in this region. In fact, the astounding variety of its resources has been the center of attraction of many a developed country. Various resources include:

- Different kinds of climatic regions replete with astounding bio-diversity.
- Plenty of rivers (both big and small) with a huge potential for hydroelectric projects.
- Rich sources of different kinds of minerals, some exclusively limited to this region only.
- Forest resources, animal resources and medicinal plants that are native to this region.

But the sad fact is that this rich diversity of resources has not been utilised properly and as a result the average living standard of people of this region is well behind the international standards. SAPTA is a step in this direction that visualises the abolition of various trade restrictions that often become impediments in the proper exploitation of the natural resources of this region. Another irony that is visible is that all the SAARC countries have maximum trade with countries like USA, Japan and Asia-pacific countries, but the proportion of mutual trade among them is negligible. Intra-regional trade is just 5 per cent of total official trade. South Asian countries have close trade relations with East Asia and other parts of Asia also. With East Asia the per cent of trade is much higher. The trade of SAARC countries with East Asian countries is 50 per cent. This is in spite of the fact that all the member countries have many common needs and desires. South Asia has cultural, linguistic, and ethnic overlap. Our history is common. Our heros are common. Moreover over villain are also common. South Asian countries are suffering with common problems too.

The question is if we have so many similarities then why South Asia is developing as a disintegrated region.

Intra-regional rivalries are the main reason of this disintegration. If we consider India and Pakistan only, 80 per cent of the GDP of all the SAARC countries gets covered. What sort of relations these two counties have is an open secret? It would not be gain saying the fact that Indo-Pak problem is a major challenge for SAARC. The problem is compounded by both countries. Both were inclined to treat their borders as fence to keep other out rather than using them as gateways for the movement of good people and ideas.[2]

After the partition of India Pakistan was still the major trader with India. However, with the passage of time sinister politics set in and trade between India and Pakistan reached a record low in 1965-66. It was just Rs110,000,000 in 1965-66 whereas the value of trade between India and Pakistan in 1948-49 was Rs 1,850,000,000[3]. This situation worsened with the passing time and both India and Pakistan adopted such economic policies as were detrimental to self-sufficiency of both the countries. To take an example, Pakistan traded with China and South Korea for coal, iron and steel. It could easily have got all these things from India at much cheaper rates. Similarly, India also had to suffer considerable loss when Pakistan denied the selling of raw jute to India.

It does not mean, however, that there is no informal trade between the two countries. According to an estimate about Rs 20 billion worth of informal trade takes place between India and Pakistan each year. What does it amount to? Naturally, it results in tremendous loss of revenue for both the countries. Not only this, Intra-SAARC trade is also very low-as low as 5 per cent. What's more the share of the SAARC region in world trade is a very dismal 1 per cent. What does it all show? It points to the fact that this region has not been able to tap its economic potential by way of economic co-operation and socio-cultural exchange.

An instrument called SAFTA, a very important tool in the hands of SAARC countries, has also been unable to lessen financial enmity between India and Pakistan. The government is apathetic about this. As a result the aspirations of the people of South Asia as a whole have not been realised. With proper regional co-operation and collective efforts the aspirations of the people can lead to significant development in South Asia. The standard of living of people belonging to this region needs to be upgraded and their welfare ensured. Even in the twenty-first century, illiteracy among the SAARC countries is very high and is a big hindrance in the achievement of success. Many areas have to be prioritised that need common attention. For this certain compromises and adjustments need to be reached at and this is possible only at the political level. SAARC vision beyond the year 2000 has already been formulated by the GEP (group of 12 eminent persons). It was agree upon that the welfare of the citizens must be given top priority so that all the persons living in South Asia region lead a life of dignity. For this, social progress and cultural development are indispensable. It was also decided that quality of life of the people of SAARC countries could be improved via accelerated economic growth. To this effect various national and regional policies need to be formulated that are complimentary. This region is also prone to various kinds of natural disasters. These also need to be tackled in a collective way. Politicians need to rise above national politics and come to the aid of the member countries by way of mutually reinforcing policies.

SAARC and Vision of Narendra Modi

India has contributed a lot to accelerate the pace of economic co-operation between the SAARC countries. An important result was the agreement called SAPTA that was adopted in December 1995. SAPTA was the first positive effort of SAARC nations in trade liberalisation and industrial reconstruction. Another historical decision that was taken when India chaired the 9th Summit in Male in May 1997 was the vision of SAFTA by the year 2001. IOR-ARC that emerged in March 1997 also was a result of active support by India. Narendra Modi government has a unique vision for south Asia. It visualises south Asian region that is free from all kinds of historical divisions. Another significant achievement of Indian foreign policy is its commitment to strength every kind of regional cooperation among SAARC countries. The invitation of Prime minster Narendra Modi to all SAARC heads to attend the swearing ceremony of Modi on 26 May 2014 was a good gesture shown by India. This effort rejuvenates life in SAARC. Arun Jetily Defense Minister of India stated that this invitation shows good intention of Modi government to maintain healthy ties with its neighbours[4].

India is the biggest and most industrialised trading member of SAARC. India has to recognise its responsibility of developing south Asian region. India should take a lead in making regional cooperation. India's present Prime Minister Narendra Modi is very much positive in his approach in this regard. He addressed the Indian space scientists at the Satish Dhawan space Centre in Sriharikota after successful launch of

PSVL C-23 carrying five foreign Satellites. He coaxed Indian scientists for developing a space satellite for south Asian countries as India's gift. He stated that "the fruits of India's space mission should reach other developing nations, especially India's neighbours[5].

Modi government also plans to establish SAARC Development bank in the line with BRICS (Brazil, Russia, India, China and South Africa) Bank to facilitate regional integration through financing of infrastructure for trade. It is a good gesture shown by India and will boost economic development of South Asia[6]. Prominent critics viewed this bank as a turning point in the history of SAARC. It will provide imputes to trade in goods, services and investment for development. Vikramjit Singh Sahney (president, SAARC Chamber of Commerce) stated that "it will manifest India's commitment towards the development of south Asian region. India has been playing the big brother for the region. It has provided duty free, quota free access to the least developed countries of the region, barring just 25 items under SAFTA agreement of 2005."[7]

Economic cooperation was the chief aim behind the formation of SAARC and that evidently has been the disappointing arena. In today's world science and technology have become indispensable for economic growth. So, efforts should be made that proper flow of science and technology is achieved among member countries. Similarly, the chamber of commerce, media, various government and private institutions and business people need to interact with each other in a freer and open way than before. The restrictions of trade should be minimised and this region as a whole should be viewed as a competitor of the developed world. NGOs can play a major role in this regard.

Any kind of regional grouping or association cannot be successful without mutual faith and understanding. It's common knowledge that much bitterness has issued forth between India and Pakistan. Similarly, Bangladesh and Sri Lanka also doubt the intentions of India and Pakistan in many areas. Such an atmosphere cannot be conducive for effective cooperation. It is not that other regional groups like ASEAN, EU etc. don't have any kind of problems with member states. The fact of the matter is that when it comes to economic cooperation the member countries of these groups keep all their differences on the back burner. For them money power is the only power that is able to rule the present world. The result is that such groups tend to become more powerful and authoritative with the passing time. Such killer instinct needs to be developed in the SAARC countries.Our region is a resourceful region of the world. There are a lot of prospects for development. The need is only to keep away the differences and focus on economic and industrial growth. SAARC countries should learn from other regional organisations like EU and ASEAN that how beautifully these organisations leave behind their differences and sharing profit with all parties. They work on the win-win policy. SAARC countries should also follow this line and should throw away their false egos.

References

1. Shveta Dhaliwal, '*Development of Regionalism in South Asia*', MD Publications, New Delhi, 2009, p. 32.
2. Ashok K Mehta, *Importance of SAARC beyond South Asia*, Pioneer, July 9, 2014.
3. Amar Nath Ram, *SAARC in Globalised era*", India Quarterly, Vol. 64, No.4, September 2009, pp. 448-49
4. The tribune, May 29, 2014, p.1
5. Times of India, June 30, 2014, p.1
6. The Economic Times, 30 July 2014.
7. The Economic Times, 2 august, 2014.

Approaches to Regionalism in the Post-Cold War Era: An Assessment

— ***Sheveta Sehgal***

Abstarct

Post-cold war world is the remarkable and deep trend towards regionalism and the strengthening of regional cooperation. Second World War may be considered a rough benchmark for mushroom growth of regional organisations and the period after second world war rightly be called an era of regional cooperation in international relations. The study of regional integration is concerned with explaining how and why states ceases to be wholly sovereign, how and why they voluntarily mingle, merge, and mix with their neighbours so as to lose the factual attributes of sovereignty while acquiring new techniques for resolving conflict between themselves. The study of regional integration is concerned with explaining how and why states ceases to be wholly sovereign, how and why they voluntarily mingle, merge, and mix with their neighbours so as to lose the factual attributes of sovereignty while acquiring new techniques for resolving conflict between themselves. The regional cooperation provide the basis for wider cooperation in many areas such as economic, arts, culture, education, and other related fields all of which combined together would go to improve the quality of human life in the member countries and the entire region.

Regionalism is the important feature of the Post-Cold War World. Post-cold war world is the remarkable and deep trend towards regionalism and the strengthening of regional cooperation. "Regionalism" refers to the proneness of the governments of a grouping of two or more states – societies to establish voluntary associations and bring together a pool of knowledge, skills and certainly, desires and expectations, in order to develop functional and structural institutional arrangements (either formal or soft, adhoc or informal) likely to forge between (or among) them the bonds of a distinct economic, social and prospectively, political entity, and/or increase their negotiating power vis-à-vis the rest of the world.

The growth of regionalism seems to be one of the most outstanding and baffling developments in the post-Second World War international relations. Both in qualitative as well as quantitative terms. It should be noted that the Second World War, notwithstanding the progress achieved towards regional coalescences. Thus, Second World War may be considered a rough benchmark for mushroom growth of regional organisations and the period after second world war rightly be called an era of regional cooperation in international relations.

Regionalism lends coherence to the history of twentieth century international relations as it draws the attention to a specific pattern of interaction and oscillation between actors in the international system. Since the end of the cold war regionalism has been carried forward by the most powerful states as a means of preserving their own self interests. Governments have recognised that regionalism is an effective political vehicle that can assist in the management of domestic and external pressures. In the present period, regionalism seems set at least to match globalisation as a primary feature of world order.

The concept of region stems from the Latin word 'Regio', which means direction. It is also derived from the Latin verb 'regere': 'to rule' or 'to command'. Subsequently, region denoted border or a delimited space, often a province. Many disciplines and discourses have maintained a strong emphasis on 'territory' and 'rule' in the study and definition of regions. This has resulted in a considerable degree of research capacity being devoted to determining that what types of regions are the most functional, instrumental and efficient (to rule).

In regard to regions, it is not a simple territorial definition. There is a need to refine regions to incorporate commonality, interaction and hence the possibility of cooperation. One perspective could be to see regions as units or 'zones' based on groups, states or territories, whose members share some identifiable traits: the Organisation for Economic Cooperation and Development. A central character of such zones is that they are smaller than the international system of states, but larger than any individual state or non-state unit; they may be permanent or temporary, institutionalised or not. Regions naturally flow into a concept of regionalism as a policy and project whereby states and non –state actors cooperate and coordinate strategy within a given region.

The study of regional integration is unique and discrete from all previous systematic studies of political unification because it limits itself to non-coercive effort. Regional integration is concerned with tasks, transactions, perceptions, and learning, not with sovereignty, military capability, and balances of power. Regional integration is often confounded with overlapping and cognate activities which however, usually address somewhat different problems.

Hague and Harrop define a regional organisation as a 'specific form of (international governmental organisation) IGO in which neighbouring countries join together for common purposes'.

The study of regional cooperation, may be considered as a part of the study of regional integration or as a separate interest. Regional cooperation is a vague term covering any interstate activity with less than universal participation designed to meet some commonly experienced need.

Regional cooperation provides for an increase in stability within regions by removing historical rivalries, settling intra-regional disputes, and promoting economic and social cooperation, it serves as a catalyst for regional peace and order.

Joseph Nye asserts that "regionalism a term that covers such diverse functional as well as geographical regional phenomena as European integration, NATO, the Commonwealth, and voting bloc in the U.N. This concept is in fact, so ambiguous that we can only agree with the recent suggestion that the time has come to replace it by more precise terms." According to one view, regionalism is the concept of organising states and dependent areas on a regional basis.

Throughout the cold war period, then, regionalism had remained on the international agenda, but its scope was limited, partly as a consequence of the continuing bipolar nature of the international system to which all regional arrangements were subordinate, but also because of the extreme tenacity with which states clung to their sovereignty, not only in most matters of high politics but in many matters of low politics as well.

According to Van Kleffens, the term, "regional" must be limited to "sovereign states within a certain area or having common interests in that area".

The 1960s and 1970s were marked by another regionalist challenge, this time from the Third World, and manifest in groupings such as Non-Aligned Movement (NAM) or the Group of 77 (G-77). Dislike of the East- West conflict and of the state of North-South relations in general prompted the rise of this broad 'Southern' coalition in world politics, which in turn, generated a school of writers advocating major structural reforms in the international system.

During the first period, from the 1950's to the 1980's, the main focal point was Western Europe. The founding of that which is now the EU in the early 1950's was explicitly linked to the conditions of the cold war, and the attendant rivalry between the USA and the USSR. Throughout the cold war period, then, regionalism had remained on the international agenda, but its scope was limited.

Present regionalism should be distinguished from historical cases of regional integration. It is 'new regionalism'. New regionalism is defined in rejection of the old; 'old' in terms of both theory and practice. The key feature of the 'new' is the sheer number of formal regional arrangements. There are few countries that are not members of at least one regional organisation and most are members of more than one. This upsurge in regional activity may be explained in several ways.

The theoretical analysis of regionalism conventionally begins with those theories that were developed explicitly to explain the creation and early evolution of the European Commuity. The theory of the study of regionalism is termed as the "regional integration theory". This area of research has exhibited an unswerving interest in the process of international changes since the mid-1950s. As regional integration developed in Western Europe and other regions in the post –Second World War period, so did attempts to understand this phenomenon through various approaches, viz: federal approach, functional approach; neo-functional approach; communication approach.

Integration theory holds that the present system cannot promote the facilities for further human growth. Rather it creates impediments to growth. Rising needs at the national and international level demand a change of the present system which was created to serve eighteenth and nineteenth century developments. Now there is a need for a global structure to organise and coordinate global and national activities. This authority should not be bound by territorial limitations.

The federalist school of thought, (solidly positioned in the ranks of idealism) conceives of integration in legal and institutional terms.(For an excellent example of the Federalist Approach Green Vill Clark and Louis B. Sohn; World Peace Through World Law, Harvard University Press, Harvard, 1966. Federalism as a theory of regional integration has been roughly handled by most contemporary theorists. Federalism envisages a direct legal, constitutional approach to world/regional unity. Theorists assume that different states can be accommodated under the federal umbrella giving sufficient autonomy to all the units, as in the case of the United States of America or Switzerland. Federalists assume that once institutional measures are taken other requirements such as community – building and people- to- people relations will automatically follow. They assume that since federations at the national level or in a limited geographical area is successful it can be transplanted to the international level. Since federalism has brought about peace and security at the national level it can do as well at the international level. Federalism has tended to be a political project, with particular goals in mind. Federalism most commonly describes political systems in which there is a division of authority between central and regional or state government: ' the federalist integration process requires the establishing of two levels of government- separate but coordinate – being the government of the whole, the federal level, and the government of the parts, the state or local level.' By implication, federalism seems to adopt institutions that operate successfully at a national level for a political union among previously sovereign and independent territories, such as was formed in the US, Australia, Canada, Former West Germany and Switzerland. The 'magic formula' for federal systems involves the optimum mixture of unity and diversity.

Federalism seeks simultaneously to meet the need for more effective governmental action in some domains (through centralisation) and the democratic postulate of local control and local autonomy (through decentralisation). They stress the importance of institutional and constitutional questions some what more than do neo- functionalists, the theorist/observers among the federalists have tended to lose their identity as a clear cut approach to questions of regional integration. Federalists assure that the domestic situation can be created at a global level to tackle the problems of the peace and security problematic. It assumes that legal and political measures are the best way to tackle international issues as is the case at the national level. Federalism sheds light on the fact that peace and security may be possible only if national are ready to give up their nationalism and sovereignty and their urge to use force against each other when opportunities arise. Federalism is an attempt at the creation of central institution for the management of relations among states with the consent of the states themselves.

Another approach to international peace and security through integration is the communication/ transaction approach. Though most of theoretical works in this approach are focused on regional contexts, the approach may be applicable at the global level. The transactionalist or communication approach pioneered by Karl .W. Deutsch and his associates. This approach (in the scientific tradition) seeks to measure the process of integration by watching the flow of international transaction, such as trade, tourist, letters and immigrants. It expects further, that such transaction will eventually lead to the development of 'security communities' or integrated socio-political system. A security community comes into existence when a regional group develops "institutions and practices" strong enough and stable enough to assure, for a 'long' time, stable expectations of 'peaceful change' within its population". Security communities could either be "amalgamated" through formal political merger of the participating unit, or remain "pluralistic", in which case the members would remain formally independent. In either case, security communities are characterised by "mutual interdependence of diverse political units; mutual responsiveness of political units; and simple pacification or the abandonment of the use of force among political units". Deutsch has identified two major sub-categories of 'security community', amalgamated and pluralist. Both characterised by the absence of intra-community wars. The United States is a good example of an example of an amalgamated security community for it has a single federal government exercising central political control over a continent sized region. For the communication school of thought, then integration can be seen both as a process leading towards political unification and as the end product of that process, amalgamated and pluralist security communities. The communication approach analysis the integration in term of numerous quantifying variables. This failed to give any yardstick to qualitative communication may foster greater integration than the mere quantified communication.

Communication approach is mainly the creation of Karl Deutsch. They believe that high levels of communication and transactions among actors are a critical indicator of, and probably a causal factor, in the formation of an integrated society. Communication theorising rests content with the demonstration of covariance among variables at the systematic level. It hypothesises that certain relationships between ratios in the case of some clusters of variables, result in a terminal conditions that is security community. A security community is considered to be a group which has become integrated, where regional integration is defined as the attainment of a sense of community, accompanied by formal and informal institutions or practices, sufficiently strong and wide spread to assure peaceful change among members of a group with 'reasonable' certainly over along 'period of time'. The systematic approach thus assumes either of the following: it may assume that transactions measure some human quality, a human perception of self- interest, and that the change in the magnitude of the measure records a change in the human behaviour to be measured; in this case the indicators becomes a proxy variable for perception that leads to behaviour.

The functional approach was formulated due to the drawbacks of the federal approach, especially in the context of twentieth century developments in non-political fields. Functionalists, especially David Mitrany, criticise federalists on many grounds. According to Mitrany, we cannot take a system which has worked well at the national and limited geographical level and transplant it to the regional or global level. The prerequisites which make such federations successful are difficult to fulfil. The theory of functionalism, which is essentially an assertion and defense of the proposition that the development of international economic and social cooperation is a major prerequisite for the ultimate solution of political conflicts and elimination of war, has been most elaborately developed and persuasively stated by David Mitrany. In Mitrany's terms, "the problem of our time is not how to keep the nations peacefully apart but how to bring them actively together". Functionalism would thus overlay political agencies in which and through which the interests and life of all nations would be gradually integrated. States usually form cooperative arrangements for specific objectives such as promoting welfare and security. The functionalism is another form of cooperation among the nations. There is vital difference between the approach of the regionalist thinkers over the goal and approach. The functional approach is based on economic, political, and cultural co-operation as a pre-requisite to political integration. It is like a tranitional path of unification. It encourages inter-governmental collaboration as an essential factor. The concept of functionalism for international cooperation in such fields as economic, social, cultural affairs and science seems to have no direct relation to the overriding political problem of regional security. The advocates of functional integration contend that the basic reasons for war are economic and social inequalities, among other things, and that regional cooperation in these spheres on a non-political level would contribute to regional peace and thus, to international security.

The importance of functionalism got considerable attention in the United Nations also. The chapter VIII of Dumbarton Oaks proposals defined the role of regional organisations in 1994, and subsequently the UN charter in articles 52 to 54. Those who favoured the "functional approach" to regionalism, however, sought a different type of relationship with the universal agency, a relationship which would be closer to mutual cooperation. The functionalist emphasised that the universal agency must provide the financial assistance to support regional functional integration in the interest of future international security. A closer political and economic integration where democratic institutions are well matured, might contribute toward greater political stability in the world.

Functionalism assumes that functions are universal. McLaren rejects this assumption. According to him, this assumption has two components. One is that all functions require translational cooperation. The other is that all states are same stage of economic development, that the solution is applicable to all. But in reality neither is valid for very few functional organisations are engaged in translational operation and among them the majority and biggest are concerned with programmes within the states and not between and among them. And in those cases where trans-border cooperation is required, universality exists in the problems and function and not in their solutions.

Inis Claude criticises the claim of functionalism that when the everybody is materially happy that will keep the peace. The argument that war is product of unsatisfactory economic and social conditions appears weak. The reparability thesis holds that economic and welfare issues can be separated and dealt with separately and economic welfare issues are more important than political issues. Claude also challenges the functionalists' reliance on human rationality, particularly the rational transfer of loyalties from national to international agencies. New institutions do not necessarily create new loyalties. Finally, Claude feels that he functionalist program for building the foundation of peace is a long- range one and he is not sure that all that time is available (presumably before another world war erupts).

No doubt functionalist explanation of international relations suffers from severe drawbacks. At the same time, functional organisations are a reality which cannot be ignored. Functional organisations came into existence to serve felt needs. They are the result of the creation of a state-system and many of them are created by states in areas where translational cooperation is necessary. -

The neo-functionalist school, following the lead of classical functionalist David Mitrany, emphasised the notion of spillover. This theory postulated that issue-based regional cooperation in areas of lesser salience could eventually move national actors towards a path of cooperation in areas of higher salience, including political and security cooperation. According to this logic, if functional regional groups could successfully foster economic integration, regional security would ensure that the actors would, over a period of time, learn to resolve their conflicts peacefully and come to cooperate on common security issues.

Neo-Functionalism is a modified version of functionalism applied at the regional level. "Basically, the neofunctionalists were federalists in functionalist clothing, pursuing federal ends through what appeared to be functionalist means." Pentland holds that, historically, though neofunctionalism is an amalgam of federalism and functionalism with certain methodological scientific additions, certain differences can be brought out among these approaches. Neofunctionalists emphasised the importance of the elements of competing interest groups of a modern pluralistic society.

The neo-functional approach, which developed under the stimulus of events in Western Europe in the late-1950s, portrays the political impact of groups and the elite and their bargaining as contributing to the incremental growth of supranational institutions. The neo-functionalists consider a supranational agency as a pre-requisite for effective problem solving which undermines the independence of the national states. Neo-Functionalists argued that high and rising levels of interdependence would set in motion an ongoing process of cooperation that would lead eventually to political integration. Supranational institutions were seen as the most effective means of solving common problems, beginning with technical and non-controversial issues, but 'spilling over' into the realm of high politics and leading to a redefinition of group identity around the regional unit. Neo-functionalist believed integration to be a cumulative and expensive process through which the organisation would slowly extend its sphere of authority so as to encompass a wider range of decision making activities. Neo-Functionalism stresses the instrumental motives of actors; it looks for the adaptability of elites in line with specialisation of roles; neo-functionalism takes self-interest for granted and relies on it for delineating actor perceptions.

Neo-functionalism has its origin in the writings of Ernst Hass and was later supplemented by Leon Lindberg, Stuart Scheingold, Phillipe Schmitter, Joseph Nye, and others. Integration theorists led by Ernst Hass (1958, 1964) and Leon Lindberg (1966) drew inspiration from two sources. From the work of Karl Deutsch, they inherited an interest in developing a social science of post-national community building that emphasised rigour over excessive normativity or idealism.

According to Hass, "political community is a condition in which specific groups and individuals show more loyalty to their central political institutions than to any other political authority in a specific period of time and in a definable geographic space."

The study of regional integration is concerned with explaining how and why states ceases to be wholly sovereign, how and why they voluntarily mingle, merge, and mix with their neighbours so as to lose the factual attributes of sovereignty while acquiring new techniques for resolving conflict between themselves. This approach to regional integration assumes that actor behaviour in a regional setting is analogous to that in a modern pluralist nation- state and takes for granted that these actors are motivated by self-interest. Ernst Hass, having identified the political community as his terminal condition, defines integration as a process whereby political actors in different countries are gradually persuaded to shift their loyalties, expectations and political activities towards a new larger centre whose institutions processes or demand jurisdiction over the nation states.

Another former student, Leon N. Lindberg, emphasised on Hass' investigation of the European community. His study begins with the analyses undertaken in Hass' '*The Uniting Europe*', and specifically attempts to apply functional theory to the level of analysis that seems most promising: regionalism, specifically the European Economic Communities (ECC). He argues that an initial contribution to the success of the ECC was the flexible framework provided by the Treaty of Rome. Following Hass' example, Lindberg conceives of political integration as a process rather than as a condition. The process is characterised by a gradual evolution toward a legitimate mechanism for the resolution of conflict for making of authoritative decisions involving the majority of interests.

By the mid of 1970s the first wave of regional integration scholarship seemed to have run out of steam. The publication of Hass' devastating *The Obsolescence of Regional Integration Theory* seemed to indicate not only that neo-functionalism had run aground, but that the very idea of producing theoretical models of regionalism was deeply misconceived. There seemed to be two major problems with the project of integration theory. First, the expectation that the European experience would be replicated elsewhere seemed to have scuppered. Ambitious analogous projects such as the Latin American Free Trade Area had failed, and there seemed to be little momentum among elites to engage in regionalist enterprises. Second, Hass acknowledged that in the European case integration theories had largely underestimated the role of national governments and the pervasiveness of nationalist sentiment.

The dissolution of integration theory was not simply a consequence of the discrepancies between theoretical predictions and empirical 'reality'. In addition, neofunctionalism was marginalised by the emerging distaste for grand predictive social scientific theories and the development of interest in 'interdependence'.

In reflecting on the achievements and problems of research on regional integration in 1970, Ernst Hass came up with a fundamental reconceptualisation of what he calls a dependent variable. In his revisionist theory in 1970, he offers a new definition: "regional integration is concerned with explaining how and why states cease to be wholly sovereign, how and why they voluntarily mingle, merge, and mix with their neighbours so as to lose the factual attributes of sovereignty while acquiring now techniques for resolving conflict between themselves". Thus emphasis is shifted from the creation of a new and larger centre to a shift of authority and legitimacy out of old centres.

In the Post old War era, regional cooperation emerged with the greater importance. The scope of regional economic cooperation is so vast that if the initiative is by the poor countries of every region can increase interdependence on each other and thereby reduce their dependence on the rich countries. Such cooperation is also beneficial to the poor countries in order to improve their cooperation with the rich countries. The study of regional integration is concerned with explaining how and why states ceases to be wholly sovereign, how and why they voluntarily mingle, merge, and mix with their neighbours so as to lose the factual attributes of sovereignty while acquiring new techniques for resolving conflict between themselves. The regional cooperation provide the basis for wider cooperation in many areas such as economic, arts, culture, education, and other related fields all of which combined together would go to improve the quality of human life in the member countries and the entire region.

References

1. Stephan C. Calleya (2000), Regionalism in the Post-Cold War World, Ashgate Publishers, U.S.A.
2. Fredrik Soderbaum and Timothy M. Shaw (2003). Theories of New Regionalism, New York, Palgrave Macmillian.
3. Mary Farrell, Bjorn Hettne and Luk Van Langenhove (ed. 2005) Global Politics of Regionalism Theory and Practice, Pluto Press, London.
4. S. Krasner (1983), International Regimes, New York, Cornell University.
5. Richard A. Falk, Saul H. Mendlovitz (ed) Regional politics and World Order, W. H Freeman and company, San Francisco.
6. Ronald J. Yalem (1962) Regionalism and World Order, International Affairs, Vol. 38, No. 4.
7. Louise Fawcett and Andrew Hurrel (ed. 1995) Regionalism in World Politics: Regional Organisation And International Order, Oxford University Press, U.K.
8. E.N. Van kleffens, Regionalism and Political Pacts, American Journal of International Law, Vol. 43, 1949.
9.
10. Shaun Breslin, Christopher W. Hughes, Nicola Phillips and Ben Rosamond (ed. 2002) New Regionalisms in the Global Political Economy, Routledge, London.
11. Bjorn Hettne, 'The New Regionalism Revisited' in Fredrik Soderbaum and Timothy M. Shaw, Theories of New Regionalism, 2003, New York, Palgrave Macmillian.
12. Fredrik Soderbaum, 'Introduction': Theories of New Regionalism in Fredrik Soderbaum and Timothy M. Shaw, Theories of New Regionalism, 2003, New York, Palgrave Macmillian.

13. Michael Smith, 'Region and Regionalism', in Brain White, Richard Little and Michael Smith, Issues in World Politics, ed.2001, Palgrave, New York.
14. Fredrik Soderbaum, Timothy M. Shaw (ed.2003). Theories of New Regionalism,Palgrave Macmillan, New York.
15. Vandna Mohla (1998) SAARC and Super Power, Deep and Deep Publications, New Delhi.
16. Thomas George (1997) The State of International Integration Theory, Anmol Publications, New Delhi.
17. Karl W. Deutsch (1968) Political Community and the North Atlantic Area, Princeton, Princeton University Press.
18. Karl. W. Deutsch et.al. "Political Communities" and the North Atlantic Area, Princeton, Princeton University, 1957.
19. Norman J. Padelford, George A. Lincoln and Lee D. Olvey, n. 45,. For details on Functionalism see, A.J.R Taylor (ed), F .G (1968) Functionalism: Theory and Practice in International Relations,1975 London.
20. Inis L. Claude (1960) Swords into Plowshares, New York, Random House.
21. Robert I. Mclaren (1985) Mitranian Functionalism: possible or Impossible, Review of International Studies Vol.11.
22. Inis L. Claude jr., Swords into Plowshares:The Problem and Progress of International Organisation, Fourth edition, New York, Random House, 1971.
23. Ernst B. Hass, The Study of Regional Integration: Reflections on the Joy and Anguish of Pretheorising, International Organisation Vol. 24,1970.
24. Ernst B. Hass and Philip C. Schmitter (1966) International Political Communities, New York.
25. Leon Lindberg (1963) The Political Dynamics of Economic Integration, Stanford.
26. Leon N. Lindberg (1970) Europe's Would be Policy: Patterns of Change in the European Community, New Jersey.
27. Roger D. Hanson (1969) Regional Integration: Reflections on a Decade of Theoretical Efforts , World Politics, Vol. 21, No. 2.
28. Ernst B. Hass, "The Study of Regional Integration: Reflection on the Joy and Anguish of Pretheorising", International Organisation, Vol. 24, No. 4, 1970.
29. Joseph Nye, Comparative regional Integration: Concept and Measurement, International Organisation, 1968, Vol. 22.
30. Paul F. Dienl (ed.2005), The Politics of Global Governance International organisations In An Interdependent World, Viva Books Private Limited, New Delhi.

31. Jacob Viner (1950) The Custom Union Issue, New York.
32. C.F. Carter, E.A. Robinson and R.C.O. Matthews, "A New Look At Custom Union Theory, Dawson and Sons Ltd, London.
33. R.G. Lipsey, "The Theory of Customs Union: Trade Diversion and Welfare", Economica. Vol. 24.
34. Murray Kemp and Henry Wan, "An Elementary Proposition Concerning the Formation of Customs Unions", Journal of International Economics, Vol. 6, 1976.
35. Charles A. Cooper and B. F. Massel, "A New Look at the Customs Union Theory", Economic Journal, Vol. 25, 1965, pp. 742-47.
36. Richard Brecher and J.N. Bhagwati, "Foreign Ownership and the Theory of Trade and Welfare", Journal of Economy, Vol. 89, 1981.
37. John Ravenhill (2005). Global Political Economy, U.K, Oxford University Press.

    Paul F. Dienl (ed.2005), The Politics of Global Governance International organisations In An Interdependent World, Viva Books Private Limited, New Delhi.

Economic Integration among SAARC Countries: From SAPTA to SAFTA

—Vipin Sharma, Dr Vinod Kumar,

Abstract

Economic Integration is a process of the abolition of tariff and non-tariff barriers to the flow of goods, services and factors of production between a group of nations. In South Asia, this process of economic integration started with formation of South Asian Association for Regional Cooperation (SAARC) in 1985. The SAARC is an International organisation of eight nations, Afghanistan, Bangladesh, Bhutan, India, Maldives, Nepal, Pakistan and Sri Lanka to promote cooperation, cultural, economic and personal development of Asian nations and mutual assistance between member nations. It was established when its charter was approved on 8 December 1985 by governments of seven founding member countries (Afghanistan became member of the union in 2007). After successful establishment of SAARC as an association for political affairs, all the seven member countries literally agreed to form a regional block for economic activities. That dream became reality ultimately when South Asian Preferential Trade Agreements (SAPTA) was founded on 11th day of April 1993. The SAPTA was envisaged primarily as the first step towards the transition to a South Asian Free Trade Area (SAFTA) leading subsequently towards a Customs Union, Common Market and Economic Union. However, trade liberalisation rounds under SAPTA were dismal due to limited product coverage and tariff preferences. Thus, SAFTA was formed with the intention to replace SAPTA, which was limited in its scope. SAFTA's ultimate aim was to put in place a full-fledged South Asian Economic Union on the lines of the European Union. The 'Contracting States' recognised that it was necessary to progress beyond a Preferential Trading Arrangement to move towards higher levels of trade and economic cooperation in the region by removing barriers to cross-border flow of goods. Thus, the SAFTA agreement was signed on 6th January 2004 and came in to effect on 1st January 2006. The available data on India's trade with SAARC countries show that India's trade with SAARC countries is very little. This shows that both SAPTA & SAFTA have failed to achieve the objectives of trade expansion among member countries. Even though SAFTA is an ambitious agreement to achieve its fundamental goal of trade liberalisation, it is being criticised because its coverage has been limited to trade in goods. Due to the existence of bilateral Free Trade Agreements (FTAs) between member countries, which benefit bilaterally, the common interest is being sacrificed. Thus, the reason behind this unsuccessful attempt is given that SAFTA is operating with the existence of a "spaghetti bowl" (Bhagwati, 1995) already prevailing in the region. For the meaningful economic integration and development of the region, SAFTA should either supersede the bilateral agreements or integrate them.

Concept of Economic Integration

Economic Integration is defined as a process and as a state of affairs. As a process, it encompasses measures designed to abolish discrimination between economic units belonging to different nations. When defined as a state of affairs, it can be represented by the absence of various form of discrimination between national economies (Balassa, 1961). Thus, Economic Integration is the abolition of tariff and non-tariff barriers to the flow of goods, services, and factors of production between a group of nations or different parts of the same nation. Balassa talked about five forms of economic integration, viz. (1) a Free Trade Area, (2) a Custom Union, (3) a Common Market, (4) an Economic Union, and (5) complete Economic Integration.

Economic Integration in South Asia

In South Asia this process of economic integration started with formation of South Asian Association for Regional Cooperation (SAARC) in 1985. The SAARC is an International organisation of eight nations, viz. Afghanistan, Bangladesh, Bhutan, India, Maldives, Nepal, Pakistan and Sri Lanka to promote cooperation, cultural, economic and personal development of Asian nation and mutual assistance between member nations. It was established when its charter was approved on 8th December 1985 by governments of seven founding member countries (Afghanistan became member of the union in 2007).

The idea of formation of SAARC as a cooperative organisation in South Asia was not new. Earlier, three conferences–the Asian Relation Conference held in New Delhi in April 1947; the Baguio Conference in the Philippines on May 1950; and the Colombo Power Conference held in Sri Lanka on April 1954,–discussed about Regional Cooperation in South Asia.

Since 1977 the Bangladesh president seemed to have been working on the idea of an ASEAN – like organisation in South Asia. During his visit to India in December 1977 Ziaur Rahman discussed the issue of regional cooperation with the new Indian Prime Minister, Morarji Desai. In the inaugural speech to the Colombo Plan Consultative Committee, which met in Kathmandu in December 1977, King Birendra of Nepal gave a call for close regional cooperation among the South Asian countries sharing river waters. This call was welcomed by President Zia-ur-Rahman during the former's visit to Bangladesh in January 1978. President Ziaur Rahman had also informally discussed the idea of regional cooperation with leaders of the South Asian countries during the Commonwealth Summit in Lusaka in 1979. Finally, the Bangladesh President Ziaur Rahman seemed to have given a concrete shape to the proposal after his visit to Sri Lanka and discussed with the Sri Lankan President, J.R. Jayawardene in November 1979. Therefore, efforts toward establishing the union were first mooted by the President of Bangladesh Ziaur Rahman on May 1980, whilst talking to the media journalist in Dhaka.

In the late 1970s, the seven Asian Nations that include Bangladesh, Bhutan, India, Maldives, Nepal, Pakistan and Sri Lanka agreed upon the creation of a Trade bloc and to provide a platform for the peoples of South Asia to work together in a spirit of friendship, trust and understanding. Thus, responding to the President Ziaur Rahman and King Birendra's convention officials of the foreign ministers of the seven countries met for the first time in Colombo in April 1981. The Bangladesh's proposal was promptly endorsed by Nepal, Sri Lanka, Bhutan and Maldives but India and Pakistan were skeptical initially. India's main concern was the proposal's reference to the security matters in South Asia. Indian policy makers also feared that Ziaur Rahman's proposal for a regional organisation might provide an opportunity to the small neighbours to regionalise all bilateral issues and to join with each other to "gang up" against India. Pakistan assumed that it might be an Indian strategy to organise the other South Asian countries against Pakistan and ensure a regional market for Indian products. However, after a series of quit diplomatic consultations between the South Asian foreign ministers at the United Nation (UN) headquarter in New York from August to September 1980, it was agreed that Bangladesh would propose the draft of a working paper for discussion among the secretaries of the South Asian countries. Between 1980 and 1983, four meetings (April 21-23, 1981, Colombo; November 2-4, 1981, Kathmandu; August 7-8, 1982, Islamabad; March 28-30, 1983, Dhaka) at the foreign secretary level took place to establish the principles of organisation and identify areas for cooperation. The foreign secretaries of inner seven countries again delegated a committee of the whole in Colombo in September 1981, which identified five broad areas of cooperation.

The first South Asian foreign ministers' conference was held in New Delhi from August 1-3, 1983, where the Integrated Programme of Action (IPA) on mutually agreed areas of cooperation (Agriculture, Rural Development, Telecommunications, Postal Services and Scientific & technical cooperation) was launched. The foreign ministers at this conference also adopted a declaration on regional cooperation, formally beginning an organisation known as The South Asian Regional Cooperation (SARC). Following the New Delhi meeting, three meetings of foreign ministers were held at Male on July 10-11, 1984; Thimpu on May 13-14, 1985 and Dhaka on December 5, 1985 to finalise detail and determine date and place for the first meeting of South Asian heads of state. At the Dhaka foreign minister's meeting, a decision was taken to change the name of the organisation from South Asian Regional Cooperation (SARC) to South Asian Association for Regional Cooperation (SAARC) based on the thinking that while SARC refers to the process of South Asian regional cooperation, SAARC mark the establishment of an association to promote and develop such cooperation. Thus, officially the union was established in Dhaka with Kathmandu being union's Secretariat–General.

Finally, the first summit meeting of the heads of state/governments of South Asian countries was held at Dhaka from December 7-8, 1985 and hosted by the President of Bangladesh, Hussain Ershad. Since its inception, SAARC has evolved slowly but continuously both in terms of institutions and programmes. Afghanistan began negotiations for joining the SAARC and applied for its membership in 2005. After two years of negotiations, Afghanistan became the eighth member of SAARC during the fourteenth SAARC summit held in New Delhi in April 2007.

China, Japan, Republic of Korea, USA, Iran, Mauritius, Australia, Myanmar and European Union have joined SAARC as observers.

SAARC provides a platform for the people of South Asia to work together in a spirit of friendship, trust and understanding. It aims to promote the welfare of the people of the South Asia and improve their quality of life through accelerated economic growth, social progress and cultural development in the region. The cooperation in SAARC is based on five principles of Sovereign Equality, Territorial Integrity, Political Independence, and Non-Interference in mutual affairs of the member states and mutual benefits.

Areas of Cooperation

At the inception of association, the Integrated Programme of Action (IPA) consisting of a number of Technical Committees (TCs) was identified as the core areas of cooperation. Over the period of years, the number of TCs was changed as per the requirements. The current areas of cooperation under the reconstituted Regional Integrated Programme of Action which is pursued through the Technical committee covers:

1. Agriculture and Rural Development;
2. Health and Population Activities;
3. Women, Youth and Children;
4. Environment and Forestry;
5. Science & Technology and Meteorology;
6. Human Resource Development; and
7. Transport.

Recently, high-level working groups have also been established to strengthen cooperation in the areas of Information, communication & technology (ICT), biotechnology, Intellectual property rights, tourism and energy.

South Asian Preferential Trade Agreements (SAPTA)

An Inter-Governmental Group (IGG) was formed by SAARC members to negotiate increment tariff reforms between member countries.

The goal is to increase trade between Asian countries and to assist less economically advantaged member through preferential treatment.

After successful establishment of SAARC as an association for political affairs, all the seven member countries literally agreed to form a regional bloc for economic activities. That dream became reality ultimately when SAPTA was founded on 11th day of April 1993. SAPTA was envisaged primarily as the first step towards the transition to a South Asian Free Trade Area (SAFTA) leading subsequently towards a Customs Union, Common Market and Economic Union.

The initiative towards the establishing SAPTA was taken during the sixth SAARC summit in Colombo in December, 1991 and agreement on SAPTA was signed in April 1993 during the 7th SAARC summit in Dhaka. This agreement was a framework "of rules providing for step-by-step liberalisation of intra-regional trade" (SAARC 1994). Under SAPTA, the member countries have agreed to exchange lists of products for seeking trade concessions. An Inter-Government Group on trade liberalisation had been established to negotiate trade concessions. The first round of trade negotiation was completed by March, 1995.

SAPTA contained provisions giving "special and favourable treatment" to the less developed countries (LDCs) in the SAARC region. It also envisaged review of trade concessions on tariff, para-tariff and non- tariff lines. The agreement stated that the member countries may conduct their negotiations for trade liberalisation in accordance with a combination of the following approaches,

1. Product –by-Product basis,
2. Across the board tariff reduction,
3. Sectoral basis, and
4. Direct trade measures

An important instrument of SAPTA, "the Rule of Origin" distinguished between two products viz. (1) product wholly produced or obtained in exporting member country; and (2) product not wholly produced or obtained in exporting member country.

With regard to product falling in second category, the rules indicate that the "local content" should be at least 50 per cent of the f.o.b. values of the products in order to claim preferential treatment.

SAPTA agreement had envisaged to introduce initially trade concessions on a product-by-product basis, although there were provisions for across the board tariff cut as well as reduction of tariff on a sectoral basis. A major constraint posed by this approach was that vested interest in individual member countries would exert pressure on the concerned governments and prevent the inclusion of certain products for trade concessions. Thus, interim trade liberalisation rounds under SAPTA were dismal due to limited product coverage and tariff preferences.

The South Asian Free Trade Area (SAFTA)

South Asian Free Trade Area was formed with the intention to replace SAPTA, which was limited in its scope. SAFTA's ultimate aim was to put in place a full-fledged South Asian Economic Union on the lines of the European Union. The 'Contracting States' recognised that it is necessary to progress beyond a Preferential Trading Arrangement to move towards higher levels of trade and economic cooperation in the region by removing barriers to cross-border flow of goods. Thus, the SAFTA agreement was signed on 6 January 2004 and came in to effect on 1st January 2006.

The process of shifting SAPTA to SAFTA was not new. It was the Sixteenth session of the Council of Ministers held in New Delhi, 18-19 December 1995 in which members agreed on the need to strive for the realisation of SAFTA. Therefore, an Inter-Governmental Expert Group (IGEG) was set up in 1996 to identify the necessary steps for progressing to a free trade area. The 10th SAARC Summit held in Colombo, from 29-31 July 1998 decided to set up a Committee of Experts (COE) to draft a comprehensive treaty framework for creating a free trade area within the region. The SAFTA Agreement was signed on 6 January 2004 during Twelfth SAARC Summit held in Islamabad, Pakistan. The Agreement entered into force on 1 January 2006, and the Trade Liberalisation Programme commenced from 1st July 2006. The agreement is to be completed by 2016 and all contracting parties will need to reduce their tariffs from 0-5 per cent at the full implementation of SAFTA.

India's Position under SAPTA and SAFTA

The main motivation behind the creation of SAFTA is to enhance intra-regional trade among SAARC members through the removal of tariff and non-tariff barriers and thereby enjoy the gains of regional integration and at the same time become more competitive in the global market. The exports under SAFTA have been witnessing considerable upward trend since the launching of the Trade Liberalisation Programme (TLP).

As of20 September 2013, the total f.o.b. value of exports by Member States under SAFTA has reached about US $ 3 billion since launching of SAFTA Trade Liberalisation Programme. Still intra-SAARC trade flows under SAFTA are far below the potential. For smooth functioning of the SAFTA, customs notifications for implementing Trade Liberalisation Programme (TLP) are issued as per the agreed timeline by the Member States. While reduction in the size of Sensitive Lists is important to increase the quantum of regional trade, efforts are being made to take out those products out of the Sensitive Lists that are of export interests to the SAARC Member States for trade within South Asia.

The Table-1 below shows the percentage share of India's exports to SAARC countries in the total exports of India. In the regime of SAPTA, this share fluctuated between the minimum 3.8776 (1999-2000) to the highest 5.5140 (2004-05). In 1996-97 the exports of India to SAARC countries were 5.15 per cent of total exports. This percentage share of exports to SAARC nations fell to 4.39 in 2000-01 and ultimately touched the highest level of 5.51 per cent in 2004-05 of this regime.

In 2006-07 when SAFTA came into existence this percentage share of India's exports to SAARC countries in total exports was 5.12 per cent. This percentage share reached the highest level 5.91 in 2007-08. But, thereafter, fell continuously till 2011-12 to 4.35 per cent. However, it was 5.03 per cent in 2012-13. Thus the data show that both SAPTA and SAFTA could not achieve their goal of trade expansion among SAARC Nations.

Table-1 India's Exports to SAARC Countries after SAPTA and SAFTA

Regime	*Years*	*Total Exports (Values in US $ Million)*	*Exports to South Asia (Values in US $ Million)*	*% share of exports to South Asia*
SAPTA	1996-97	33,646.95	1,724.39	5.1521
	1997-98	34,784.98	1632.20	4.6923
	1999-2000	36,822.49	1427.83	3.8776
	2000-01	44560.29	1954.41	4.3860
	2004-05	83535.94	4606.14	5.5140
	2005-06	103090.53	5547.65	5.3813
SAFTA	2006-07	126414.05	6473.81	5.1211
	2007-08	163132.18	9637.76	5.9079

Contd..

2008-09	185295.36	8567.12	4.6235
2010-11	251136.19	11659.14	4.6426
2011-12	305963.92	13296.47	4.3458
2012-13	300400.68	15110.70	5.0302

Source: Department of Commerce, Ministry of Finance GOI.

Table-2 below gives information about the percentage share of imports from SAARC countries in total imports of India. During the regime of SAPTA i.e. 1996-97 to 2005-06, it was volatile and moving in the range of 0.5906 (1997-98)-0.9754 (2000-01) per cent. It was 0.6192 in 1996-97, reached to the highest of the SAPTA regime i.e. 09754 in 2000-01.

But in the regime of SAFTA, this percentage share was continuously falling and reached to 0.55 per cent in 2012-13.

Table-2 India's Imports from SAARC Countries after SAPTA and SAFTA

Regime	*Years*	*Total imports (Values in US$ Million)*	*Imports from South Asia (Values in US$ Million)*	*% share of imports from South Asia*
SAPTA	1996-97	39132.41	1242.31	0.6192
	1997-98	41484.49	245.00	0.5906
	1999-2000	49738.06	418.70	0.8418
	2000-01	50536.45	492.49	0.9745
	2004-05	111517.43	997.19	0.8942
	2005-06	149165.73	1413.31	0.9475
SAFTA	2006-07	185,735.24	1,507.45	0.8116
	2007-08	251654.01	2117.35	0.8414
	2008-09	303696.31	1817.89	0.5986
	2010-11	369769.13	2173.37	0.5878
	2011-12	489319.44	2524.74	0.5160
	2012-13	496736.65	2679.95	0.5461

Source: Department of Commerce, Ministry of Finance GOI.

Thus the data in both tables shows that India's trade with SAARC countries is very little. Even though SAFTA is an ambitious agreement to achieve its fundamental goal of trade liberalisation, it is being criticised because its coverage has been limited to trade in goods. Due to the existence of bilateral Free Trade Agreements (FTAs) between member countries, which benefit bilaterally, the common interest is being sacrificed. Thus, the reason behind this unsuccessful attempt is given that SAFTA is operating with the existence of a "spaghetti bowl" (Bhagwati) already prevailing in the region. For the meaningful economic integration and development of the region, SAFTA should either supersede these bilateral agreements or integrate them.

References

Balassa, bela (1962): "The Theory of Economic Integration", George Allen & Unwin, London.

Batra, Amita (2007): "South Asia's Free Trade Agreement: Strategies and Options", Economic & Political weekly, Vol. 42, No. 38, pp. 3878-3885.

Bhagwati, Jagdish(1995): "U.S. Trade Policy: The Infatuation with Free Trade Agreements", Discussion Paper Series No. 726.

Dash, Kishore c. (1996): "The Political Economy of Regional Cooperation in South Asia", Pacific Affairs, Vol. 69, No. 2, pp. 185-211.

Sejuti, Jha (2013): "Utility of Regional Trade Agreements? Experience From India's Trade Regionalism", Foreign Trade Review, Vol. 48, No. 2, pp. 233-245.

S Perera, M.S. (2009): "The South Asian Free Trade Area: an analysis of Policy Options for Sri Lanka", Journal of Economic Integration, Vol. 24, No. 3, pp. 530-562.

Weerakoon, Dushni (2001): "Does SAFTA Have a Future", Economic & Political Weekly, Vol. 36, No. 34, pp. 3214-3216.

Weerakoon, Dushni and Tayanthi Thennakoon (2006): "SAFTA Myth of Free Trade", Economic & Political Weekly, Vol. 41, No. 37, pp. 3920-3923.

Department of Commerce under the Ministry of Finance, Government of India.

SAARC's Official website.